HOW TO UPCYCLE NEARLY EVERYTHING

FOR THE OUTDOORS

CALIN DUKE

To Donnie:

The outdoors is not the same without you.

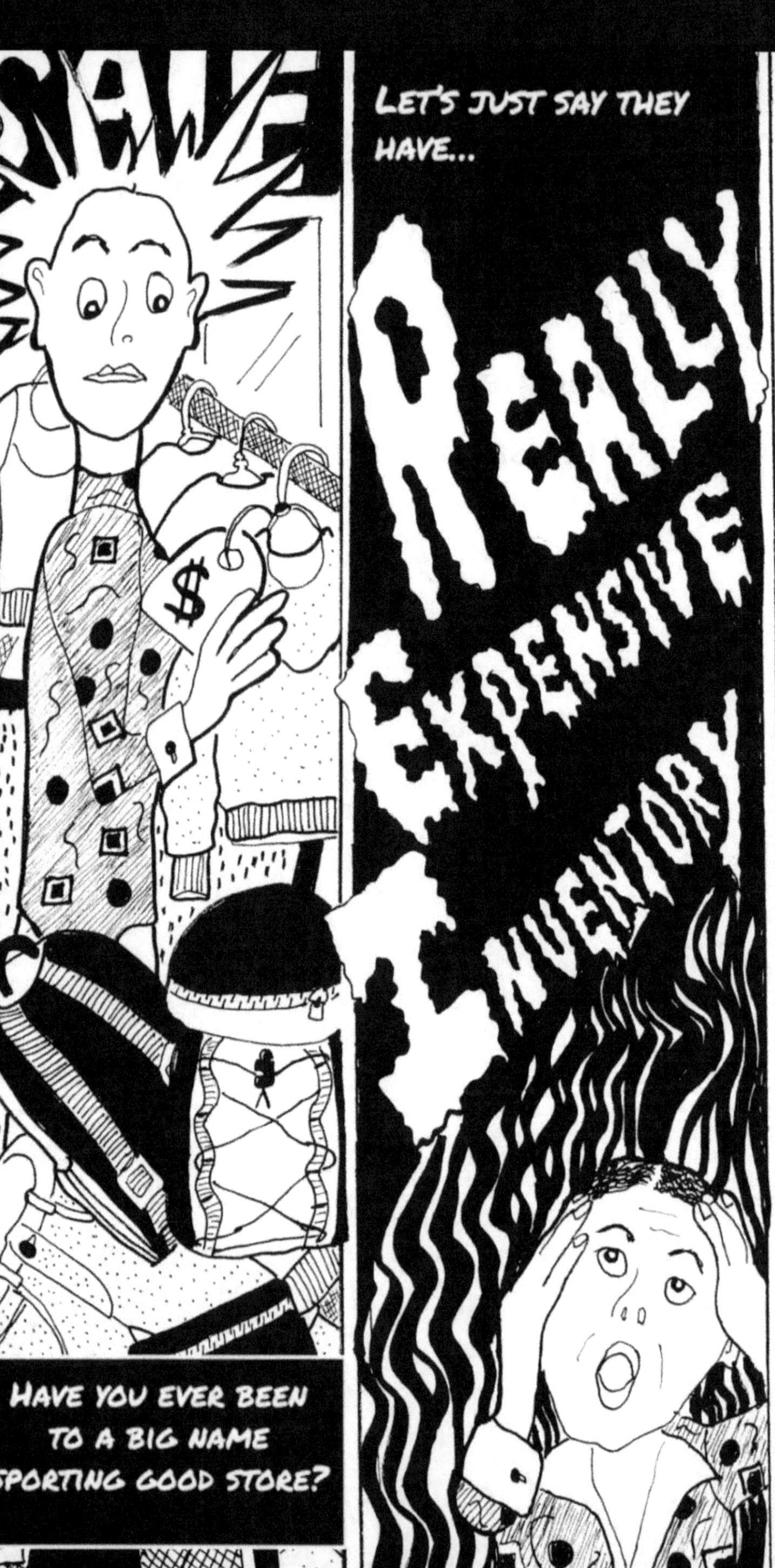

DEAR UPCYCLERS-

AS AN OUTDOOR ENTHUSIAST, I LOVE GETTING NEW GEAR BECAUSE OFTEN IT HELPS ME DO WHAT I LOVE...BETTER.

WARM SOCKS IN A WET TENT? HEAVEN!

HIKING POLES ON A BRUTAL DOWNHILL? YES, PLEASE!

AND YET...LET'S BE HONEST. THERE IS A PART OF ME THAT LIKES NICE GEAR BECAUSE IT SIGNALS, "HEY, LOOK AT HOW OUTDOORSY I AM!"

HERE'S THE THING: A LOT OF THE GEAR FOR SALE TODAY IS COOL...BUT NOT ESSENTIAL.

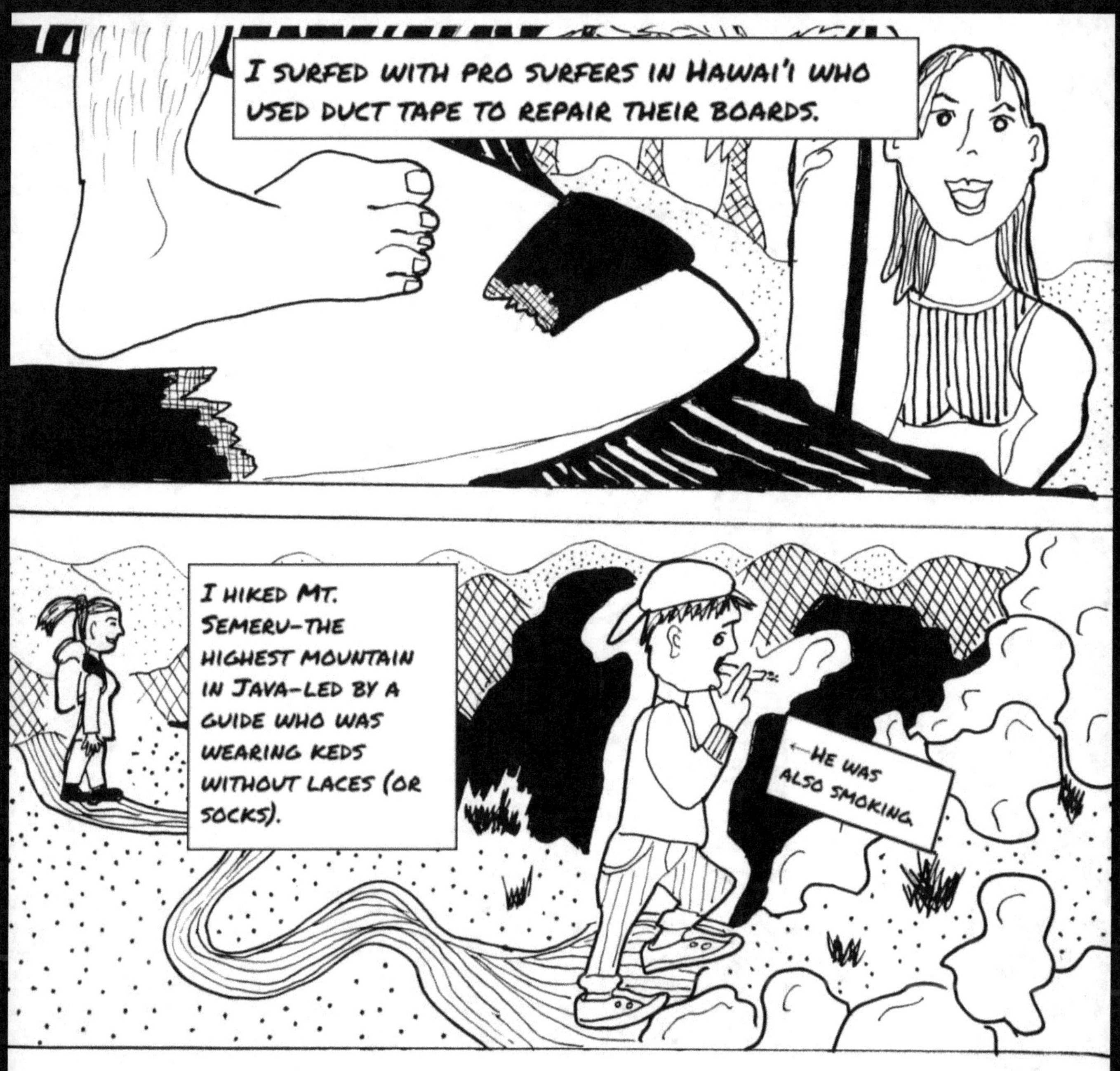

AND HOW ABOUT THE STORY OF MARÍA LORENA RAMIREZ? THE ULTRAMARATHONER WHO WON IN SANDALS AND TURNED DOWN A NIKE DEAL WITH: "EVERYONE WHO WEARS YOUR SHOES IS BEHIND ME."

YESSS!!

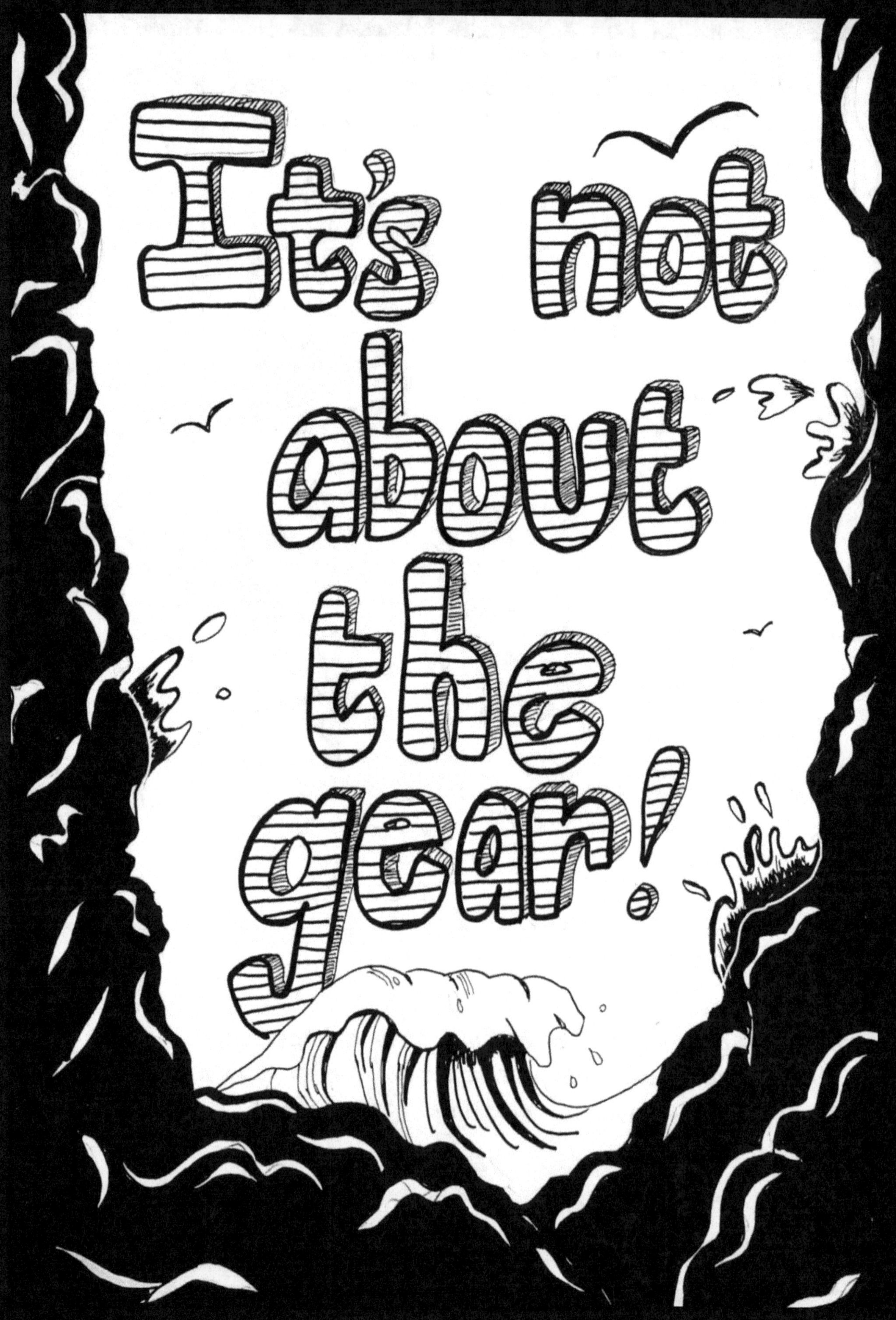
It's not
about
the
gear!

Okay, I realize stating that "it's not about the gear" is a weird way to kick off a book about making outdoor gear. But here's the thing- maybe only a few of the projects in this book appeal to you. If that's the case, skip what you don't need and use the time you saved in the OUTDOORS: take a walk, hug a tree, feel the sun on your face.

BEING OUTSIDE IS WHAT IT'S ABOUT!

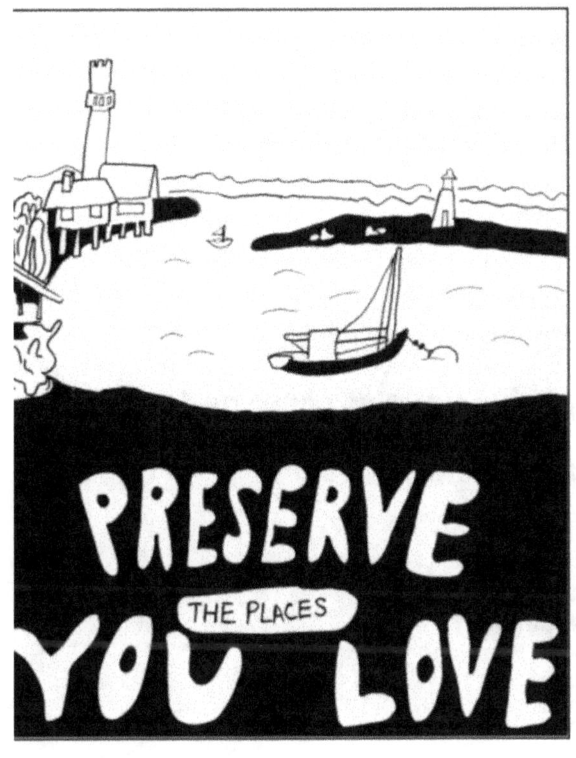

And when it's time to work on some of these projects? Raid your closet and discover forgotten treasures to repair, reuse, or transform. It's basically shopping—without the shopping.

Also, check out my drawings throughout the book of wild places I love. Each is accompanied by quick action tips (with more detailed ideas in the final section of the book). Because—let's face it—admiring nature is wonderful but protecting her is even better!

I wrote this book with love for you. I hope it makes you smile and inspires you to make something useful. If you want to share your creations with me, I'd LOVE to see them—email me at calin@calinduke.com.

Okay, time to hit the waves...now where did I put my duct tape?

Love,
Calin

If you end up LOVING this book (which I hope you do!!) please give a review on any of the following platforms:

Amazon
Ingramspark
Good Reads
Please give five stars and say what you loved.
I appreciate you!

Also, join my newsletter to become a part of the calinduke.com community, get monthly upcycling tips and get free step by step project pages!

HAPPY UPCYCLING!

www.calinduke.com

HOW TO READ THIS BOOK

All projects–some with multiple variations–have been rated to reflect their complexity.

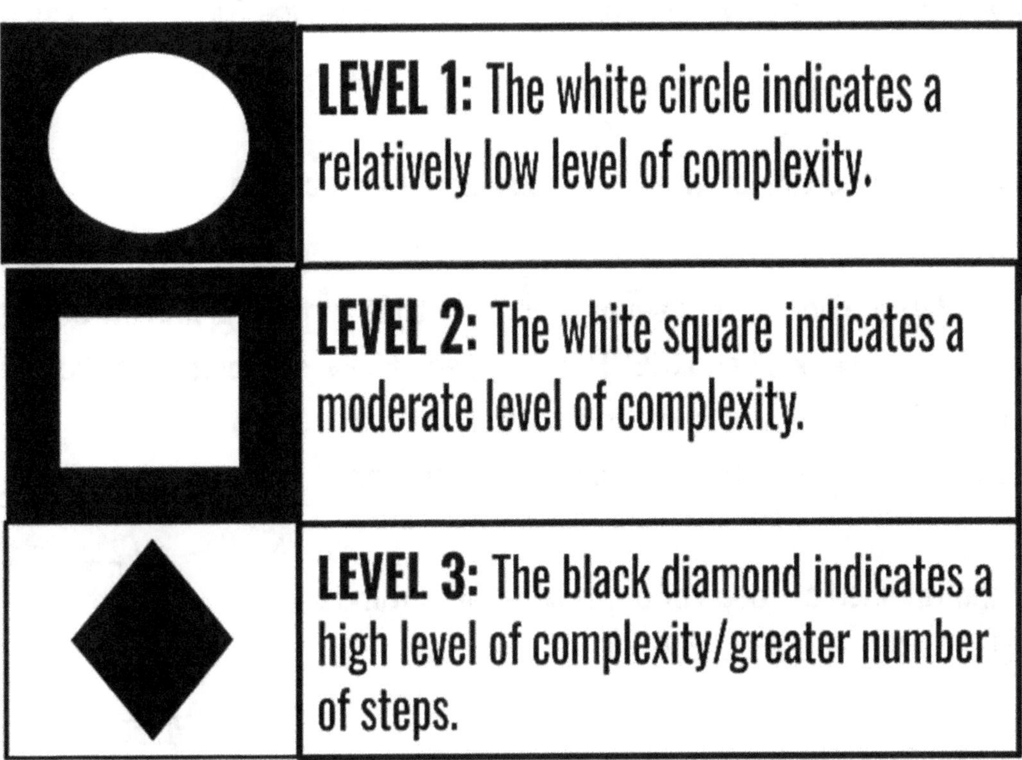

PAIRS NICELY WITH ← You will see this occasionally. This is how I point out other projects that will help you use up your scraps so that you can upcycle AND minimize waste!

Mwha ha ha! You Eco-Warrior, You!

VOCABULARY

BASTING: to hold fabric in place with long loose stitching before sewing down–often done by hand. Basting holds fabric in place more substantially than pinning and is often done with slippery or hard–to–manage fabric at a hem or seam.

CASING: a fabric tunnel where you feed elastic or cording

FREE ARM: the part of the sewing machine that forms the narrow base once the rest of the base has been (GENTLY!) popped off. Every machine is slightly different. Refer to manufacturer instructions if you are not sure how to detach the base of your machine,

HEM: the finished off edge of a garment, oftentimes created by folding fabric over itself.

RAW EDGES: unfinished/unsewn edge of fabric, often left after cutting.

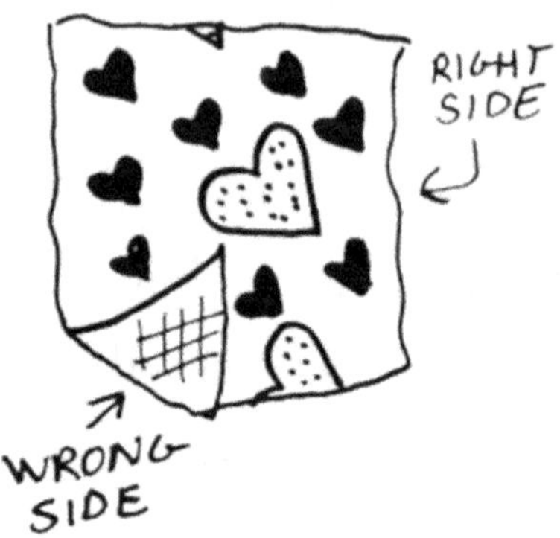

RIGHT SIDE (OF THE FABRIC): the side of the fabric intended to be seen. Think of a bright cotton print or fake fur and "right side" becomes pretty obvious.

SEAM: the stitching holding two (or more) pieces of fabric together. In garments these are usually inside and at the sides.

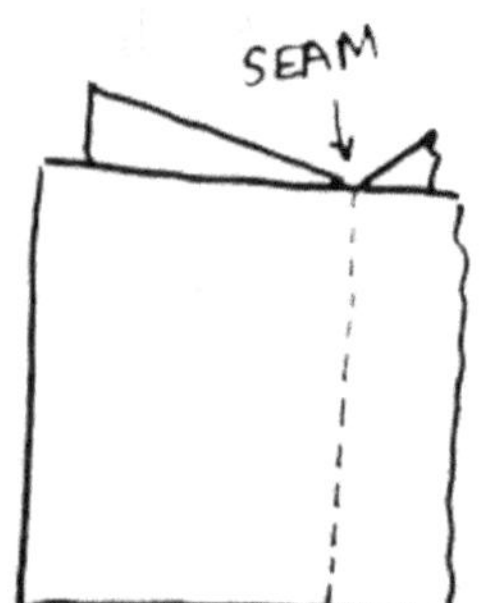

**NOTE: I used to get 'seam' and 'hem' confused for an embarrassingly long time. Give yourself a mnemonic device that works for you (E.G: "<u>seams</u> like there are two pieces of fabric held together here!").

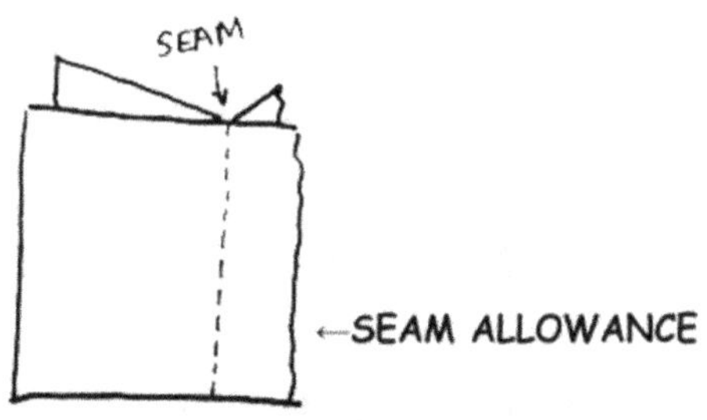

SEAM ALLOWANCE: extra amount of fabric you leave when you cut something so there is enough fabric to make a seam.

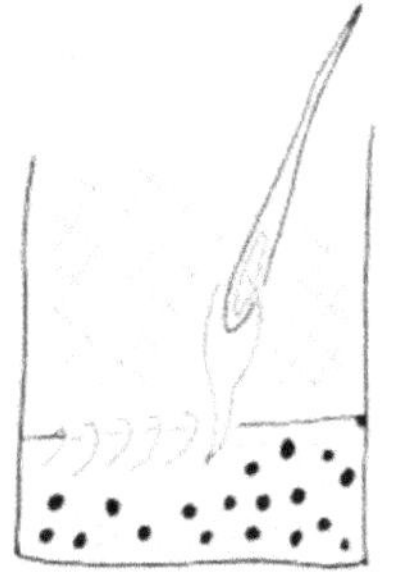

SLIP STITCH: a loose handstitch used to join layers of fabric. A slip stitch is ideally not visible from the right side of the garment.

SEWING SUPPLIES: unless otherwise indicated, this means: Scissors, pins, and either a sewing machine or thread and needle.

TACK: to hold fabric in place or several pieces of fabric together by making one or two stitches by hand. For example, you might fold over a cuff and tack it down to hold it in place.

TAKE IN: to make something smaller by creating a larger seam allowance

TAPER: to sew in a gradual diagonal to meet up with a seam, hem or fabric edge

WHIP STITCH: a handsewn stitch created by sewing around the edge of fabric

WRONG SIDE (OF THE FABRIC): the side of the fabric NOT intended to be seen (although, such a judgey name, no?).

CONTENTS

◁◁ HOW TO MAKE STUFF ▷▷

◁◁ HOW TO CHANGE STUFF ▷▷

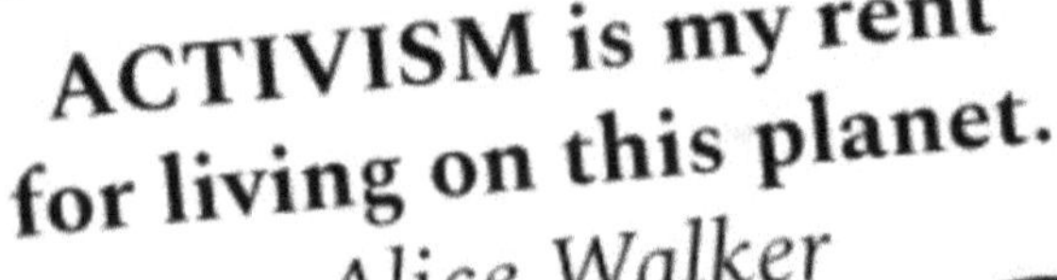

Buy Less,
Choose Well,
Make it Last.
—Vivienne Westwood

Only when the last tree has died and the last river been poisoned and the last fish been caught will we realize we cannot eat money.
—Cree Proverb

This is our last chance.
This is our last dance.
This is ourselves under pressure.
–Freddie Mercury

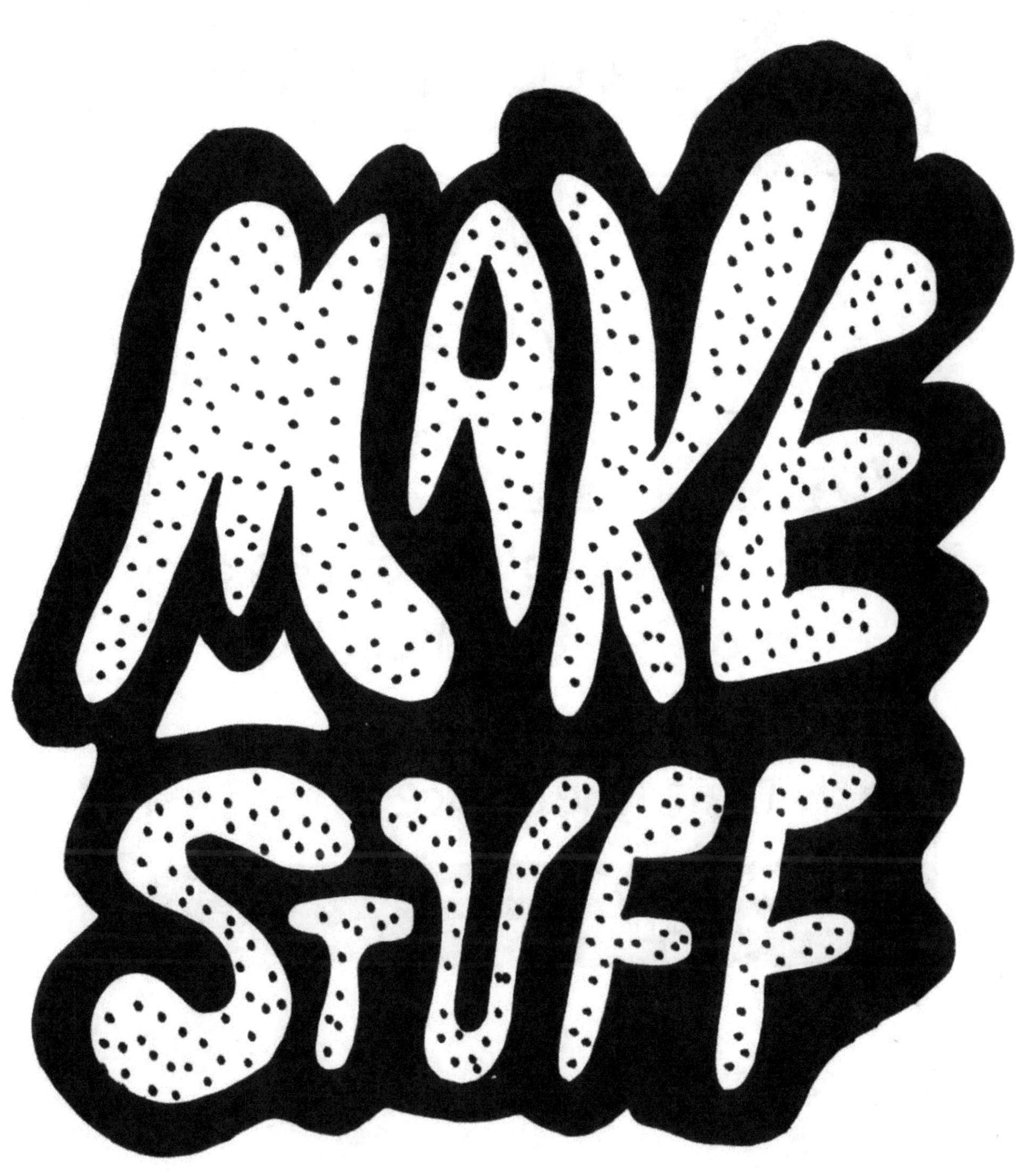
MAKE
STUFF

CROAKIES

Neoprene Shorty Version

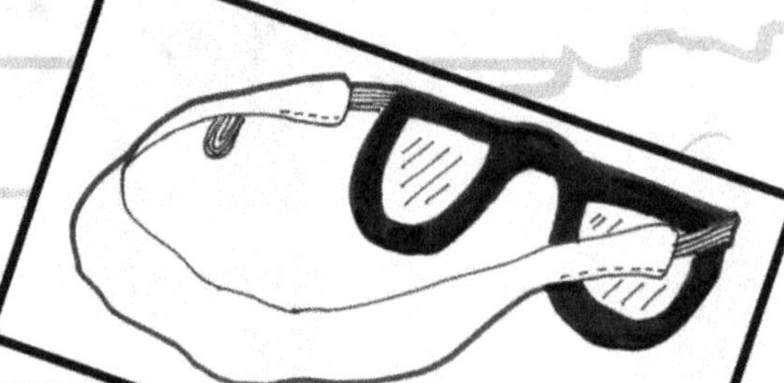

You will need:

- A scrap of neoprene that is 18 inches by 1 inch
- Tape measure

PAIRS NICELY WITH (if using spandex): Level 1 Fanny Pack, Fingerless Gloves, Leggings to Shorts

1

Fold over one end of your scrap about 1.5 inches and pin. With a heavy duty needle sew close to the raw edges. Repeat this on the other side.

1 ½ inches

1 ½ inches

2

Using some muscle, shove the end of your sunglasses into one end of the croakie. Slide it down the sunglasses until the sunglass foot pops out the end of the croakie. Repeat this on the other side.

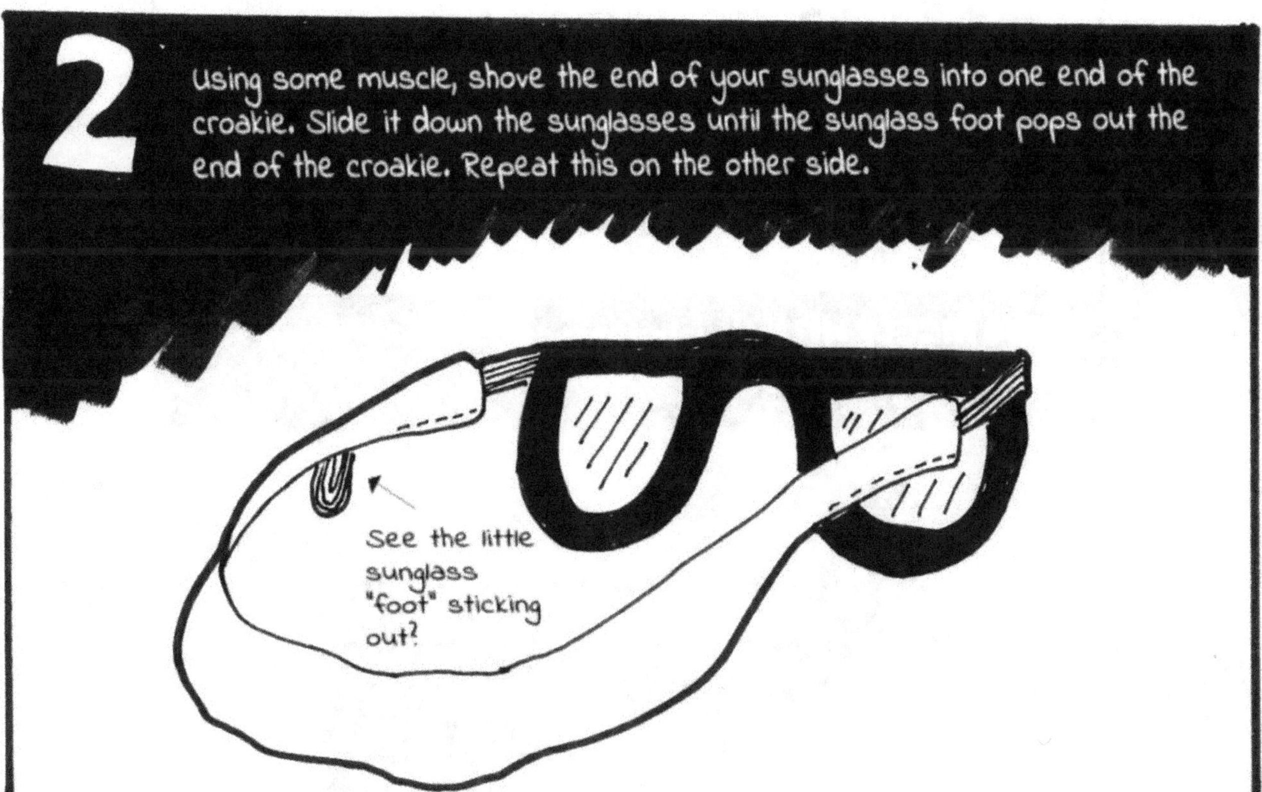

CROAKIES

Long Ropey Version

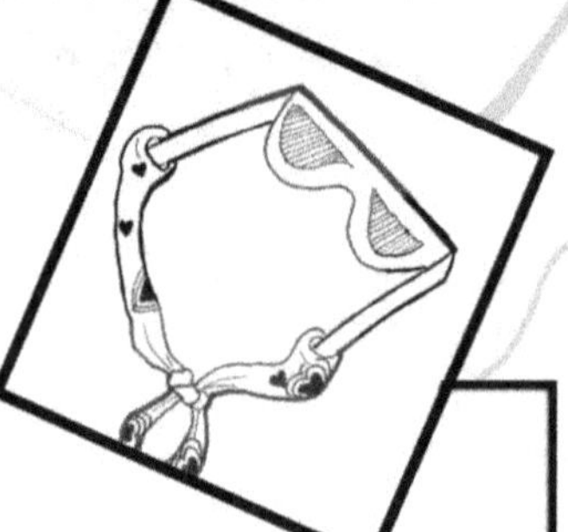

You will need:

- one strip of spandex that is 27 inches long
- A tape measure
- OPTIONAL: big bead with a wide opening

PAIRS NICELY WITH (if using spandex): Level 1 Fanny Pack, Fingerless Gloves, Leggings to Shorts

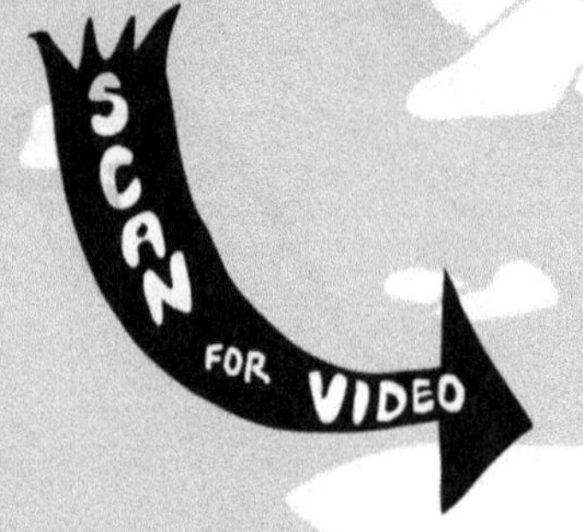

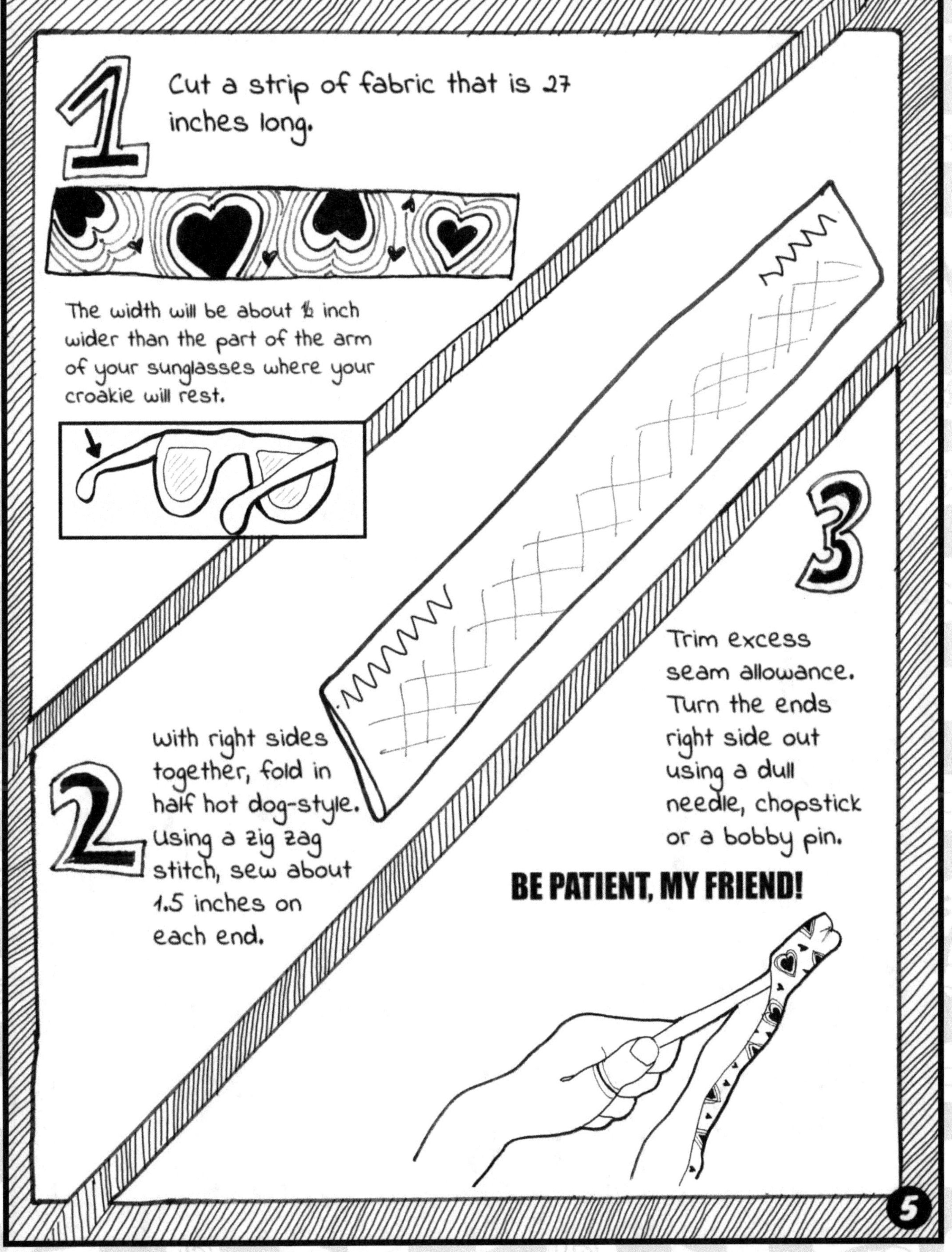
1
Cut a strip of fabric that is 27 inches long.
The width will be about ½ inch wider than the part of the arm of your sunglasses where your croakie will rest.
2
With right sides together, fold in half hot dog-style. Using a zig zag stitch, sew about 1.5 inches on each end.
3
Trim excess seam allowance. Turn the ends right side out using a dull needle, chopstick or a bobby pin.
BE PATIENT, MY FRIEND!

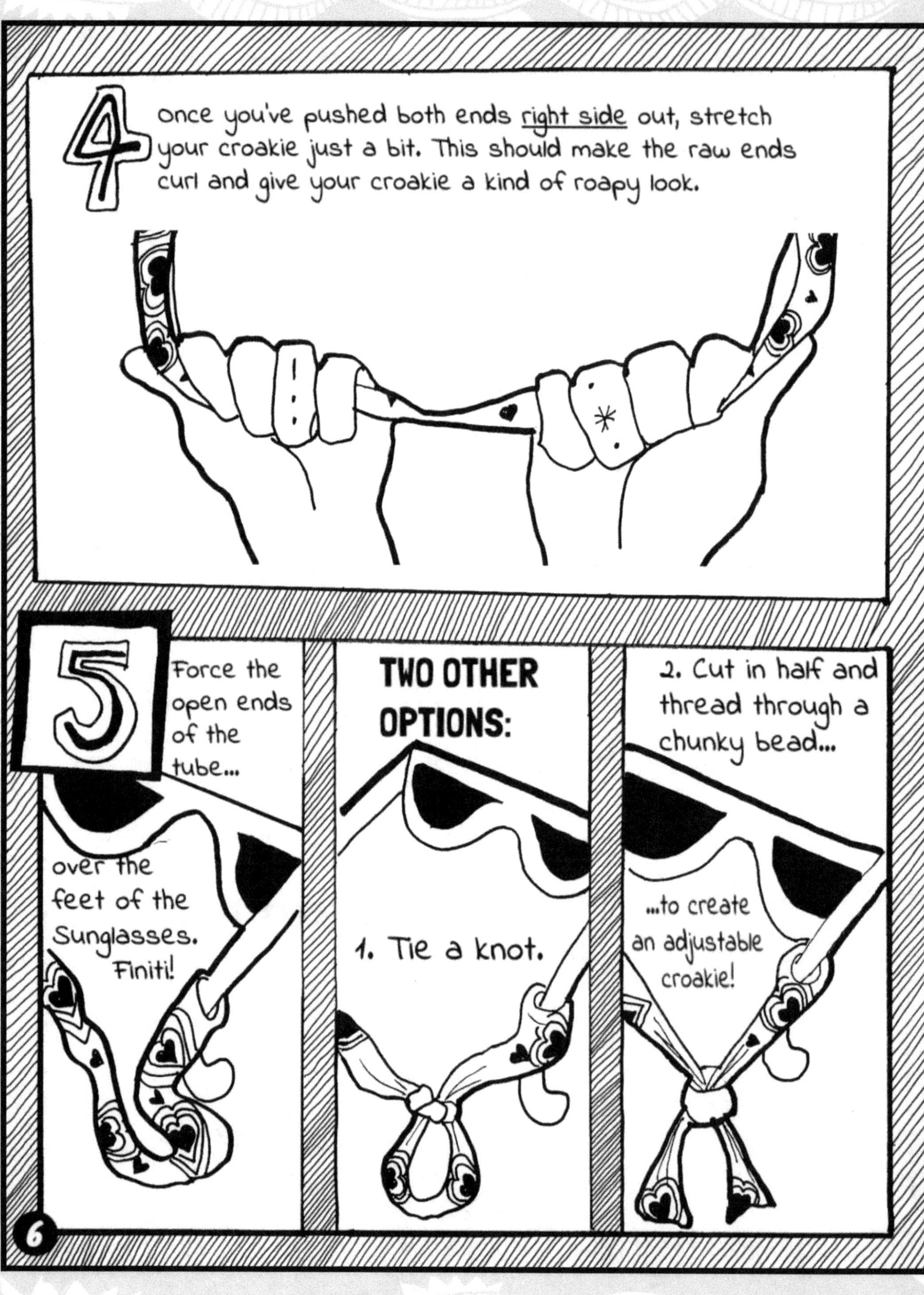
4
once you've pushed both ends right side out, stretch your croakie just a bit. This should make the raw ends curl and give your croakie a kind of roapy look.
5
Force the open ends of the tube...
over the feet of the Sunglasses. Finiti!
TWO OTHER OPTIONS:
1. Tie a knot.
2. Cut in half and thread through a chunky bead...
...to create an adjustable croakie!

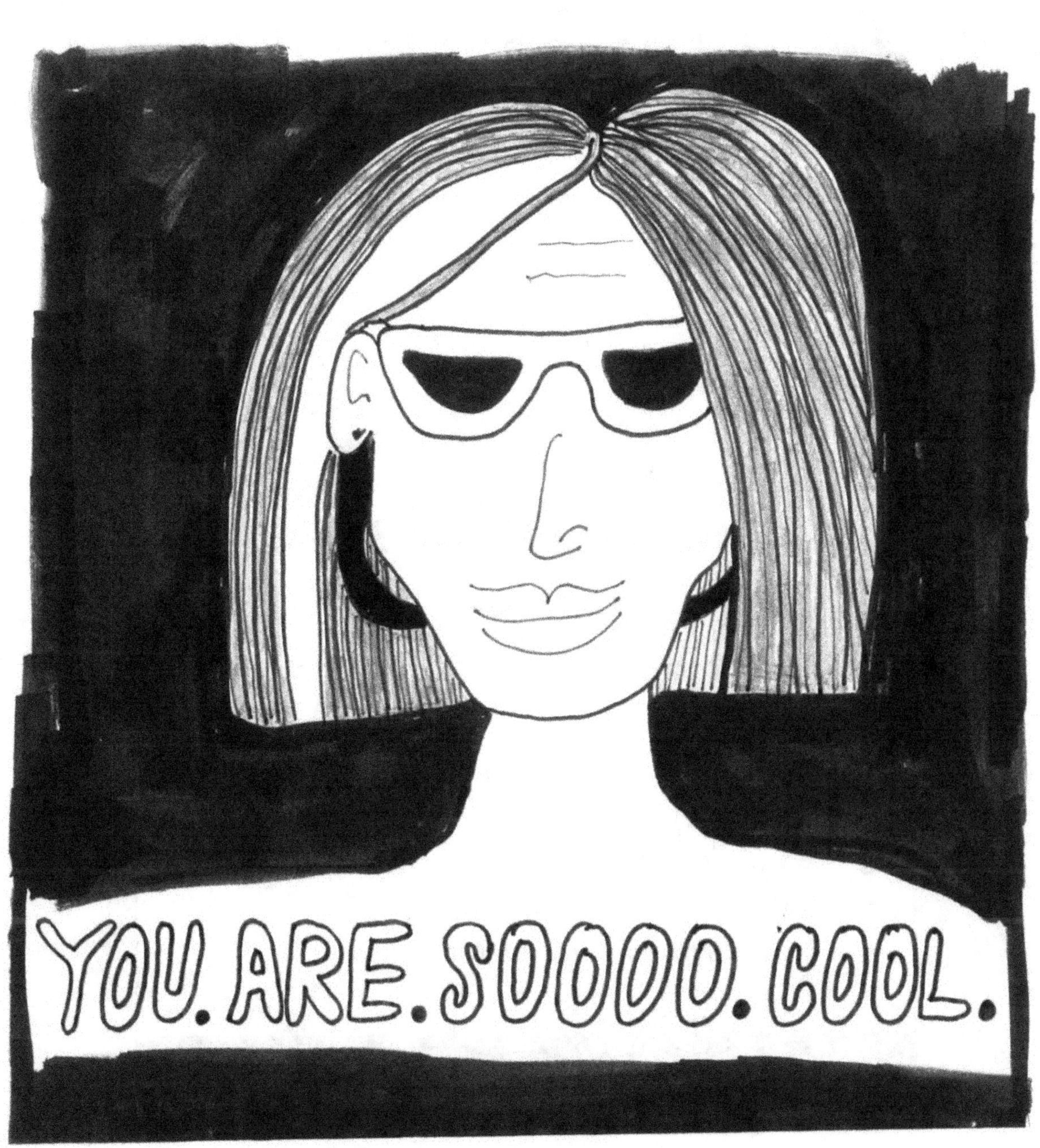
YOU. ARE. SOOOO. COOL.

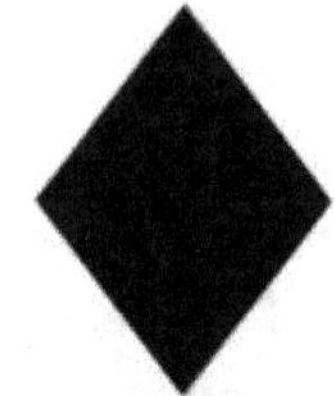

DOG TREAT BAG/ CHALK BAG

You will need:

- A raincoat (canvas, heavy nylon or gortex)
- ½" wide webbing, appx. 12 inches
- Zip tie, boning or any stiff but narrow material that you can bend (a wire hanger?)
- Elastic cording
- A toggle ---->
- Scrap paper
- Seam ripper

OPTIONAL:

- Alternating color of similar fabric
- A compass

PAIRS NICELY WITH: Fanny Pack Level 2

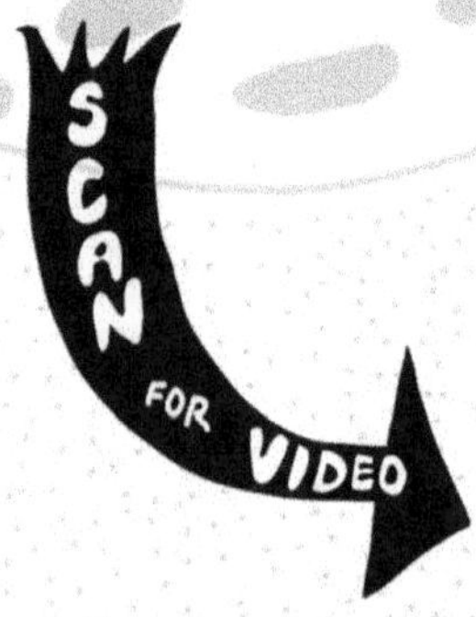

1 Create a circle on scrap paper that is 5 inches in diameter (see the making circles page at the end of this project).

Using your pattern as a guide, cut two of these circles (either from the same fabric or one of each color).

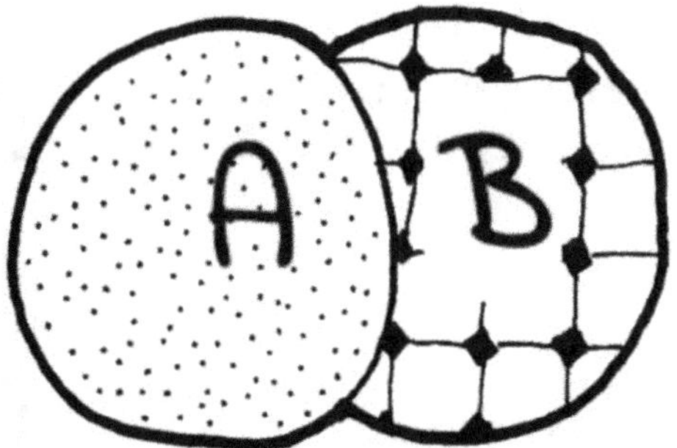

2 From Fabric A cut a rectangle that measures 16 x 7 inches.

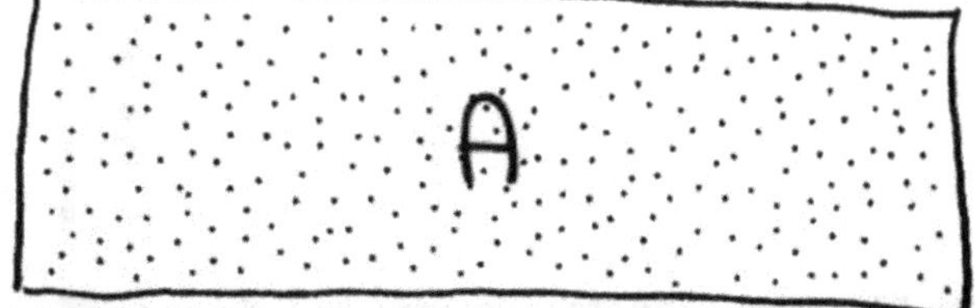

3 From Fabric B cut a rectangle that measures 16 x 11.5 inches. If using only one fabric...cut this piece from that fabric.

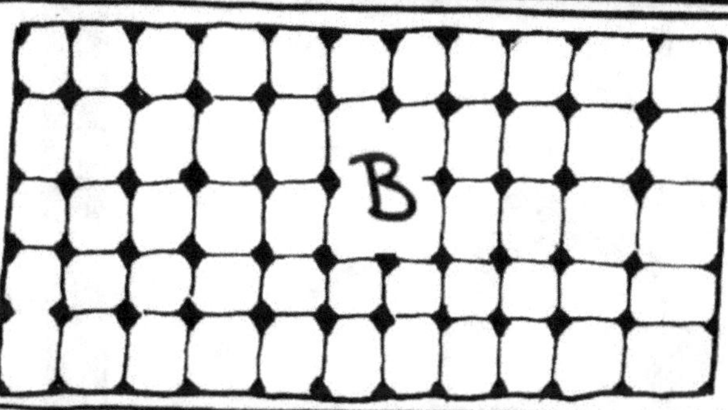

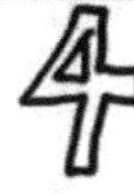

On PIECE A, sew together short ends, right sides together.

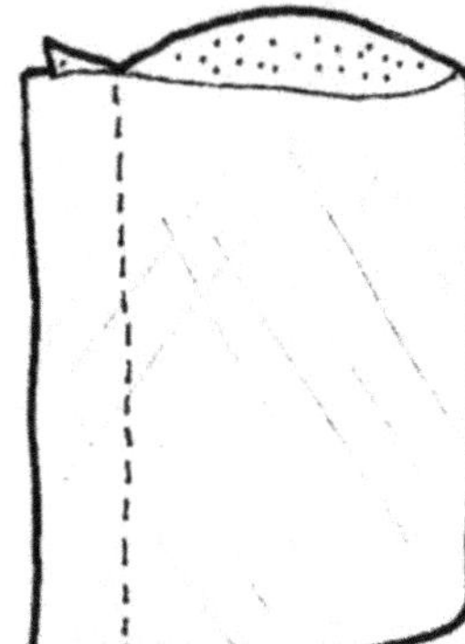

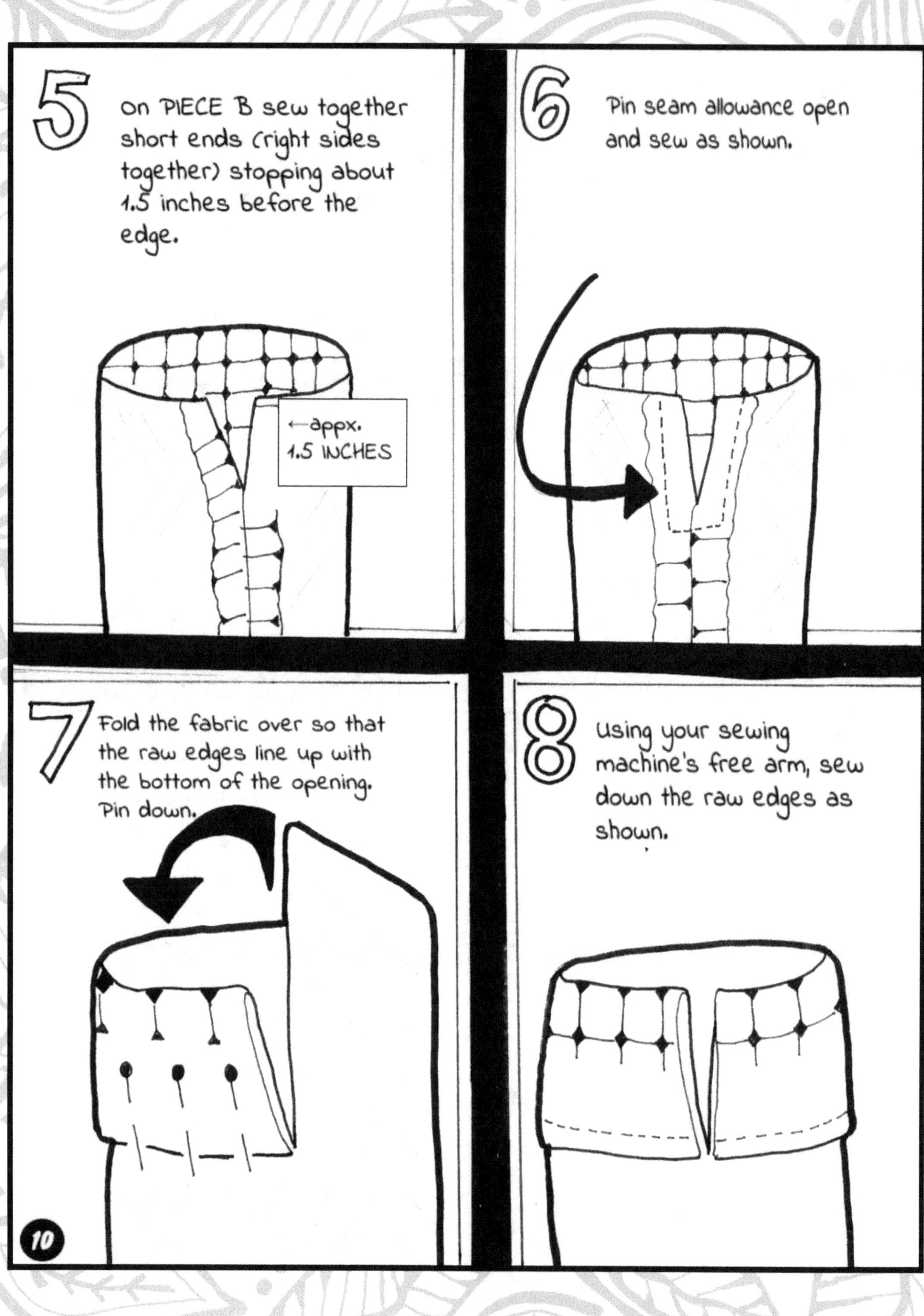
5
On PIECE B sew together short ends (right sides together) stopping about 1.5 inches before the edge.
←appx. 1.5 INCHES
6
Pin seam allowance open and sew as shown.
7
Fold the fabric over so that the raw edges line up with the bottom of the opening. Pin down.
8
Using your sewing machine's free arm, sew down the raw edges as shown.

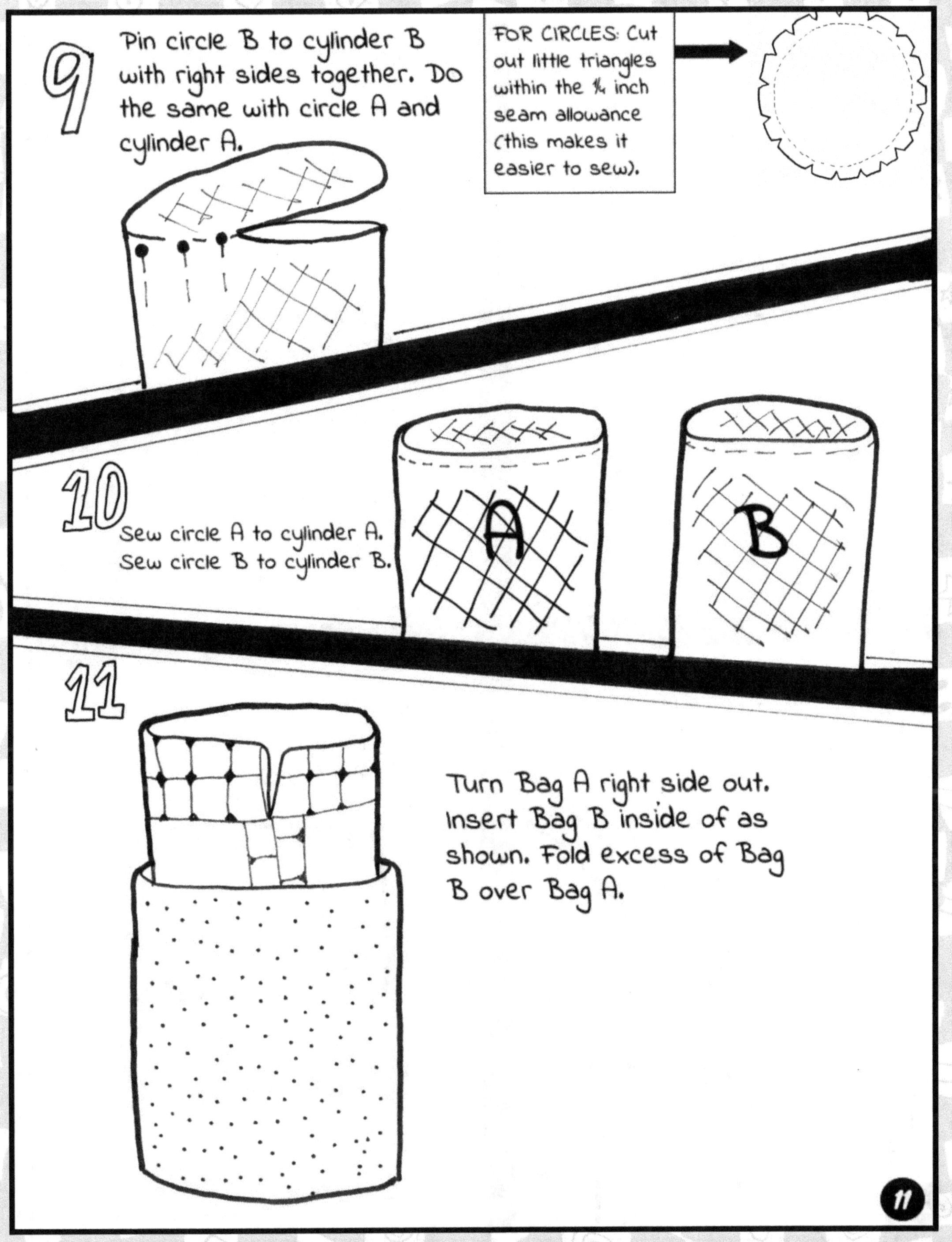
9
Pin circle B to cylinder B with right sides together. Do the same with circle A and cylinder A.
FOR CIRCLES: Cut out little triangles within the ¼ inch seam allowance (this makes it easier to sew).
10
Sew circle A to cylinder A. Sew circle B to cylinder B.
A
B
11
Turn Bag A right side out. Insert Bag B inside of as shown. Fold excess of Bag B over Bag A.

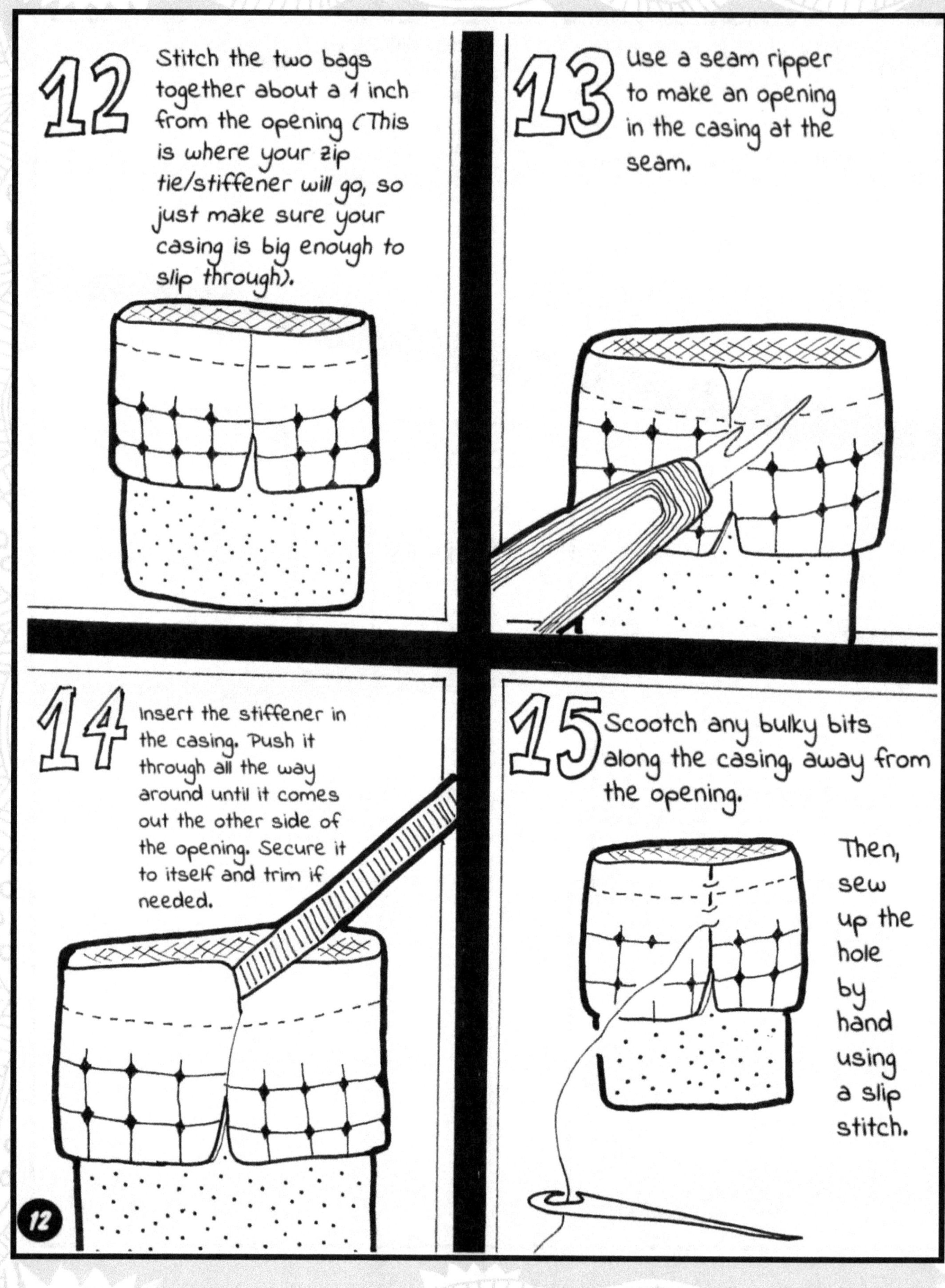
12
Stitch the two bags together about a 1 inch from the opening (This is where your zip tie/stiffener will go, so just make sure your casing is big enough to slip through).
13
Use a seam ripper to make an opening in the casing at the seam.
14
Insert the stiffener in the casing. Push it through all the way around until it comes out the other side of the opening. Secure it to itself and trim if needed.
15
Scootch any bulky bits along the casing, away from the opening.
Then, sew up the hole by hand using a slip stitch.

16 Now sew the folded over bit of Bag B to Bag A as close to the edge as possible.

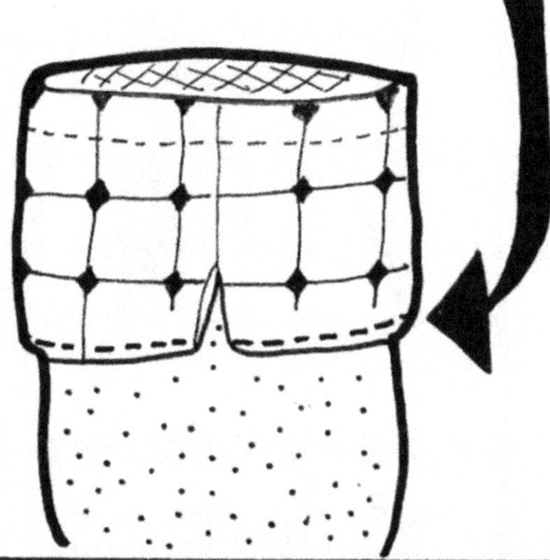

17 Insert the elastic into the casing until it comes out the other side.

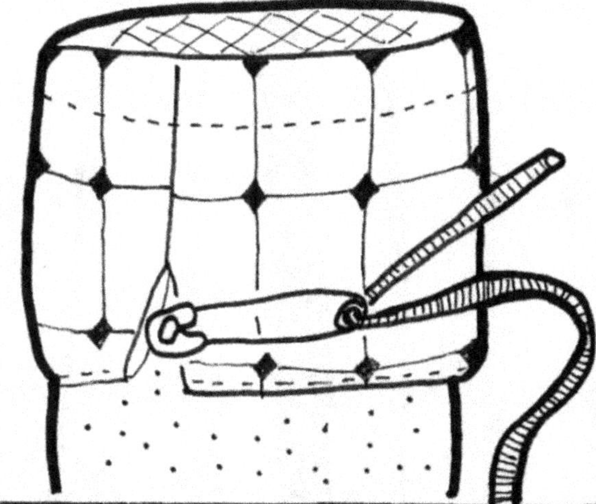

18 Insert both ends of the elastic into a little toggle thing-y until they come out the other side. Don't stretch the elastic as you do this-keep it as loose as possible.

19 Tie the ends together in a double knot.

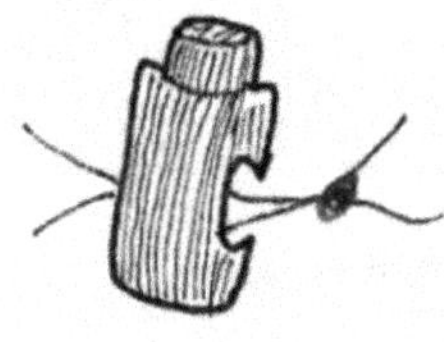

SEWING THE LOOP

20 Sew down the ends of your webbing using a zig zag stitch.

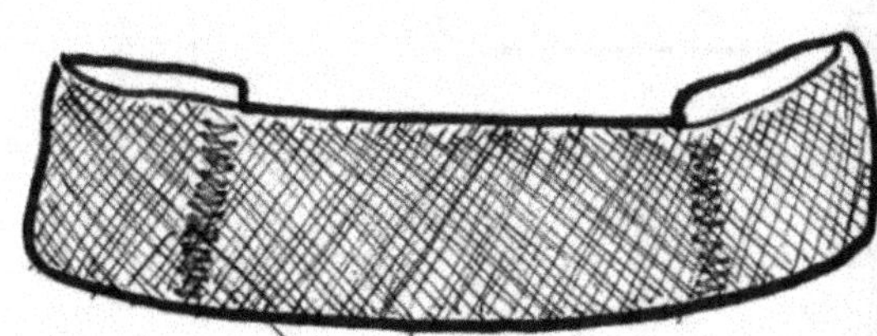

21 Sew the ends of the webbing together, sandwiching the bag in between them.

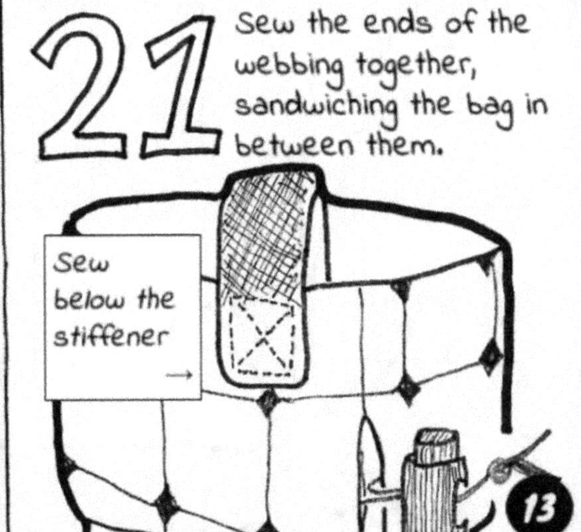

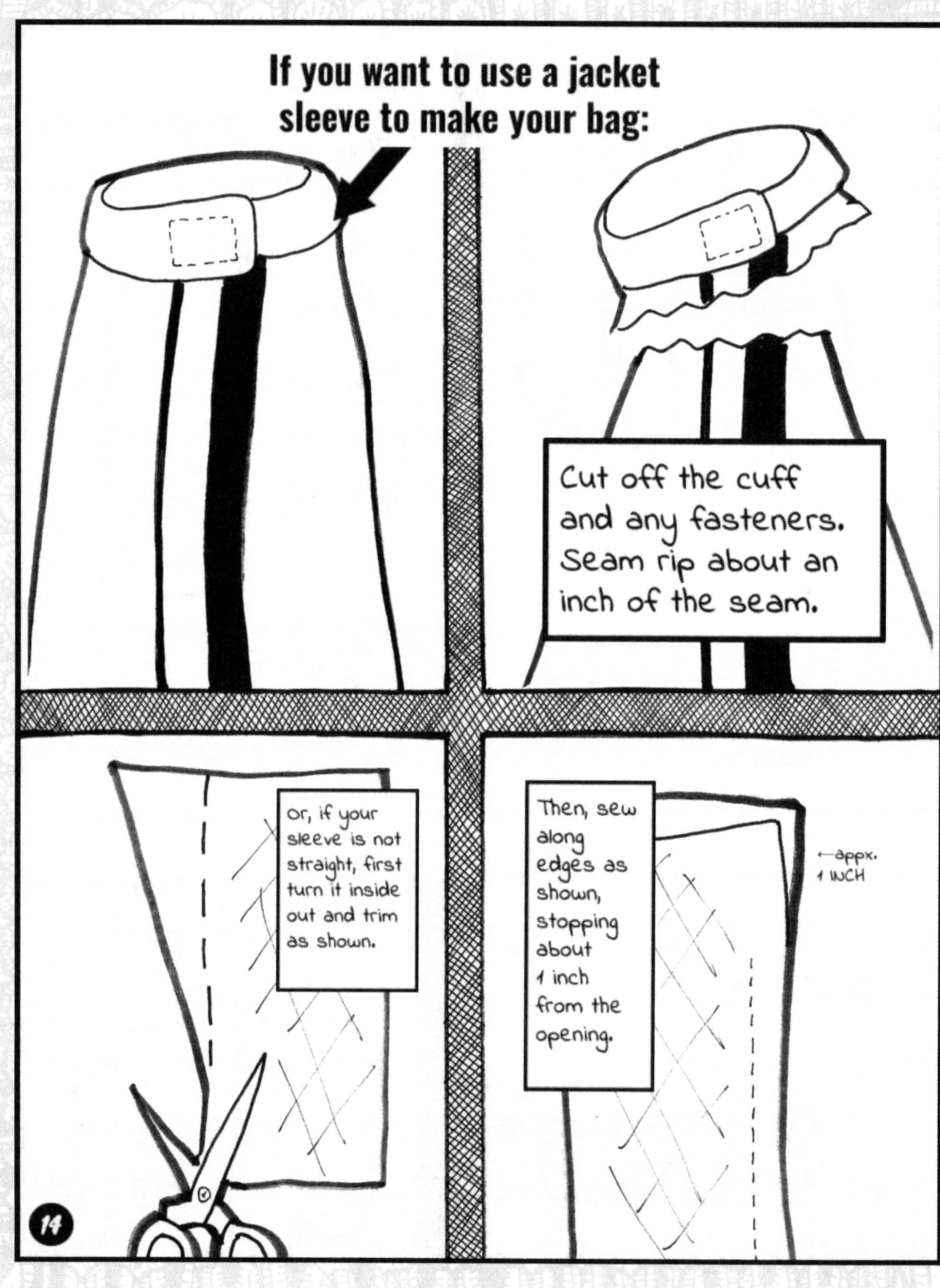
If you want to use a jacket sleeve to make your bag:
Cut off the cuff and any fasteners. Seam rip about an inch of the seam.
Or, if your sleeve is not straight, first turn it inside out and trim as shown.
Then, sew along edges as shown, stopping about 1 inch from the opening.
←appx. 1 INCH

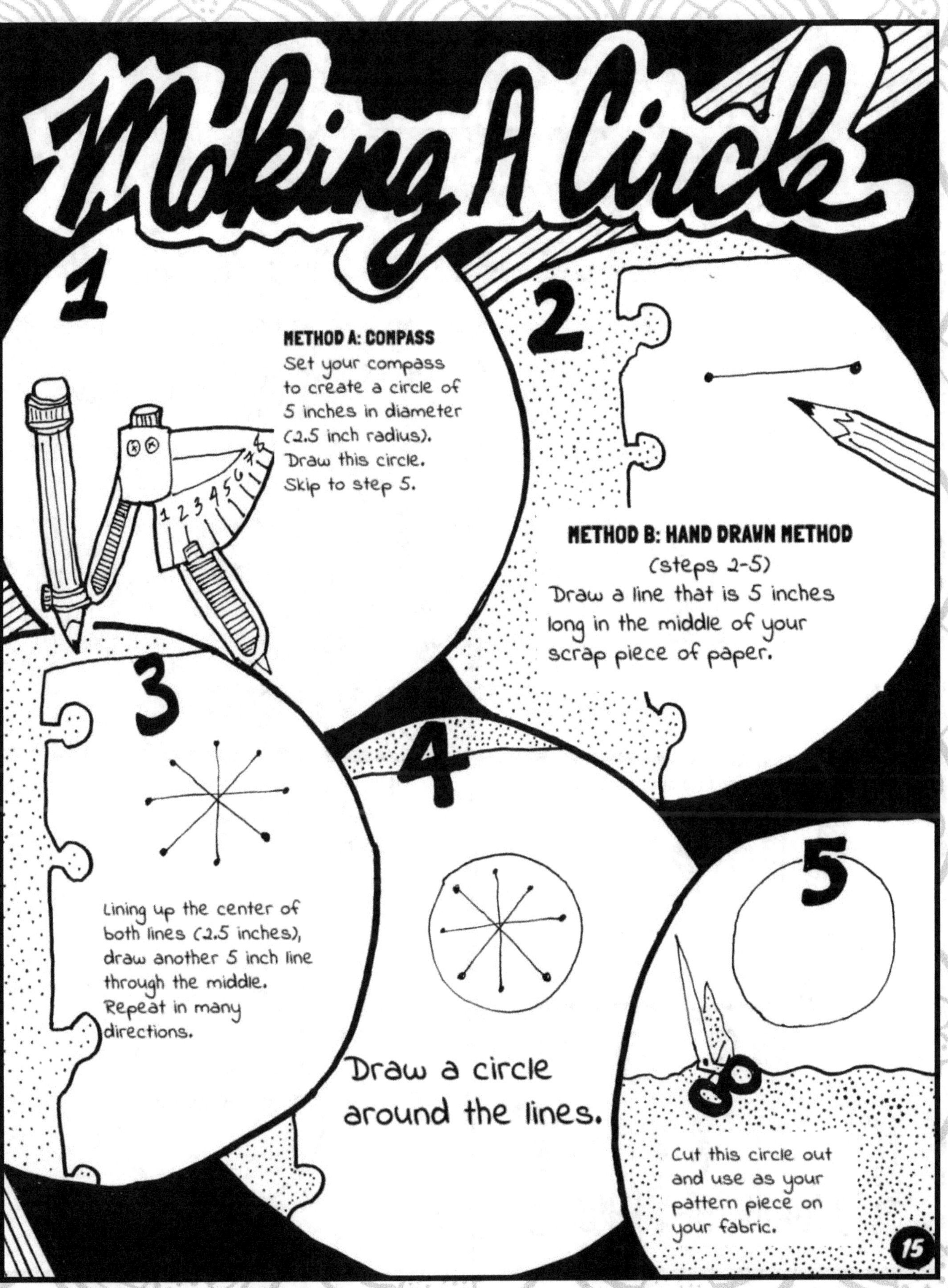
Making A Circle
1
METHOD A: COMPASS
Set your compass to create a circle of 5 inches in diameter (2.5 inch radius). Draw this circle. Skip to step 5.
2
METHOD B: HAND DRAWN METHOD
(steps 2-5)
Draw a line that is 5 inches long in the middle of your scrap piece of paper.
3
Lining up the center of both lines (2.5 inches), draw another 5 inch line through the middle. Repeat in many directions.
4
Draw a circle around the lines.
5
Cut this circle out and use as your pattern piece on your fabric.

How to CALCULATE THE CIRCLE PATTERN PIECE FOR ANY CYLINDER PROJECT

1. How big around do you want your cylindrical shape to be? ***(Write this number down!)***

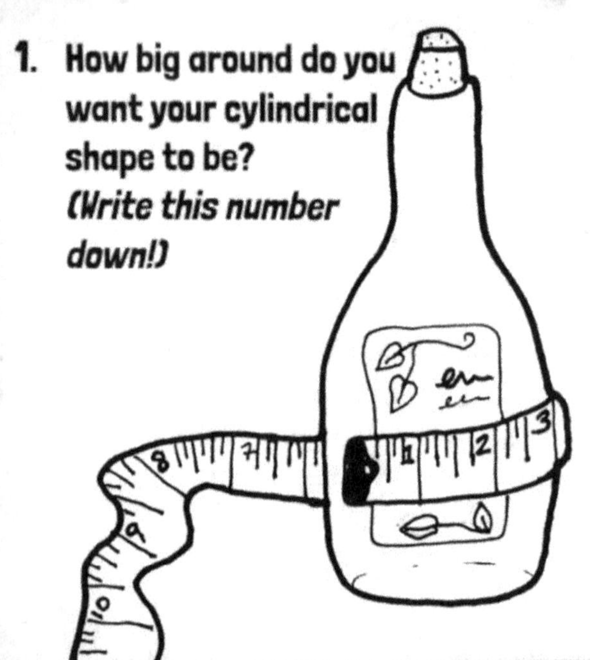

2. To find the diameter of the circle: Divide the number from STEP 1 by 3.14 ***(remember your old friend pi from high school math?).***

3. Type the following into any search engine:

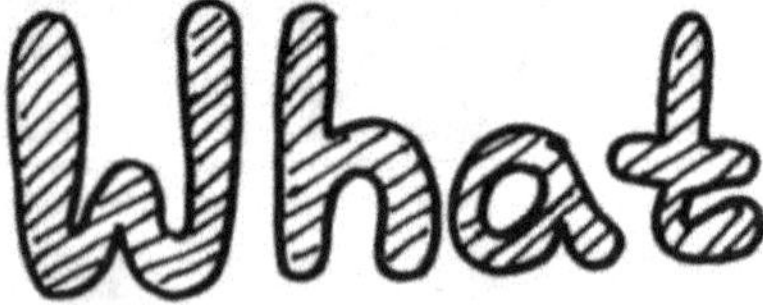

is ______ (your weird number from STEP 2)

as a

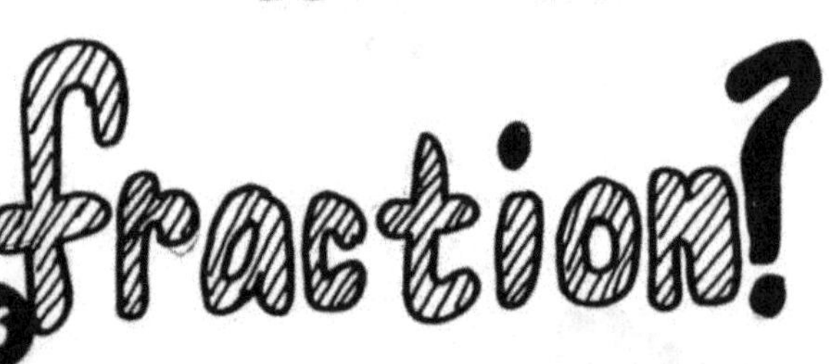

4. Draw a circle with a diameter as close to the answer in STEP 3 as possible.

THIS IS YOUR CIRCLE PATTERN PIECE!

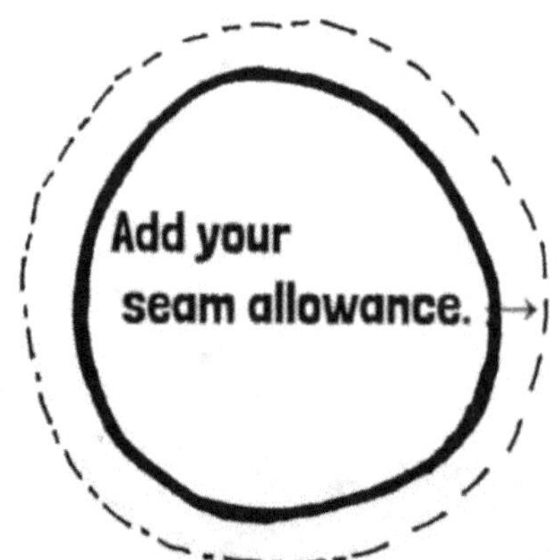

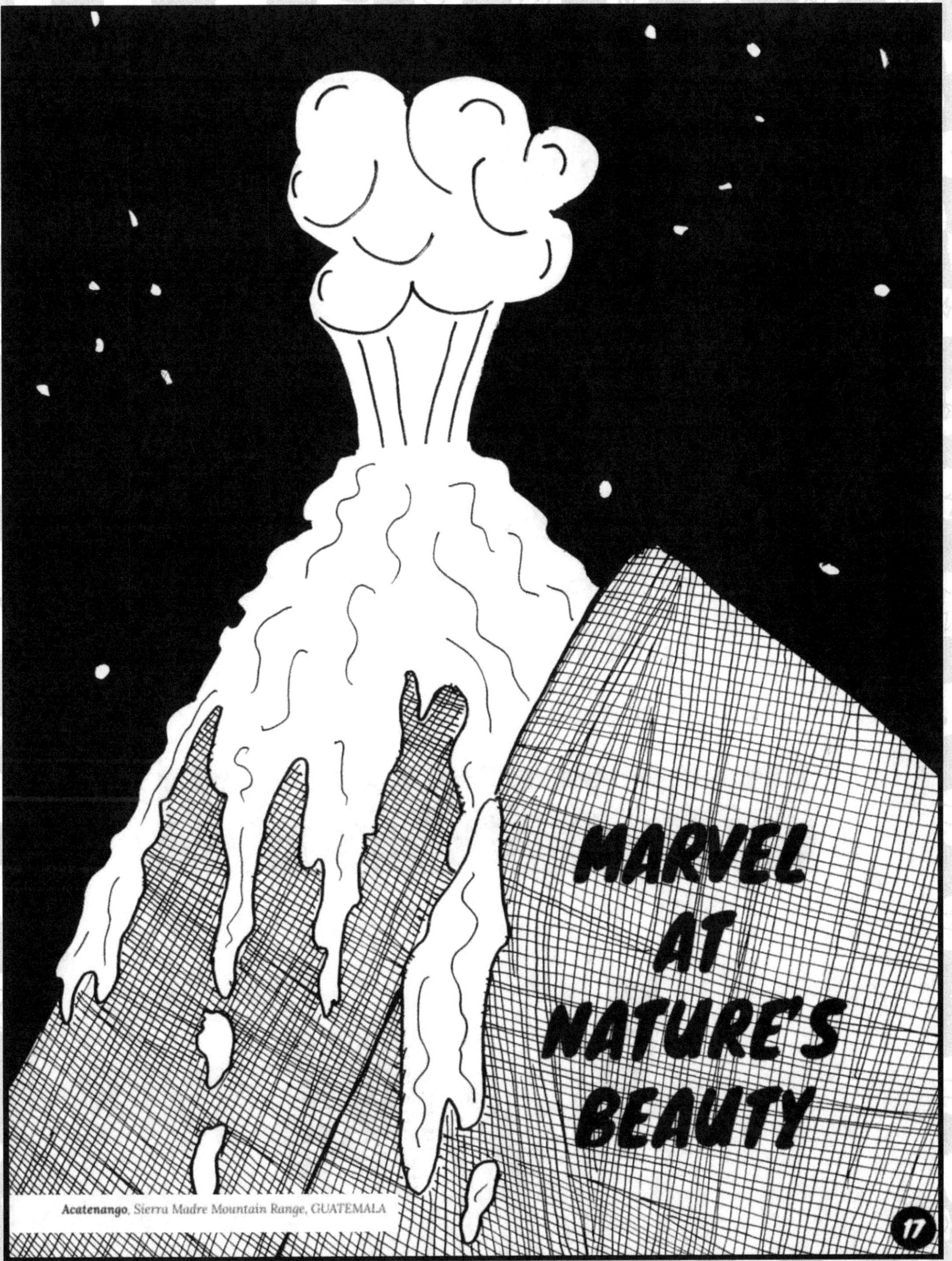

***Acatenango**, Sierra Madre Mountain Range, GUATEMALA*

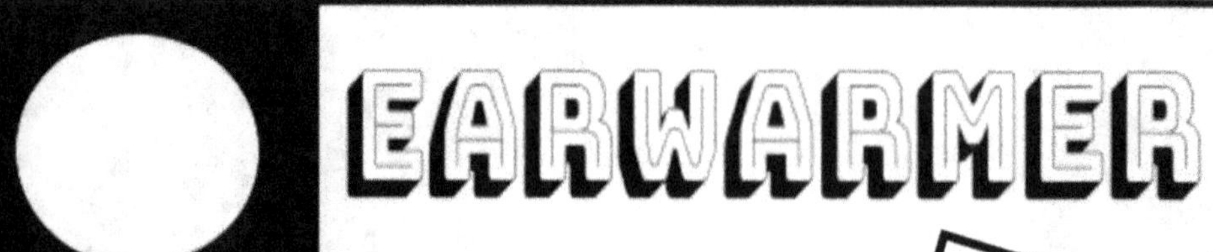

EARWARMER

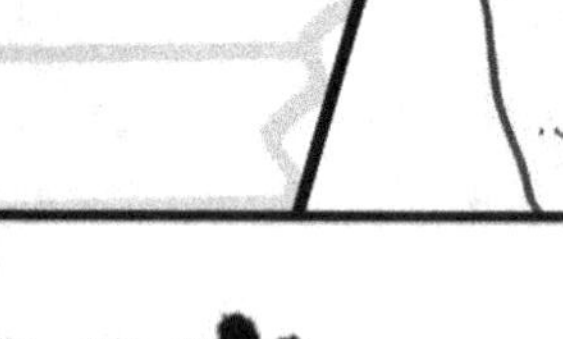

You will need:

- An upcycled sweater (preferably wool)
- A tape measure

PAIRS NICELY WITH: MITTENS-*If your sweater is big enough*

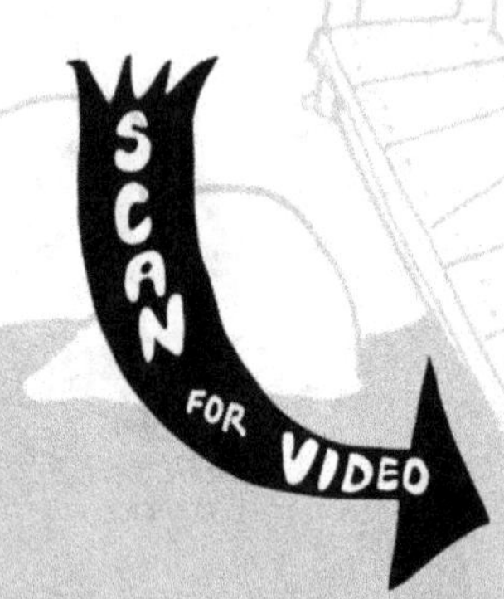

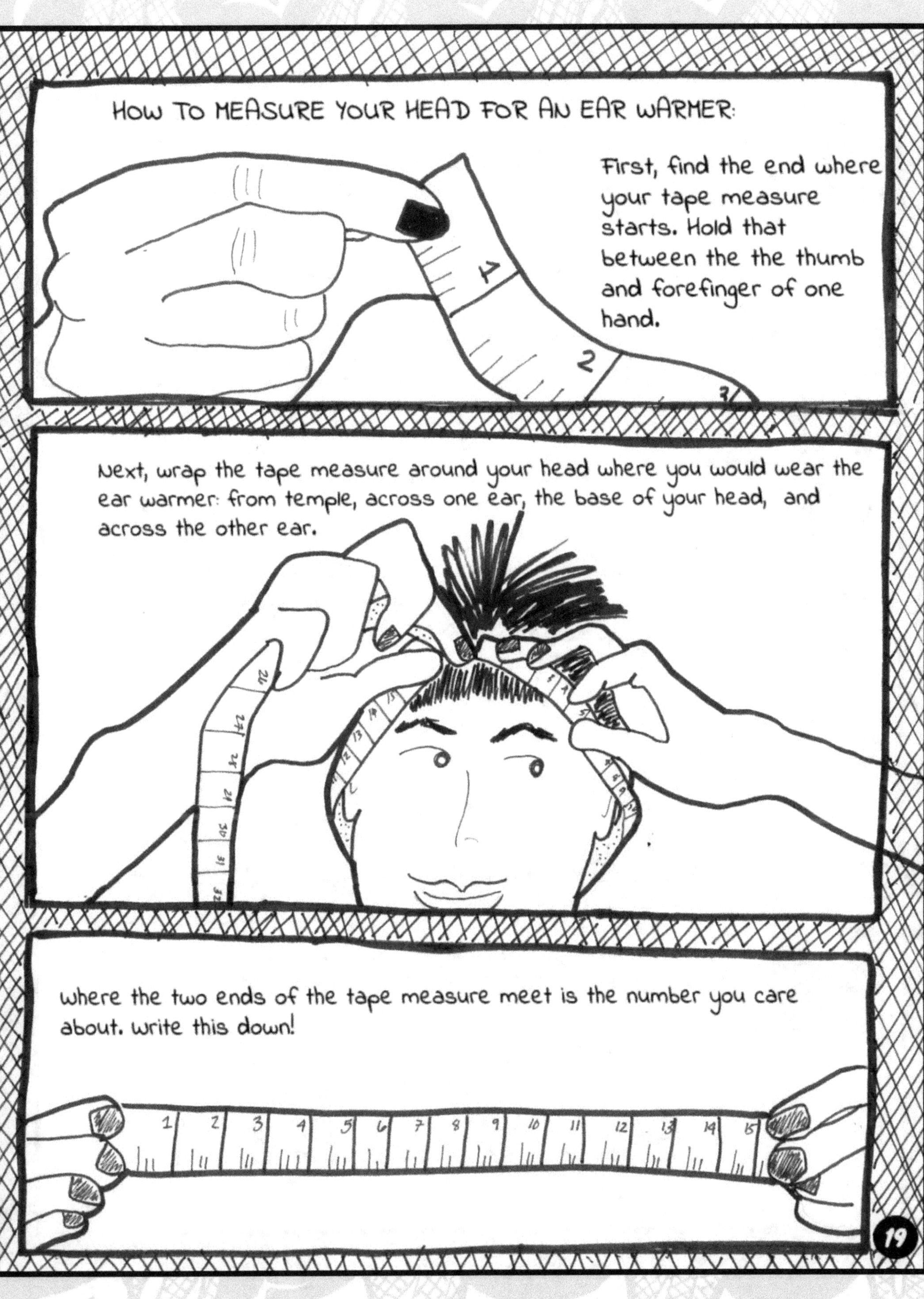
HOW TO MEASURE YOUR HEAD FOR AN EAR WARMER:
First, find the end where your tape measure starts. Hold that between the the thumb and forefinger of one hand.
Next, wrap the tape measure around your head where you would wear the ear warmer: from temple, across one ear, the base of your head, and across the other ear.
where the two ends of the tape measure meet is the number you care about. write this down!

1

Cut a strip out of your sweater that is 11 inches wide and the length from page 19.

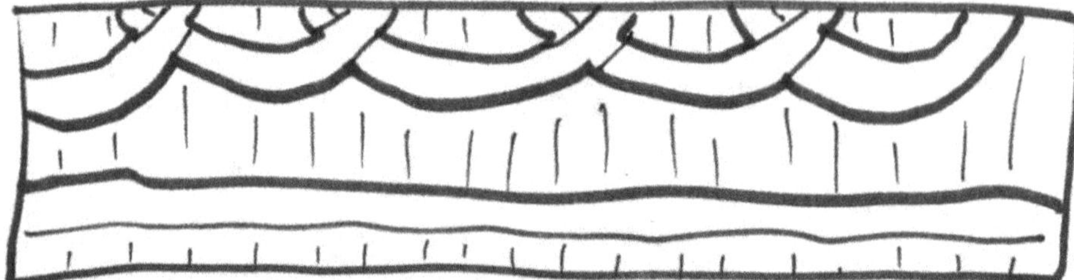

2

With right sides together, fold in half hot dog-style.
Stitch together across the long end, leaving about 1 inch on either end unsewn.

3

With right sides together, sew the short ends together.

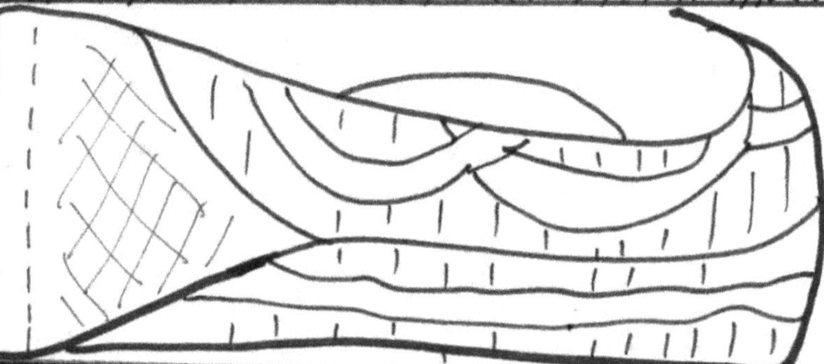

4

To make the seam lay flat, iron the seam open on a gentle setting. You should now have something that looks like this almost-done ear warmer.

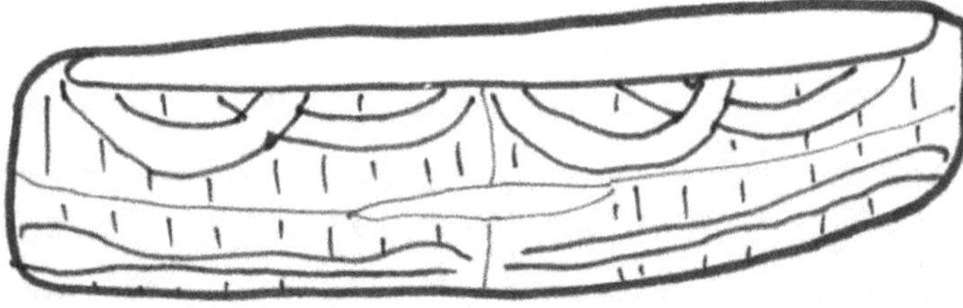

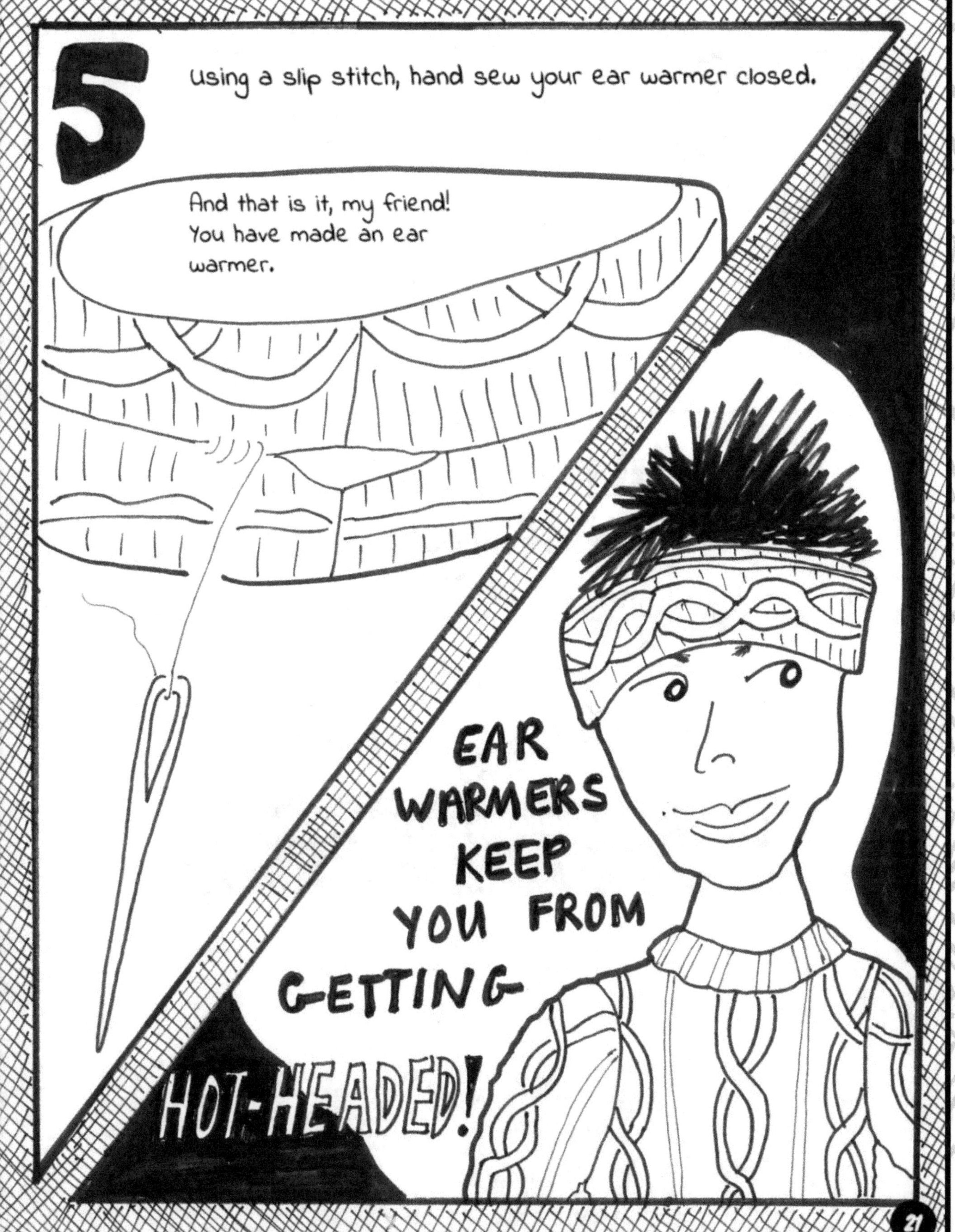
5
Using a slip stitch, hand sew your ear warmer closed.
And that is it, my friend!
You have made an ear
warmer.
EAR
WARMERS
KEEP
YOU FROM
GETTING
HOT-HEADED!

FANNY PACK

Flat

You will need:

- A pair of leggings or polyester sports jersey that fit you or are just slightly larger

PAIRS NICELY WITH: CROAKIES Level 2, FINGERLESS GLOVES

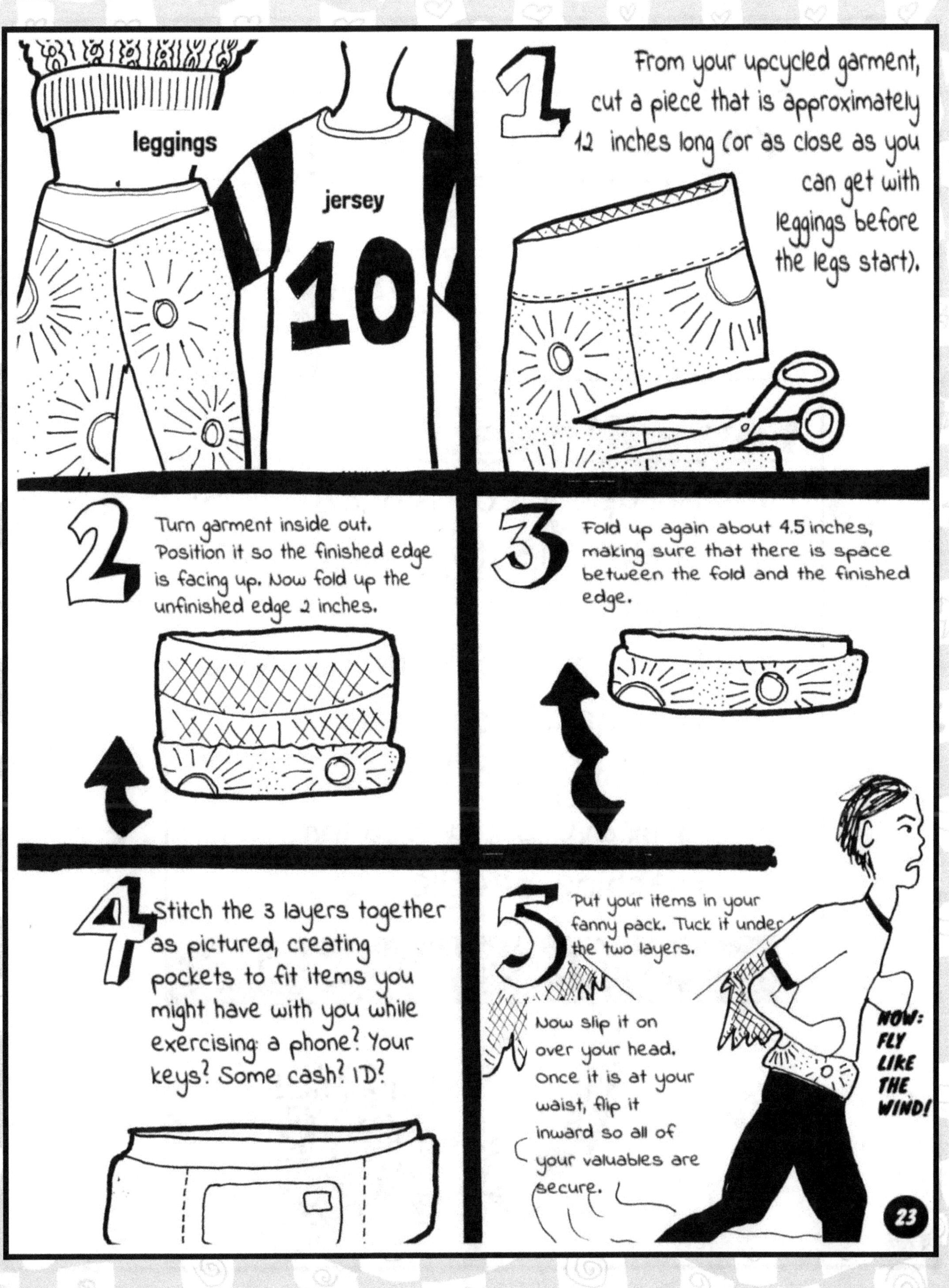
leggings
jersey
10
1
From your upcycled garment, cut a piece that is approximately 12 inches long (or as close as you can get with leggings before the legs start).
2
Turn garment inside out. Position it so the finished edge is facing up. Now fold up the unfinished edge 2 inches.
3
Fold up again about 4.5 inches, making sure that there is space between the fold and the finished edge.
4
Stitch the 3 layers together as pictured, creating pockets to fit items you might have with you while exercising: a phone? Your keys? Some cash? ID?
5
Put your items in your fanny pack. Tuck it under the two layers.
Now slip it on over your head. Once it is at your waist, flip it inward so all of your valuables are secure.
NOW: FLY LIKE THE WIND!

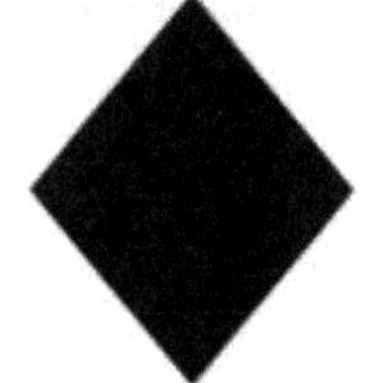

FANNY PACK

Deeper

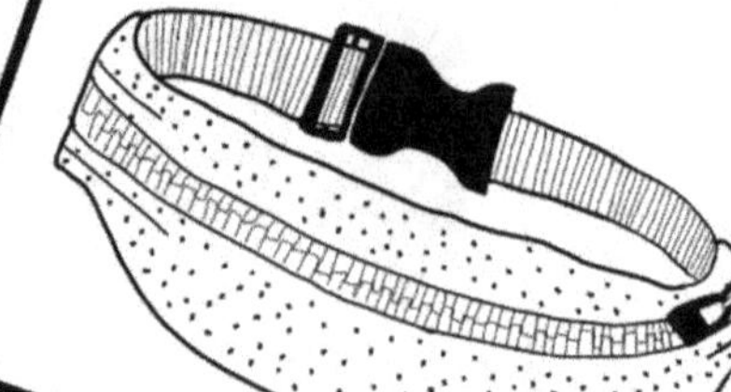

You will need:

- An upcycled raincoat (nylon, ripstop, gortex all work great)
- An upcycled belt that fits you or 2 inch wide webbing and buckle
- A heavy duty sewing machine needle

PAIRS NICELY WITH: DOG TREAT BAG/ CHALK BAG

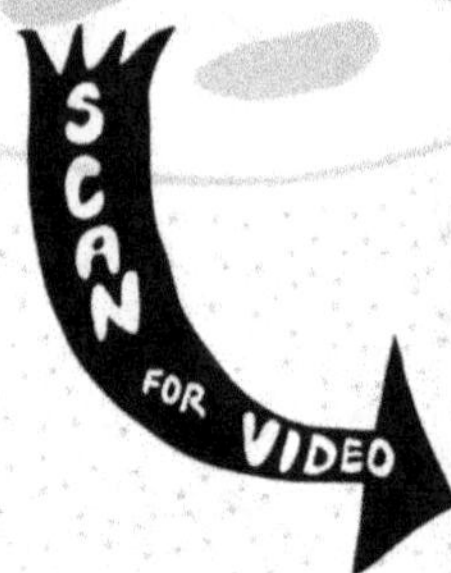

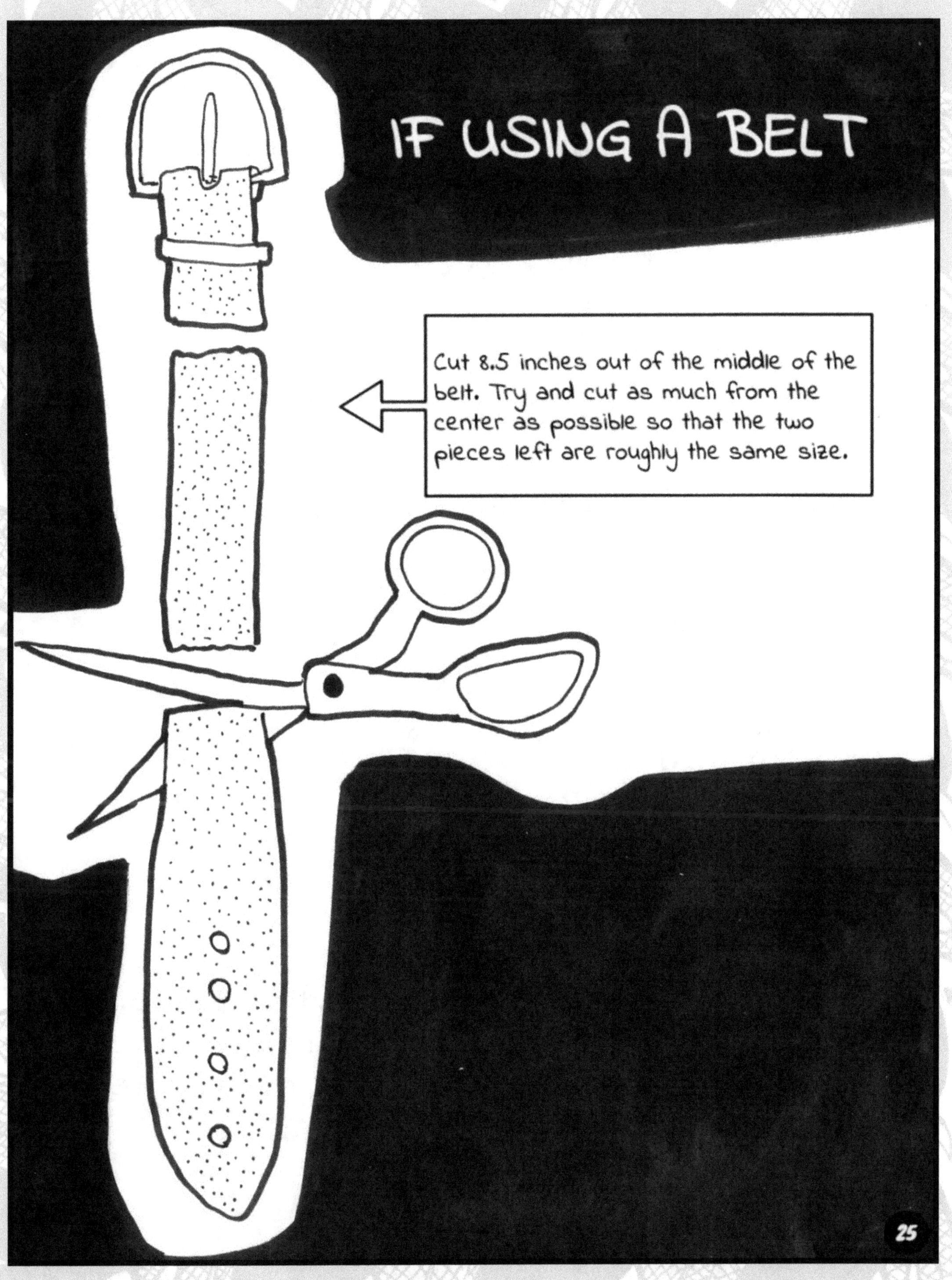
IF USING A BELT
Cut 8.5 inches out of the middle of the belt. Try and cut as much from the center as possible so that the two pieces left are roughly the same size.

1

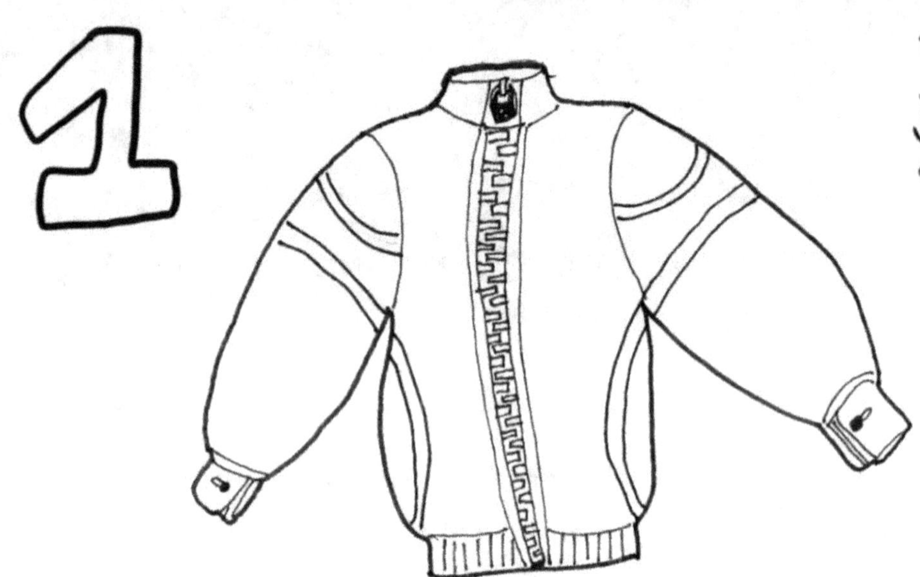

Zip up your jacket and lay it flat.

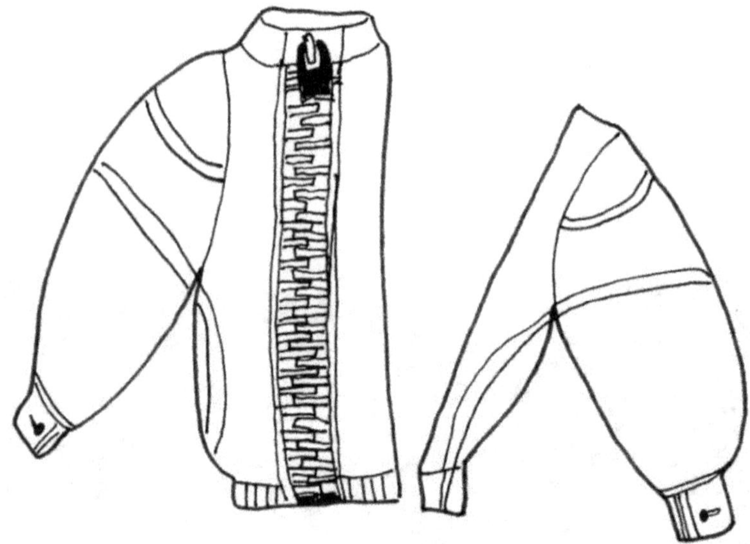

2

Cut through both the front and the back 5.5 inches on the right side of the zipper. If you have a rotary cutter and mat, now is a great time to use it!

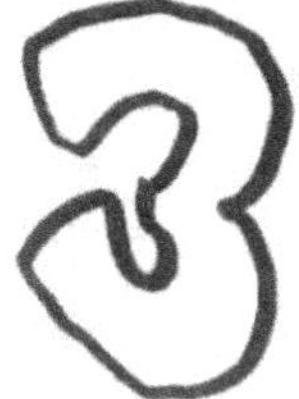

Checking that the front and back are still lined up straight, cut another 1 inch from the left of the zipper.

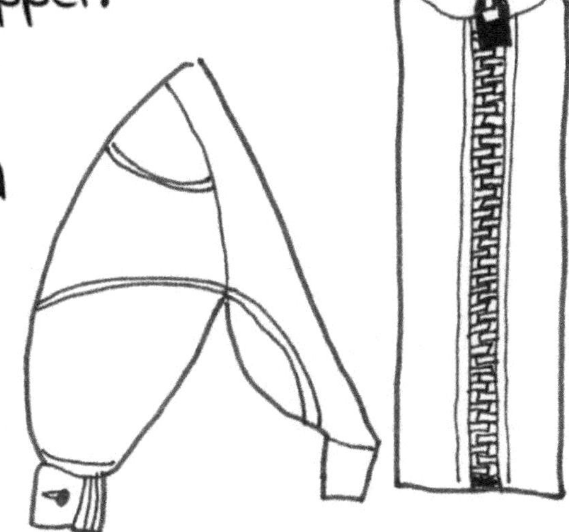

Again, cutting through both the front and the back of the jacket.

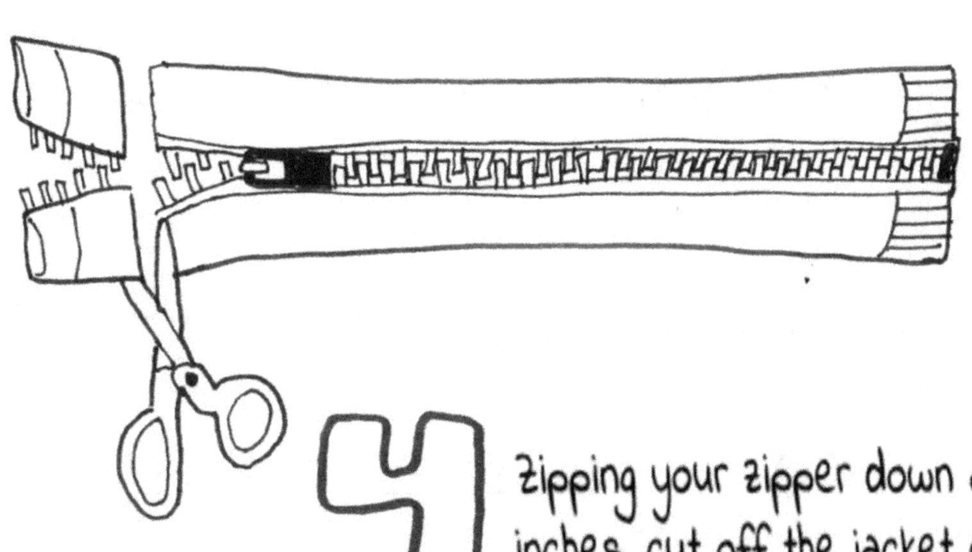

4

Zipping your zipper down a few inches, cut off the jacket collar to make a straight edge about 10.5 inches from any ribbing or waistband.

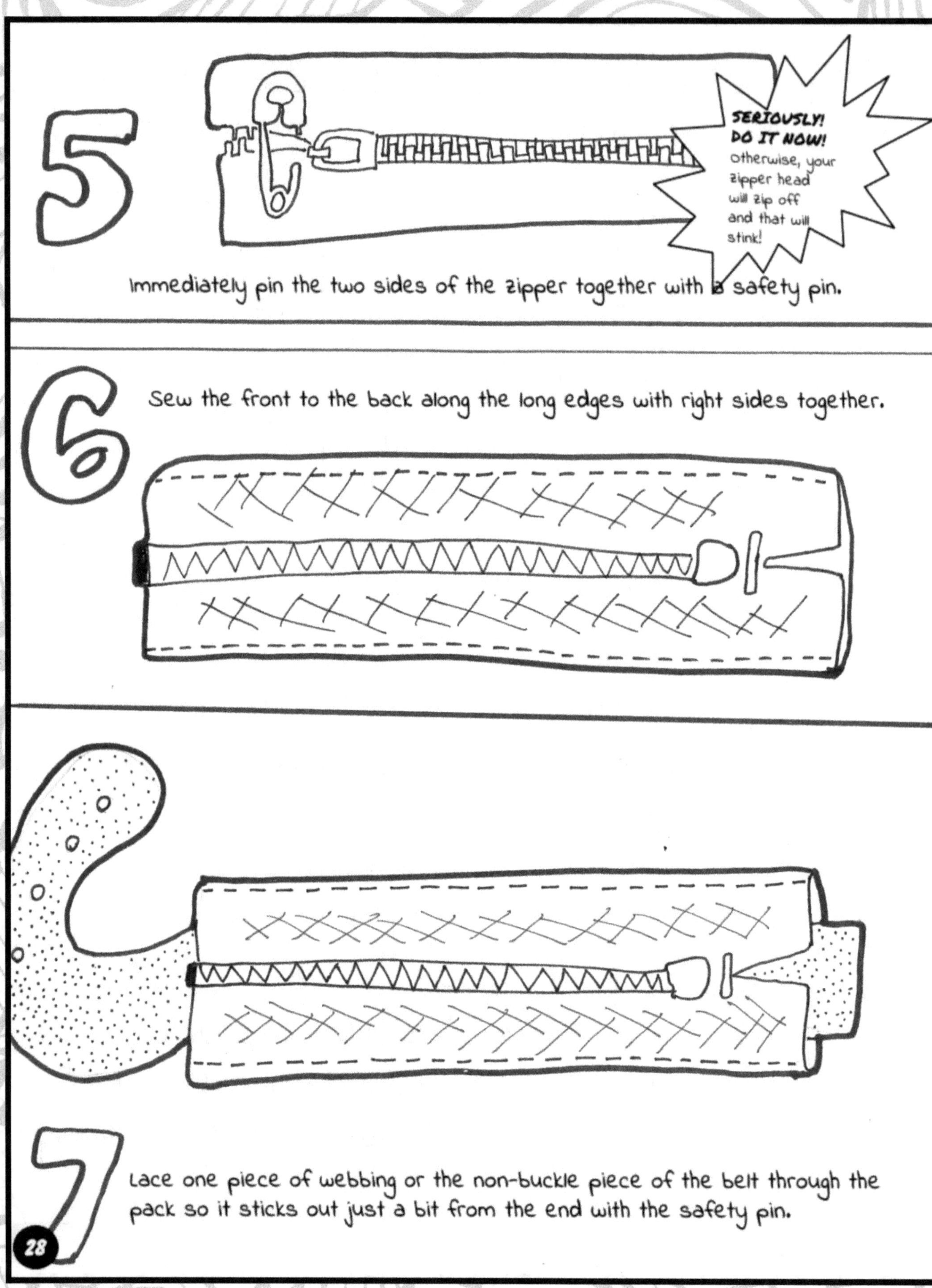
5
SERIOUSLY! DO IT NOW!
otherwise, your zipper head will zip off and that will stink!
Immediately pin the two sides of the zipper together with a safety pin.
6
Sew the front to the back along the long edges with right sides together.
7
Lace one piece of webbing or the non-buckle piece of the belt through the pack so it sticks out just a bit from the end with the safety pin.

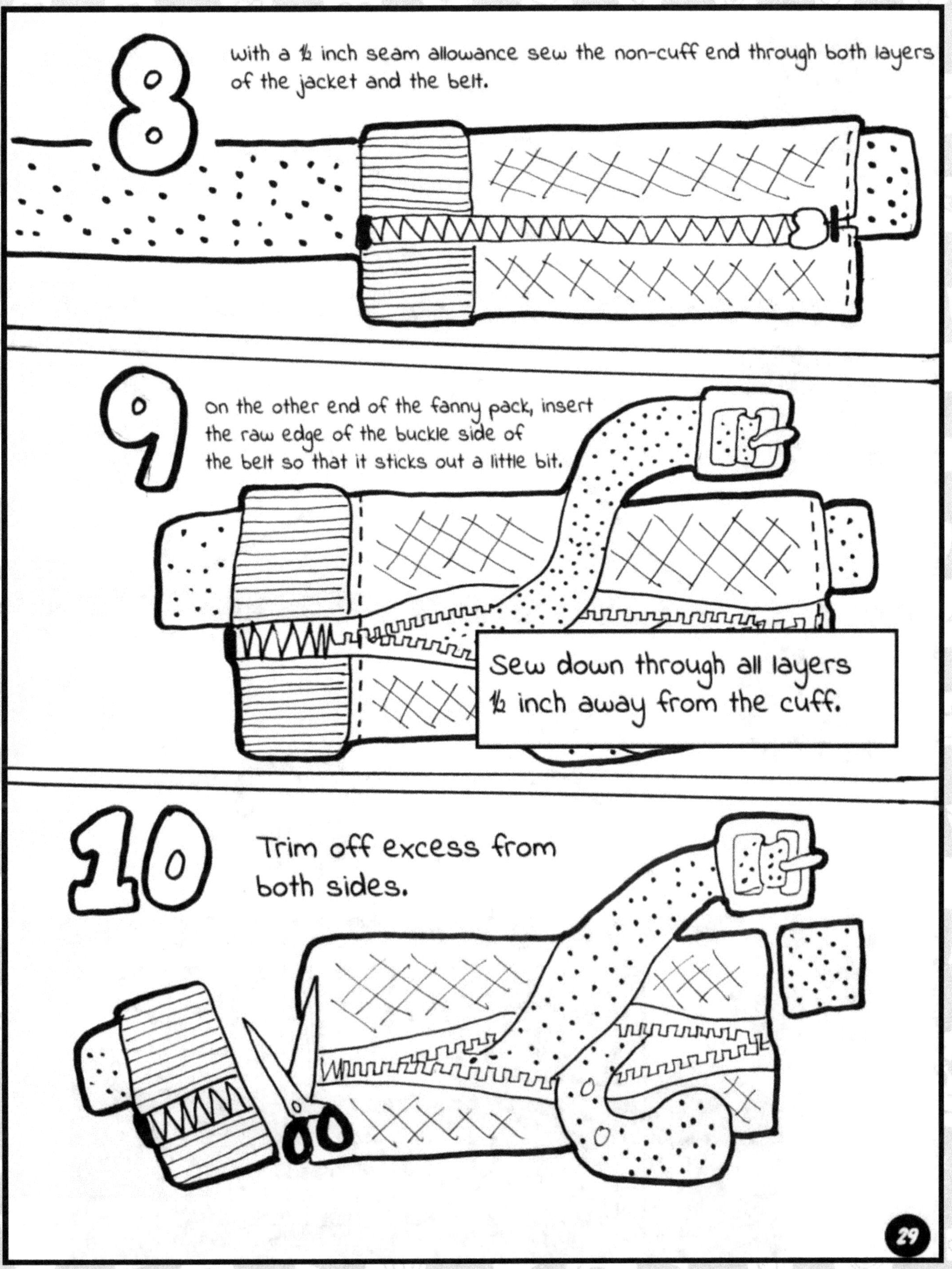
8
with a ½ inch seam allowance sew the non-cuff end through both layers of the jacket and the belt.
9
on the other end of the fanny pack, insert the raw edge of the buckle side of the belt so that it sticks out a little bit.
Sew down through all layers ½ inch away from the cuff.
10
Trim off excess from both sides.

11

Open up one bottom corner so that the seams are lined up, creating a little triangle.

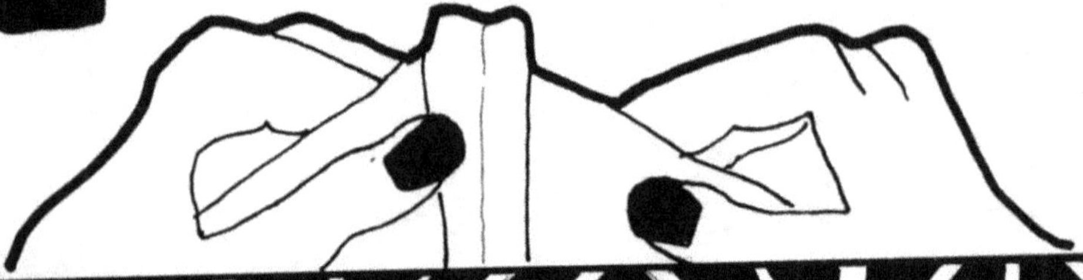

12

Measure an inch from the tip of the triangle and then pin and sew a straight line across.

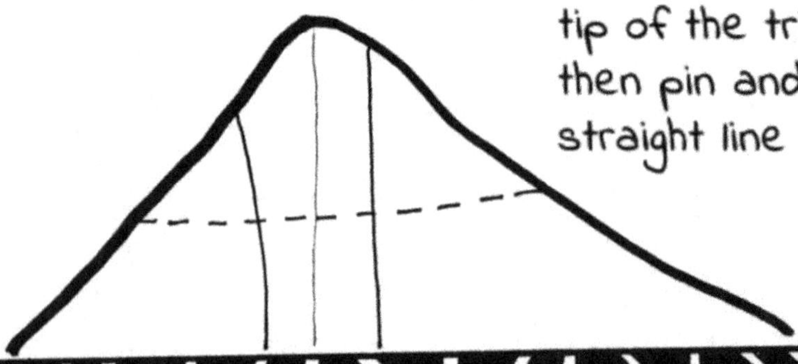

13

Trim the tip off of the triangle close to where you sewed.

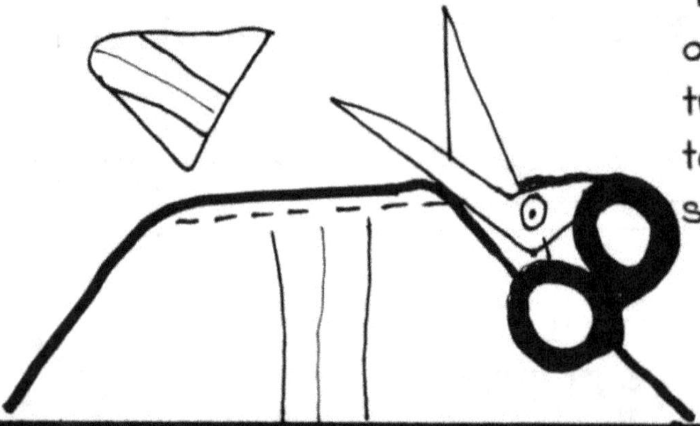

14

REPEAT

STEPS 11–14 ON THE OTHER BOTTOM CORNER.

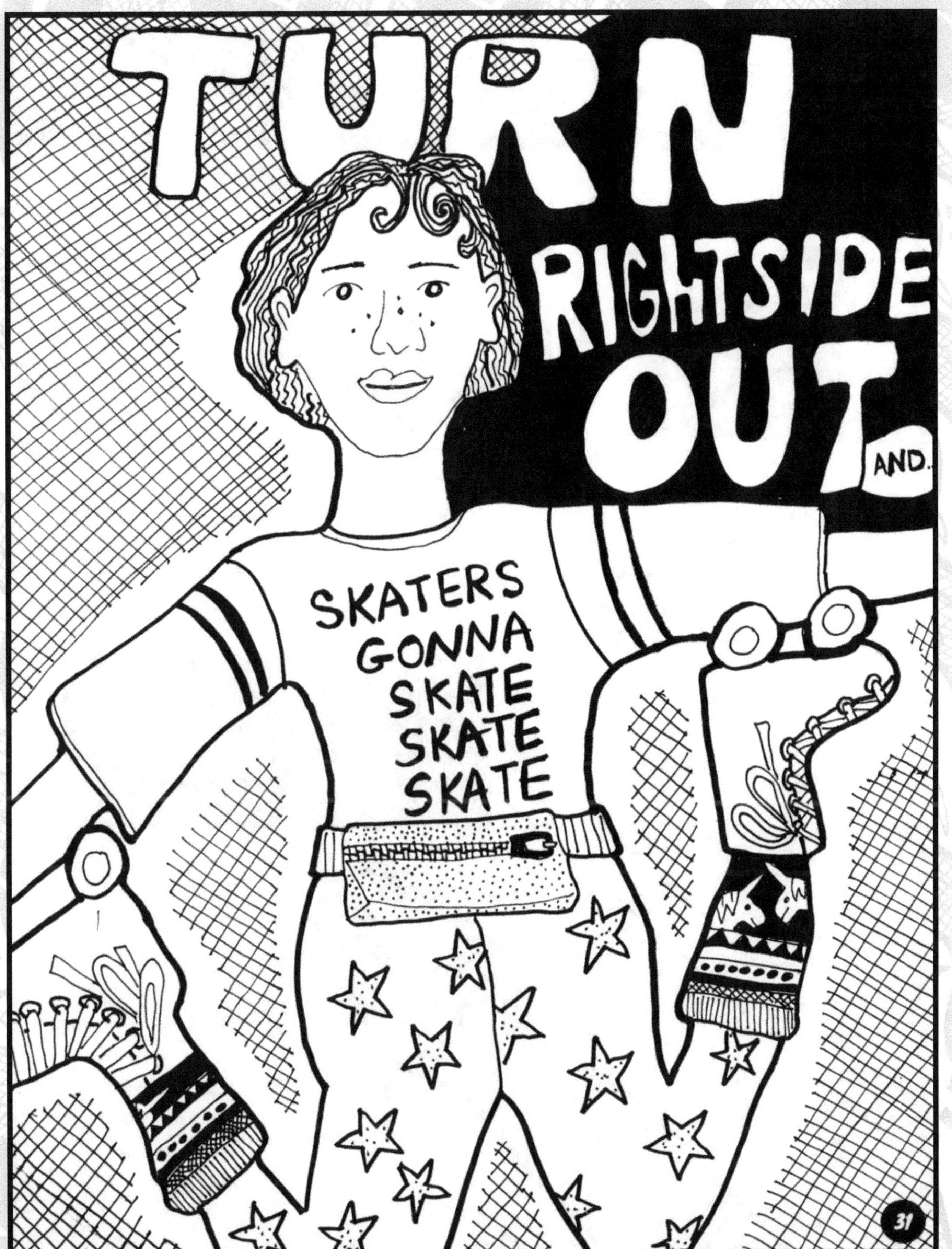
TURN
RIGHTSIDE
OUT
AND...
SKATERS
GONNA
SKATE
SKATE
SKATE

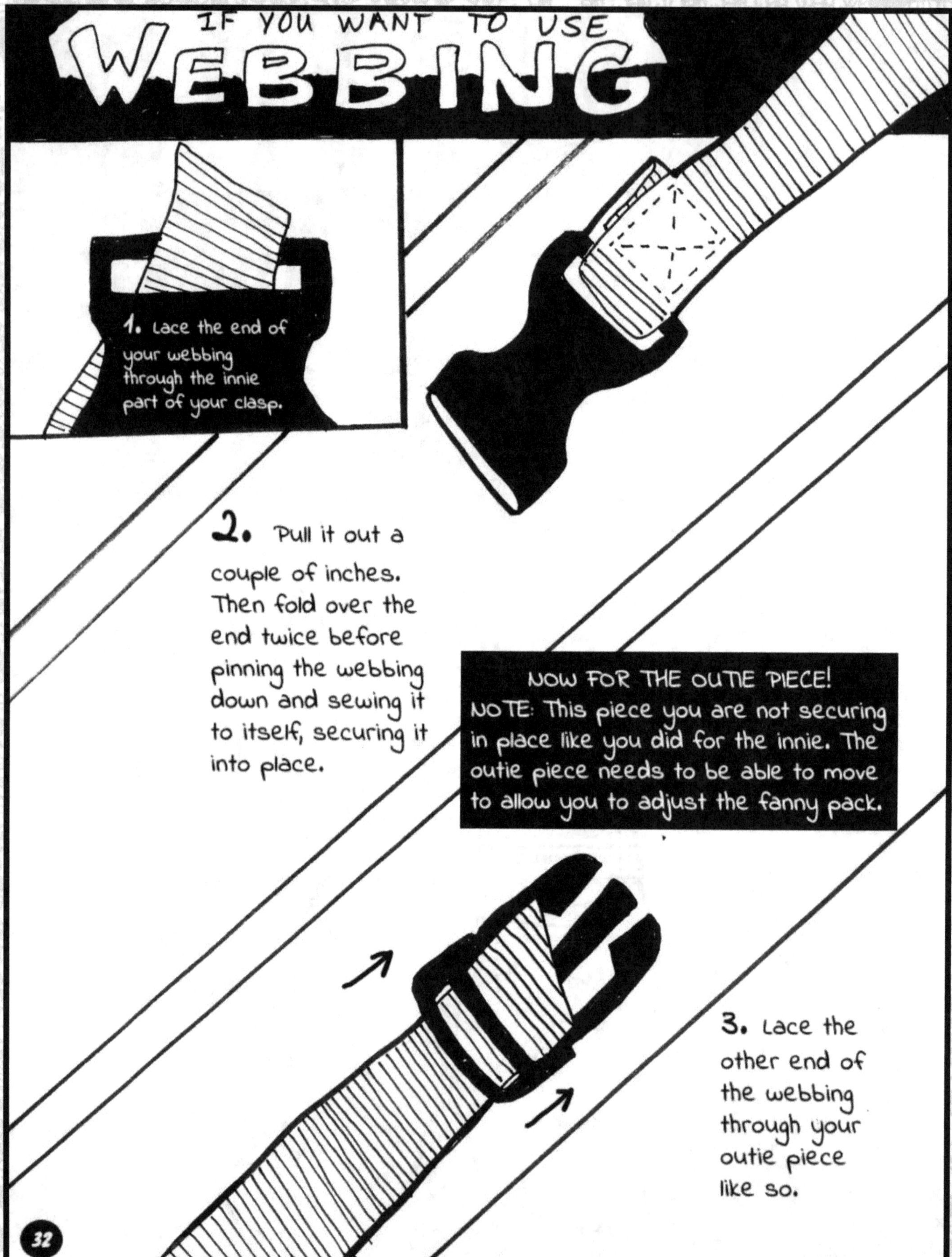
IF YOU WANT TO USE
WEBBING
1. Lace the end of your webbing through the innie part of your clasp.
2. Pull it out a couple of inches. Then fold over the end twice before pinning the webbing down and sewing it to itself, securing it into place.
NOW FOR THE OUTIE PIECE!
NOTE: This piece you are not securing in place like you did for the innie. The outie piece needs to be able to move to allow you to adjust the fanny pack.
3. Lace the other end of the webbing through your outie piece like so.

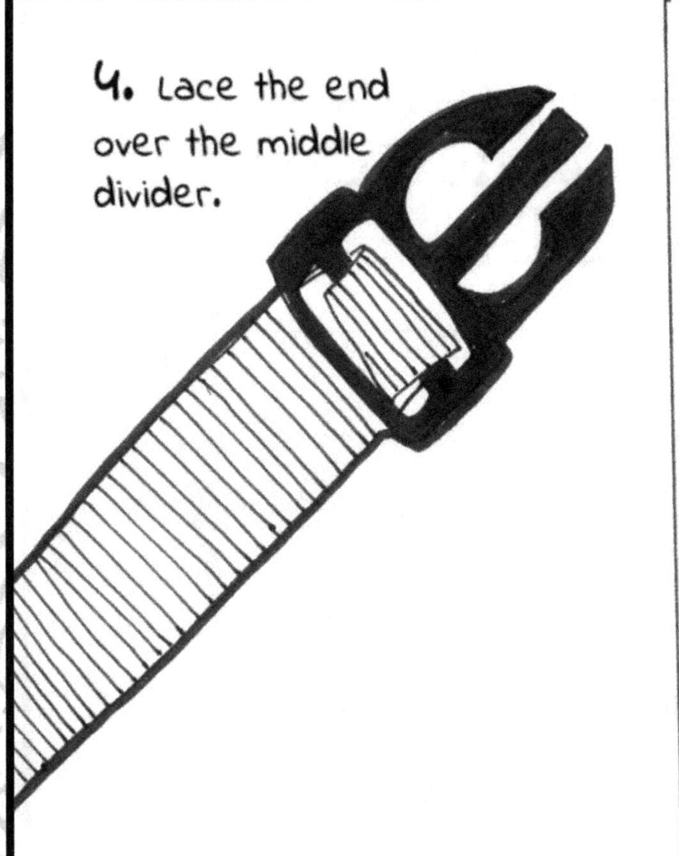
4. Lace the end over the middle divider.

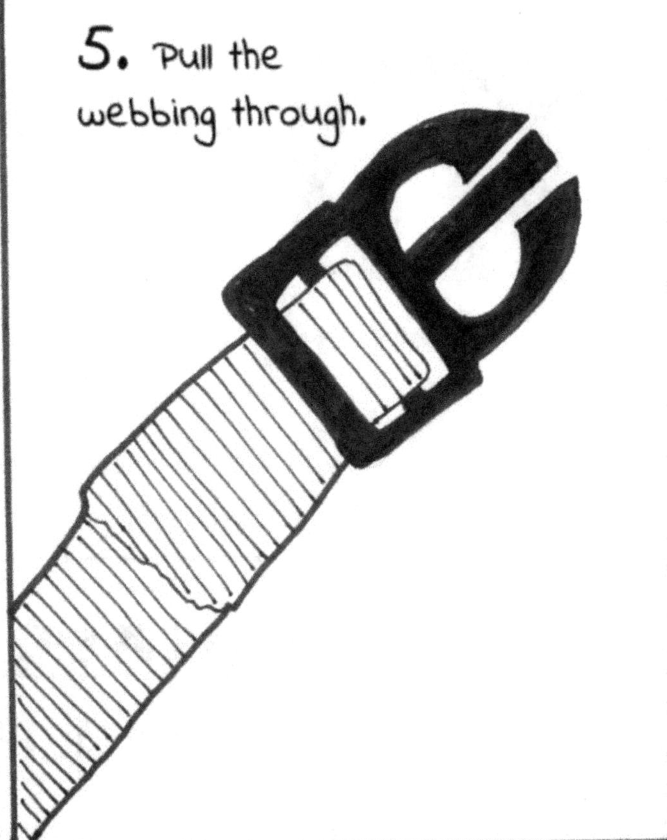
5. Pull the webbing through.

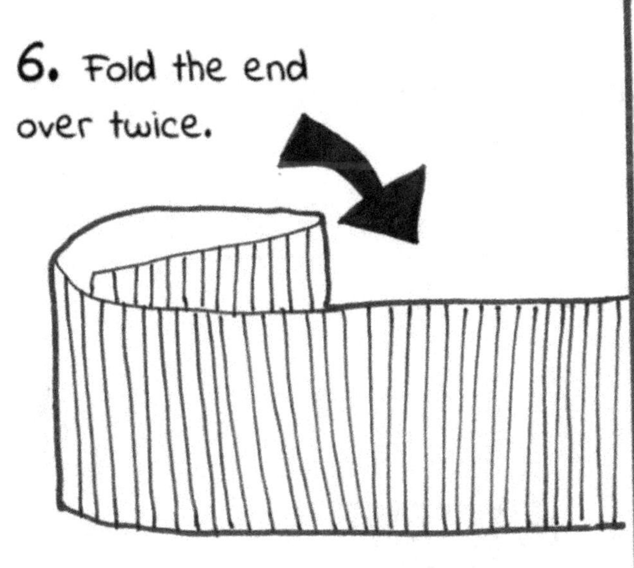
6. Fold the end over twice.

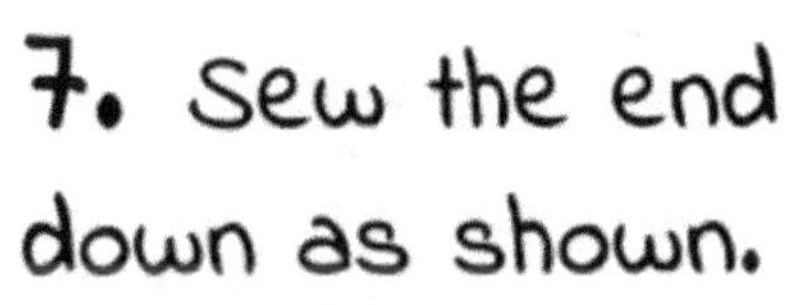
7. Sew the end down as shown.

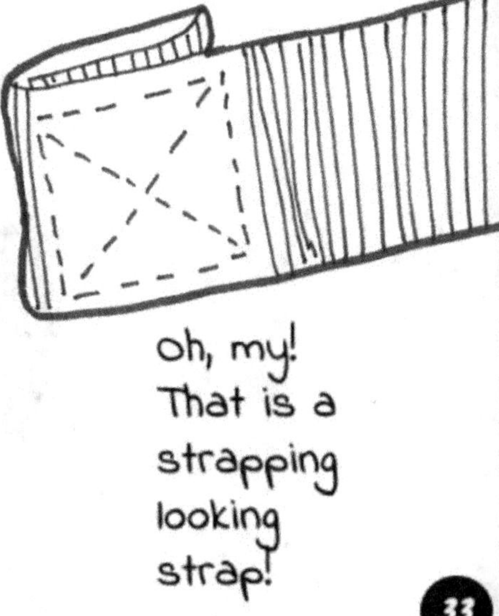
Oh, my! That is a strapping looking strap!

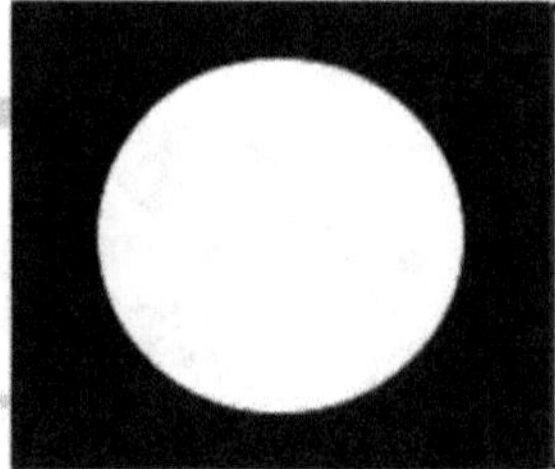

FINGERLESS GLOVES

From Boxer Briefs

You will need:

- An upcycled (CLEAN!) pair of boxer style brief underwear (ideally more spandex-y than cotton-y)

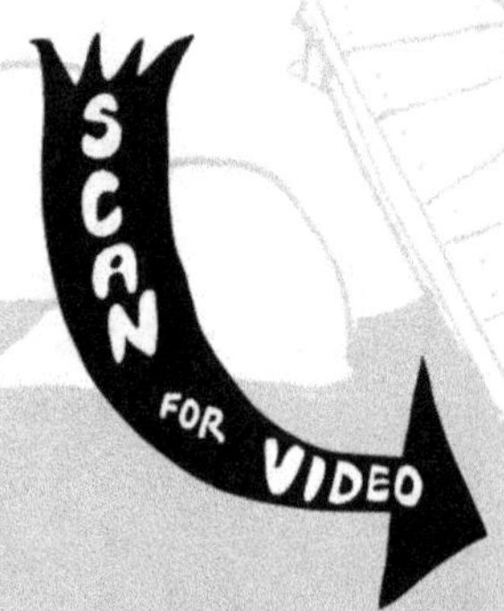

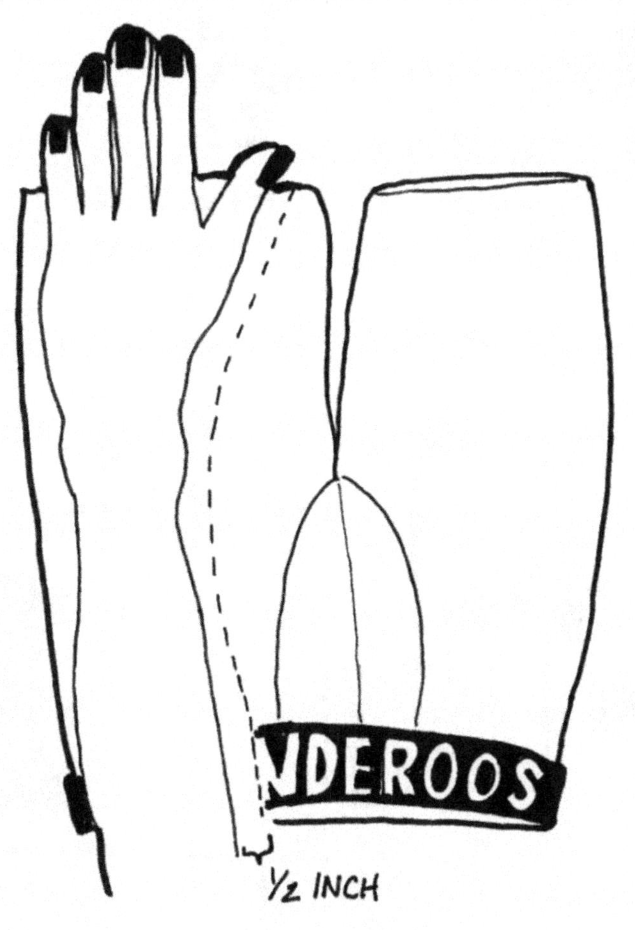

1

Position your left hand and forearm on the left leg of the boxer briefs as shown. Make sure that your fingers and thumb will be covered to your liking. Next, trace a line about ¼ inch away from your arm and hand.

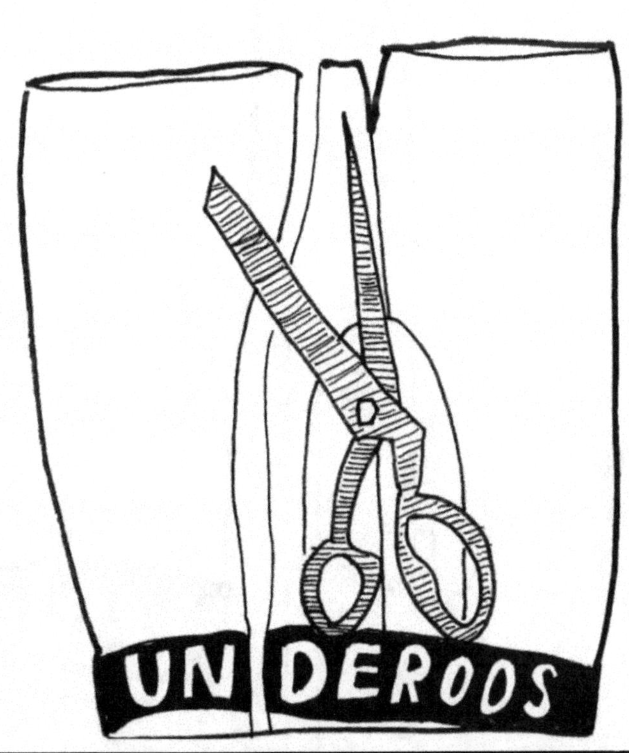

2

Cut along the line.

3

with right side to right side, sew the raw edges together either by gently pulling and using a wide straight stitch or by using a zig zag stitch.

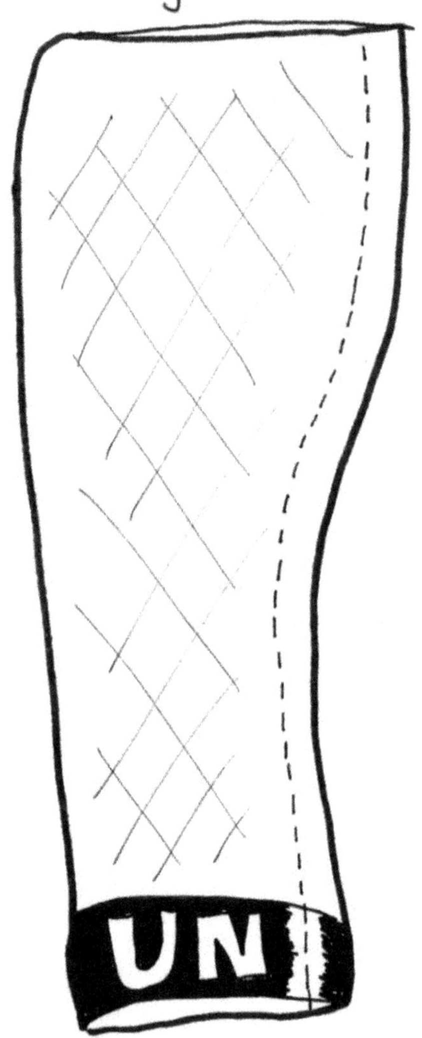

4

Position your fingers and thumb where they will be in the finished glove.

Mark by drawing a V between your fingers and thumb.

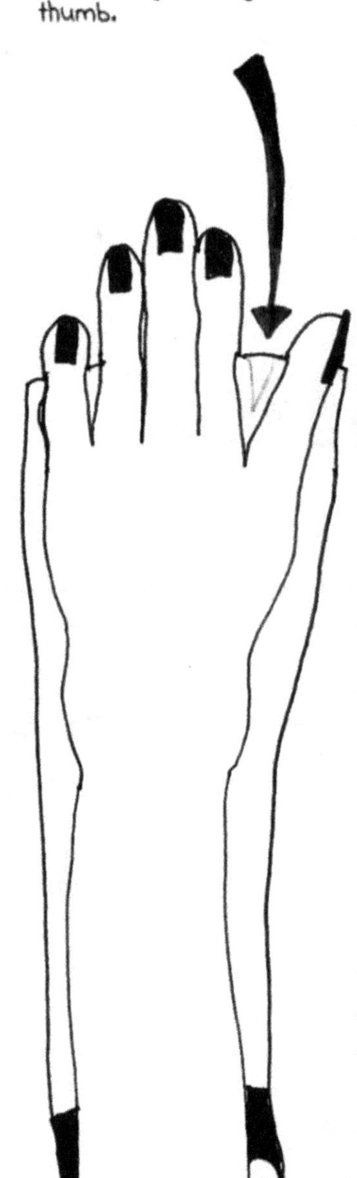

5

Sew where you marked (again, using a wide straight stitch and slightly pulled fabric OR a zig zag).

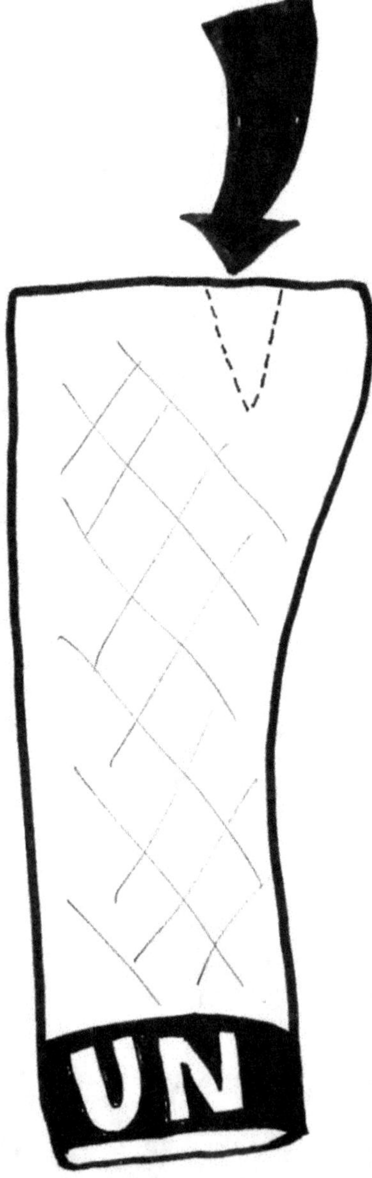

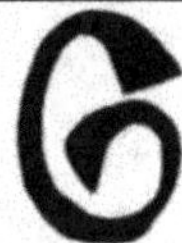

Cut out the little v-shape leaving a very tiny seam allowance around your stitching.

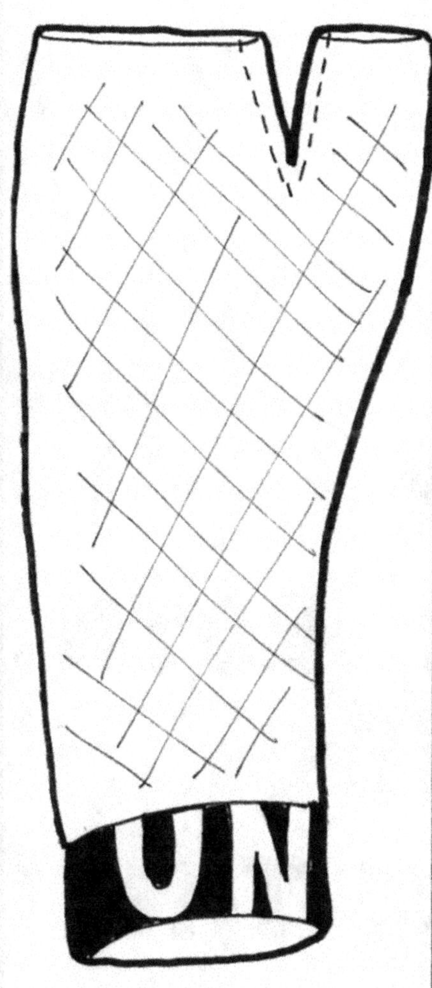

REPEAT
STEPS 1–6

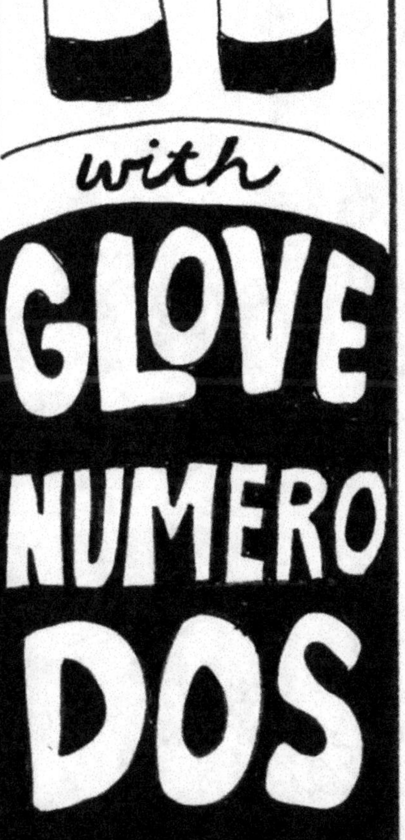

Now it's time to use your fingerless gloves!

They are great for gardening or cycling but...

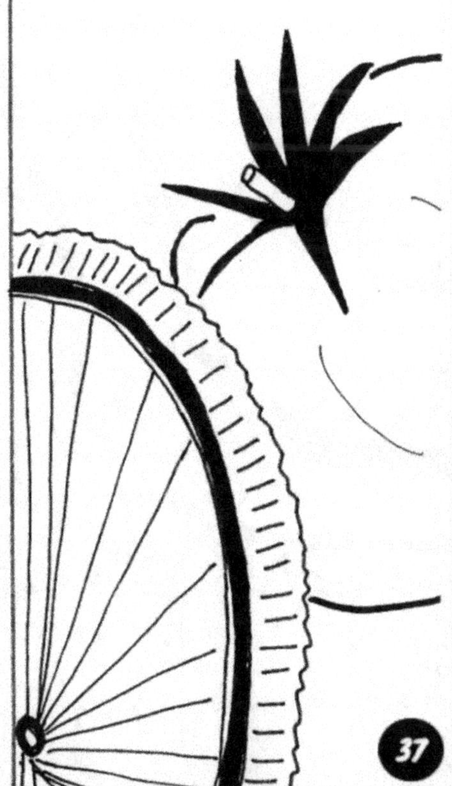

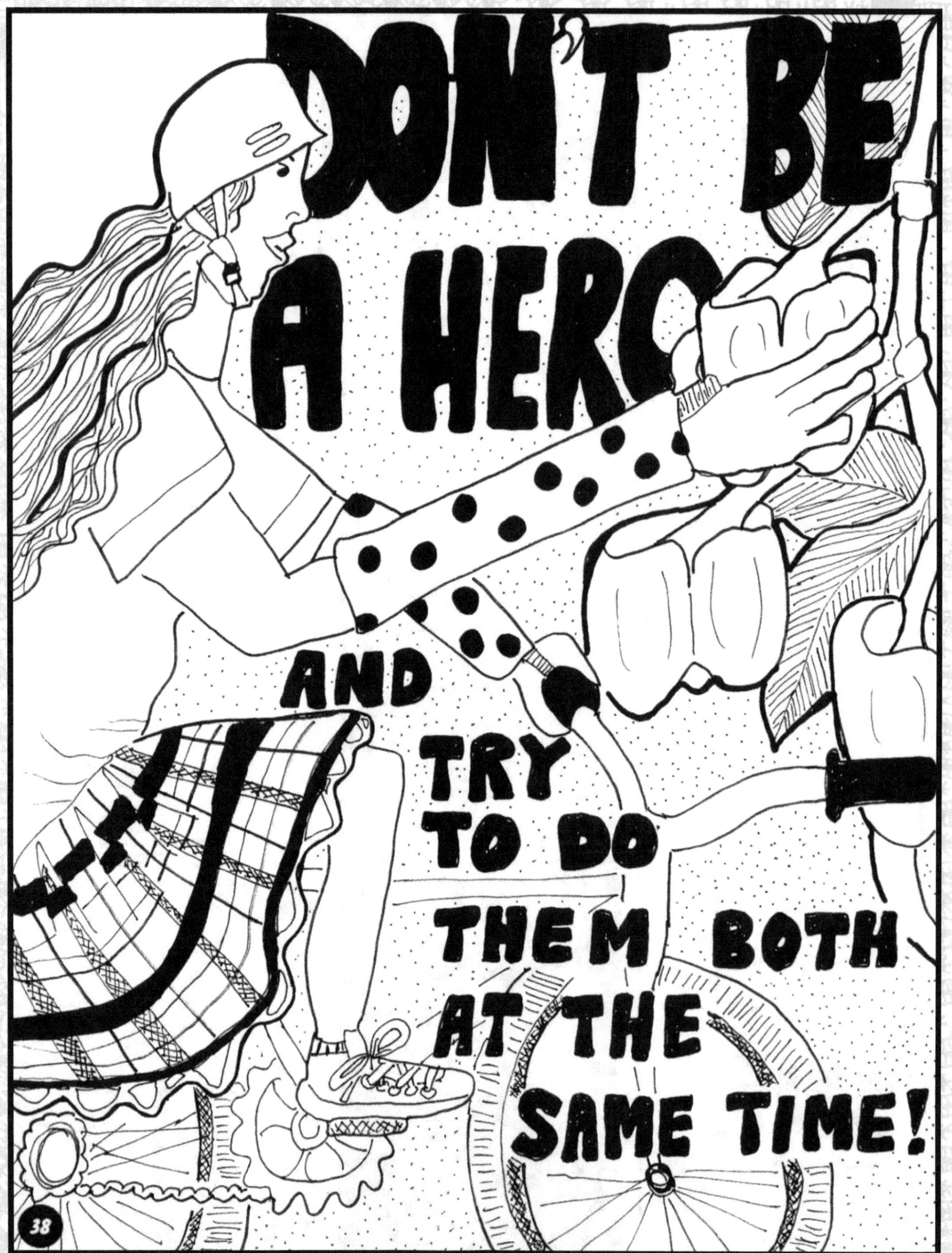
DON'T BE
A HERO
AND
TRY
TO DO
THEM BOTH
AT THE
SAME TIME!

Follow The Rules

Yeah, we get it. You're a Maverick.

But when you're in a national park, a sensitive ecological area or anywhere in nature, follow the posted rules or the Leave No Trace Rules.

It's good to be a rebel sometimes but this isn't one of those times.

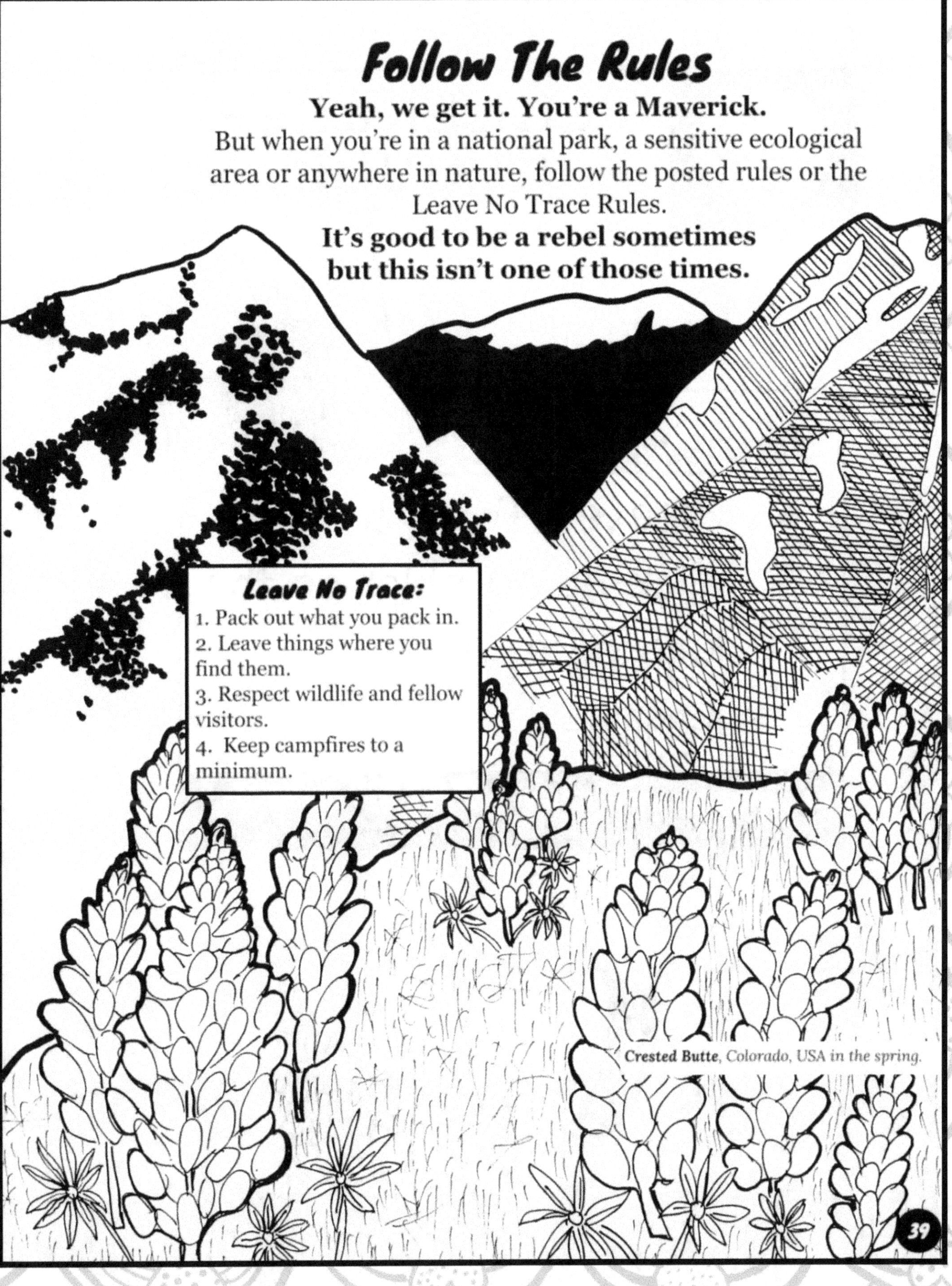

Leave No Trace:

1. Pack out what you pack in.
2. Leave things where you find them.
3. Respect wildlife and fellow visitors.
4. Keep campfires to a minimum.

Crested Butte, *Colorado, USA in the spring.*

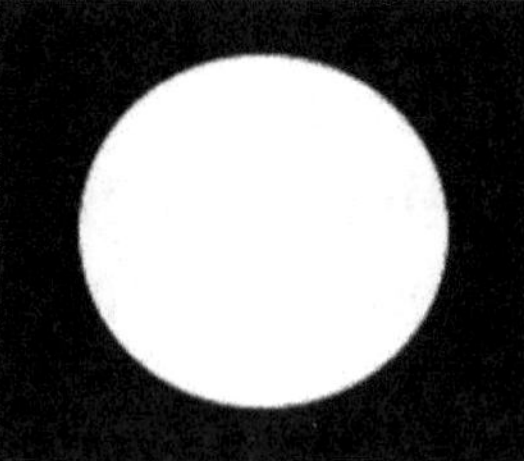

FINGERLESS GLOVES

Standard

You will need:

- Sleeves from a wick-away shirt or the legs of spandex leggings

PAIRS NICELY WITH: *FANNY PACK Level 1 and TOWEL*

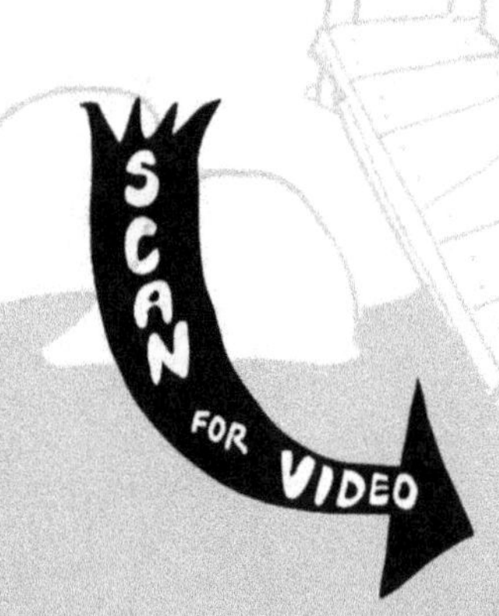

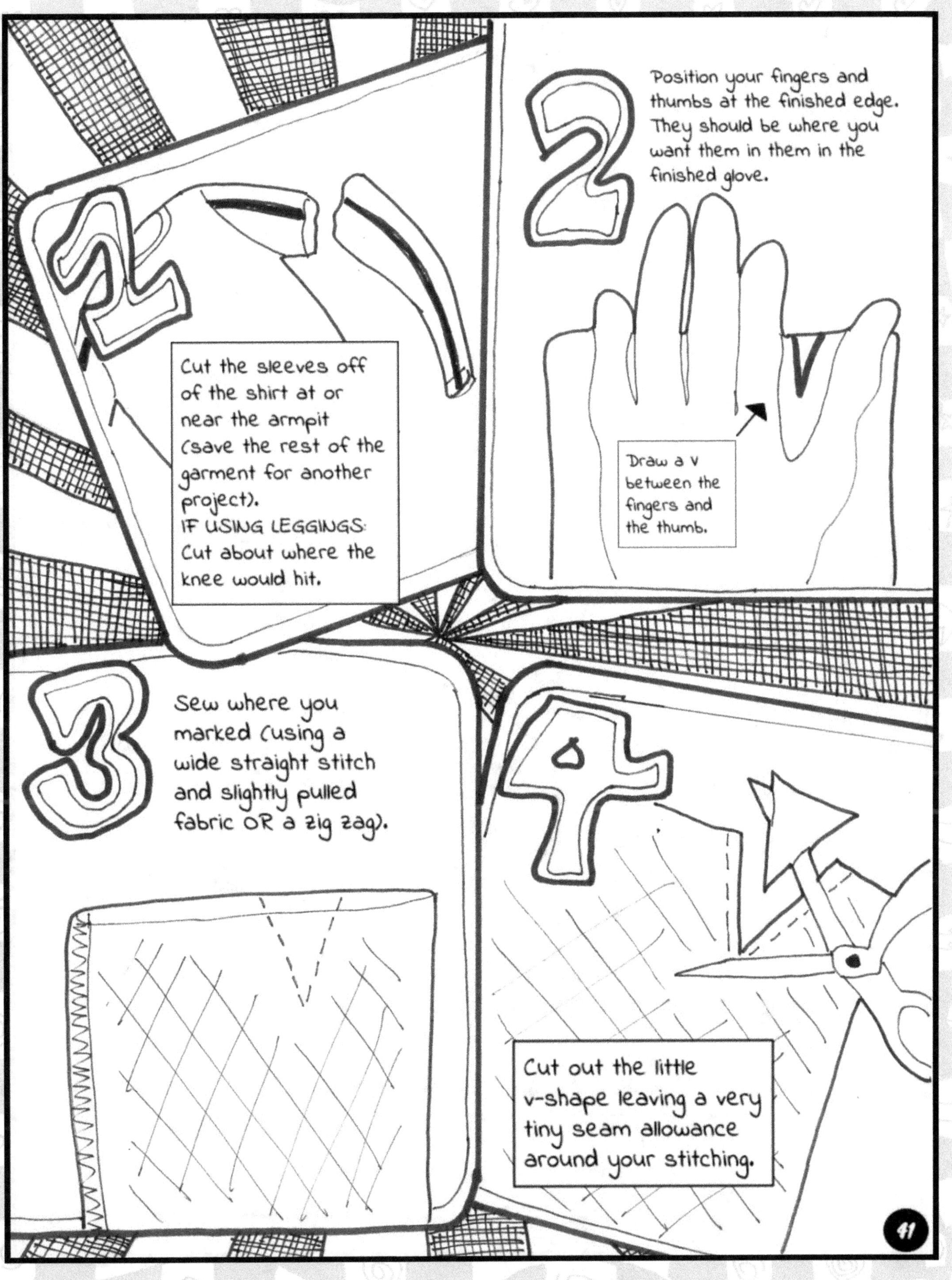
1
Cut the sleeves off of the shirt at or near the armpit (save the rest of the garment for another project).
IF USING LEGGINGS: Cut about where the knee would hit.
2
Position your fingers and thumbs at the finished edge. They should be where you want them in them in the finished glove.
Draw a V between the fingers and the thumb.
3
Sew where you marked (using a wide straight stitch and slightly pulled fabric OR a zig zag).
4
Cut out the little v-shape leaving a very tiny seam allowance around your stitching.

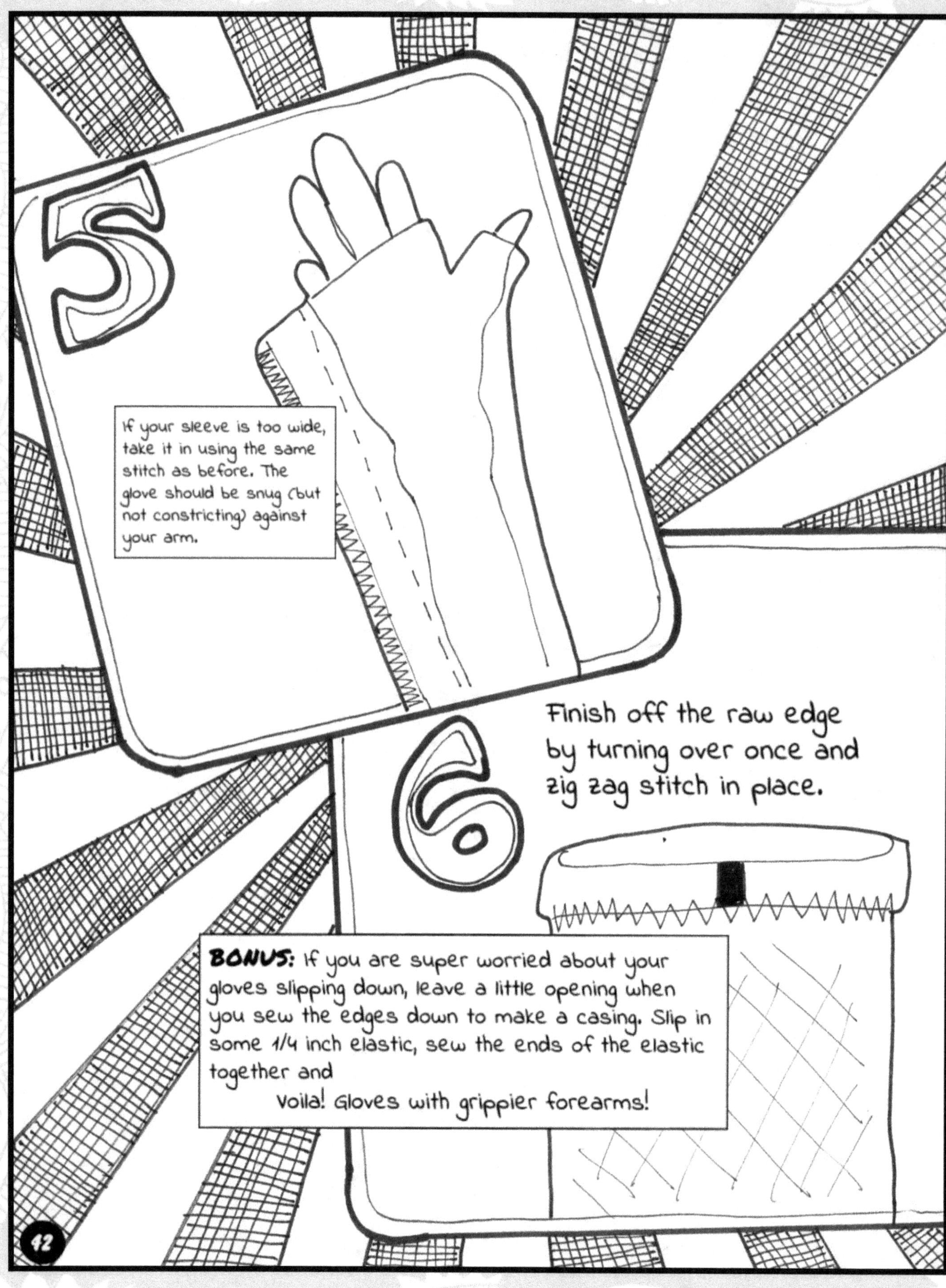
5
If your sleeve is too wide, take it in using the same stitch as before. The glove should be snug (but not constricting) against your arm.
6
Finish off the raw edge by turning over once and zig zag stitch in place.
BONUS: If you are super worried about your gloves slipping down, leave a little opening when you sew the edges down to make a casing. Slip in some 1/4 inch elastic, sew the ends of the elastic together and
Voila! Gloves with grippier forearms!

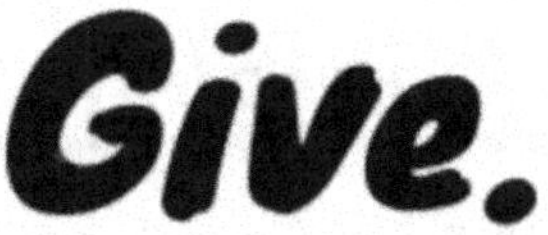

Your time by volunteering.
Your money to organizations, causes or people you believe in.

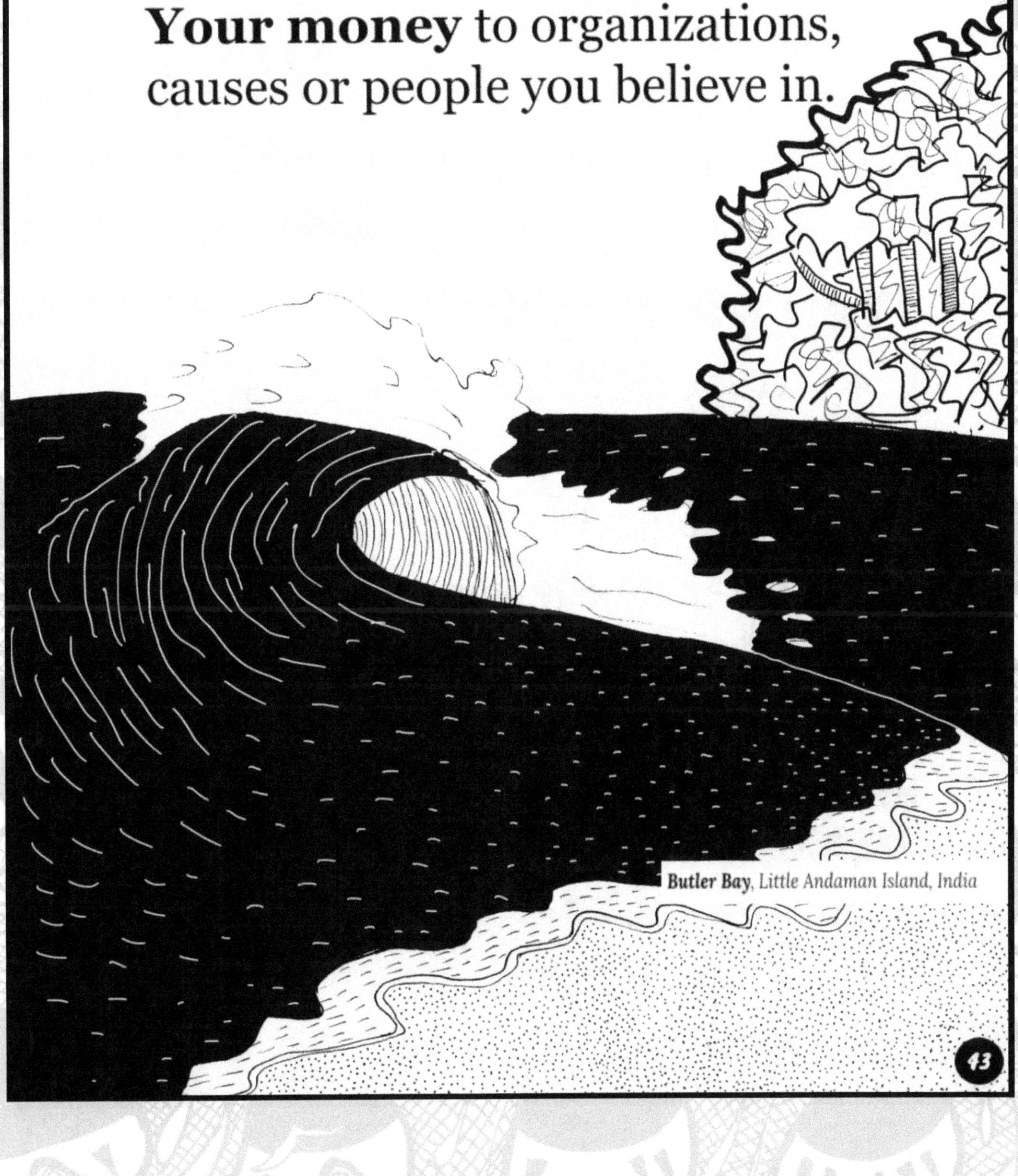

Butler Bay, Little Andaman Island, India

FINGERLESS GLOVES

Sun Sleeves

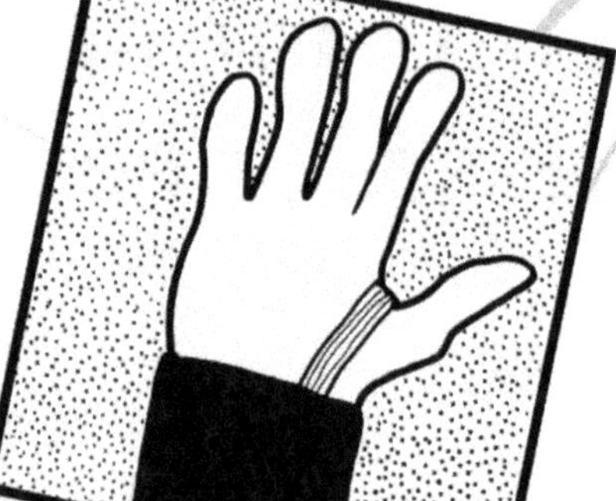

You will need:

- Upcycled sleeves of a wick-away shirt or the upcycled legs of spandex leggings
- ¼" elastic, about 2 feet

PAIRS NICELY WITH: *FANNY PACK Level 1 and TOWEL*

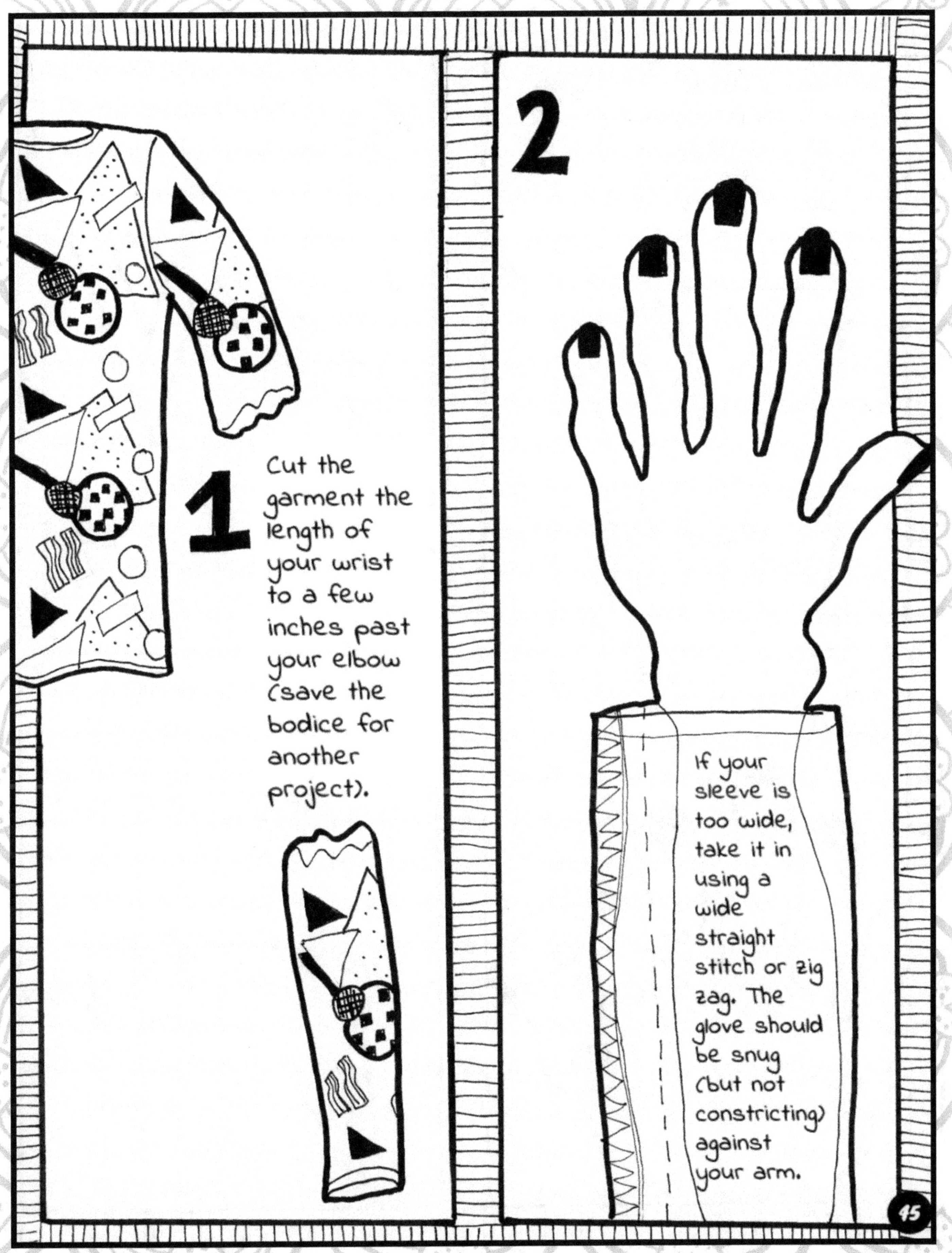
1
Cut the garment the length of your wrist to a few inches past your elbow (save the bodice for another project).
2
If your sleeve is too wide, take it in using a wide straight stitch or zig zag. The glove should be snug (but not constricting) against your arm.

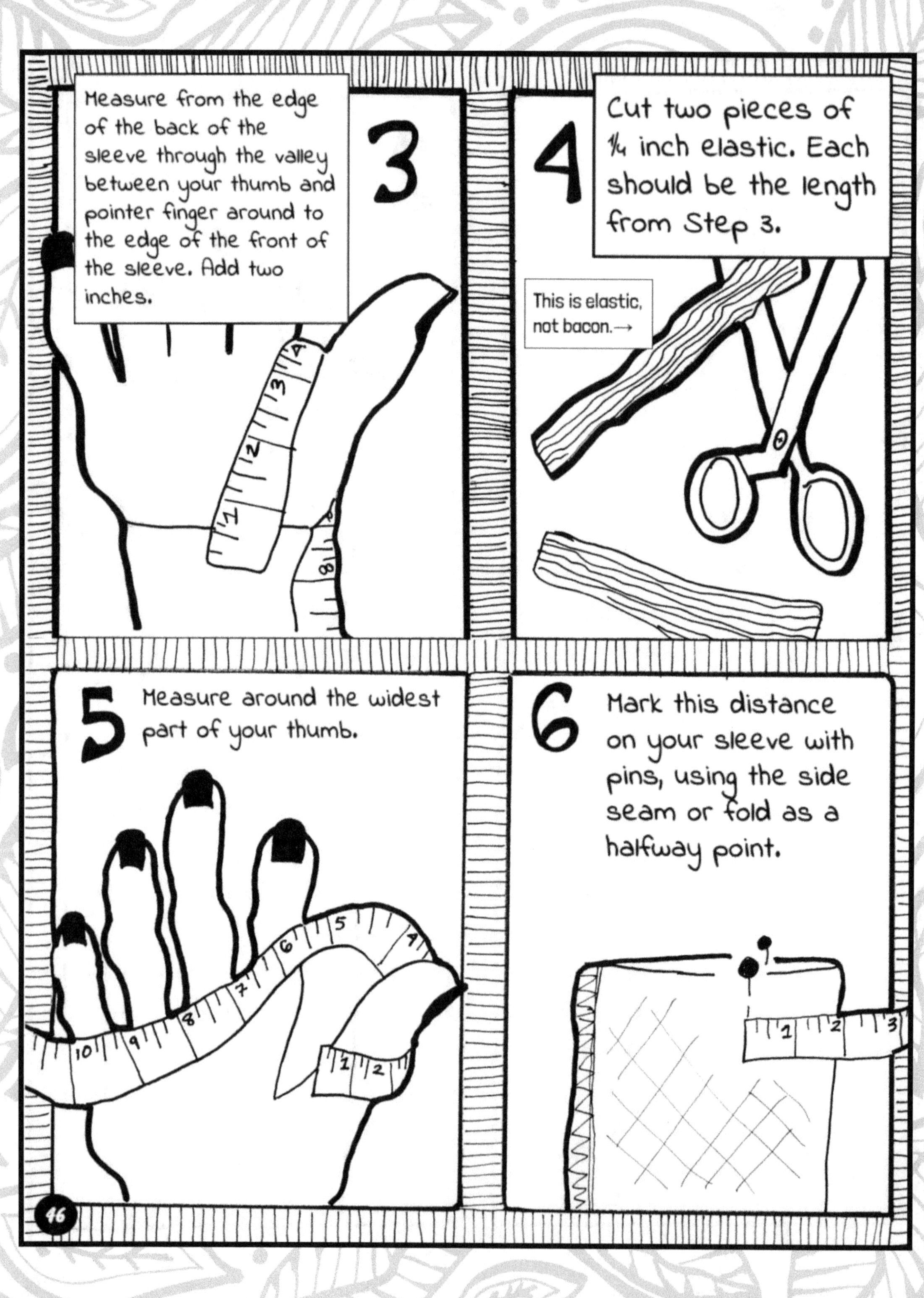

3
Measure from the edge of the back of the sleeve through the valley between your thumb and pointer finger around to the edge of the front of the sleeve. Add two inches.
4
Cut two pieces of ¼ inch elastic. Each should be the length from Step 3.
This is elastic, not bacon.→
5
Measure around the widest part of your thumb.
6
Mark this distance on your sleeve with pins, using the side seam or fold as a halfway point.

7 Fold over 1/2 inch of the end of an elastic piece, pin to your mark on the wrong side and sew down with a zig zag stitch. On the second side, turn over ½ inch of the elastic, pin and try on. Adjust as needed before sewing down.

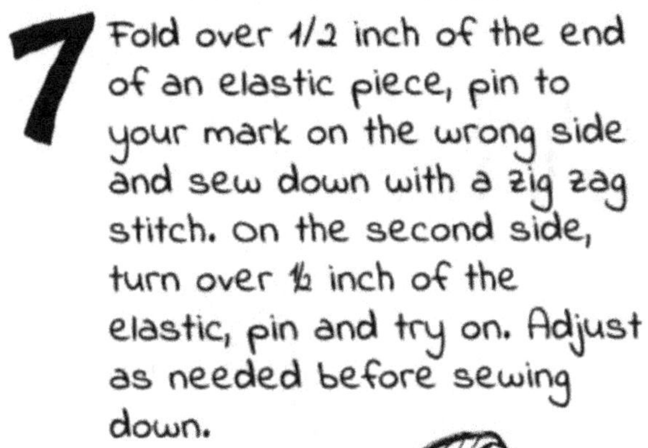

Do this for both gloves.

8 Finish off the raw edges by turning over once and zig zag stitching it down or...

9

BONUS:
MAKE YOUR GLOVE GRIPPIER

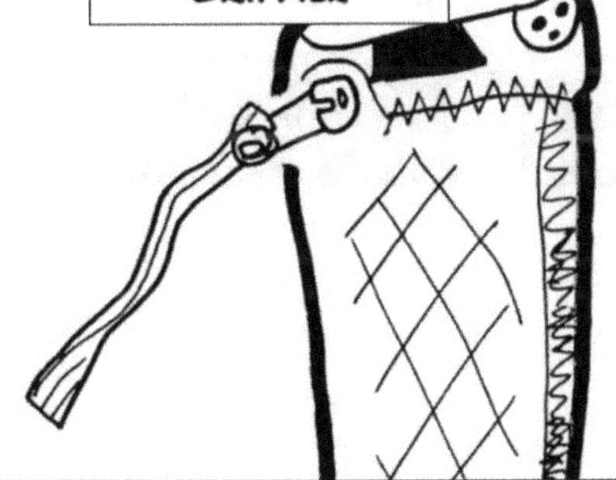

You can make the forearm of your glove grippier. Slip in some 1/4 inch elastic, sew the ends together and voila!

♪ ALL YOU NEED is GLOVE ♪

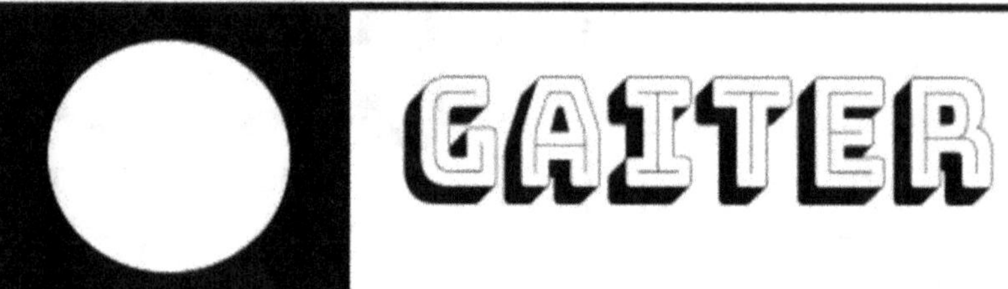

You will need:

- An upcycled spandex skirt or shirt

NOTE: I prefer types that also contain cotton because I like how soft they are against my skin. But if you are concerned about your gator getting wet and staying wet (running in the rain, maybe?) then I recommend upcycling a wick-away or quick drying shirt with stretch.

PAIRS NICELY WITH: BEANIE

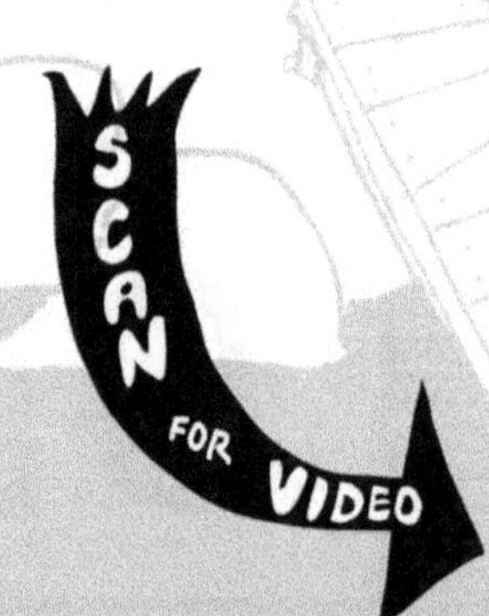

1 Cut a piece of fabric that is 17.5 inches by 14 inches. TWO THINGS: 1) Cut the piece so that the stretchiest direction is lengthwise. 2) If possible, use a finished hem to create one of the long edges.

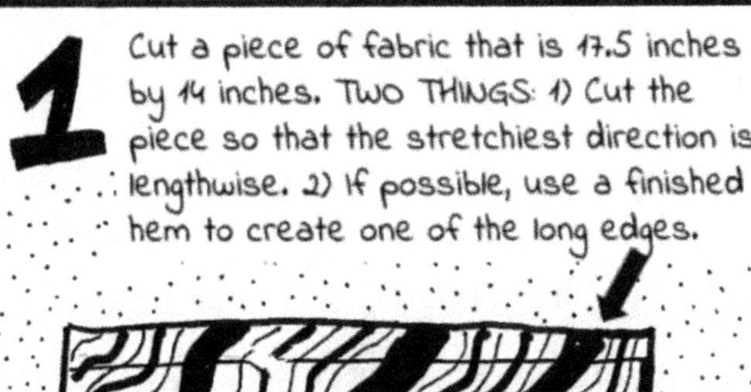

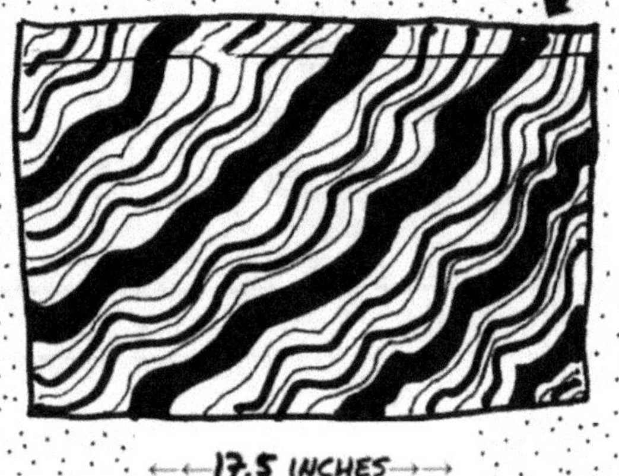

2 Sew the two short ends together. You can use a zig zag stitch or a straight stitch while slightly stretching the material as you sew.

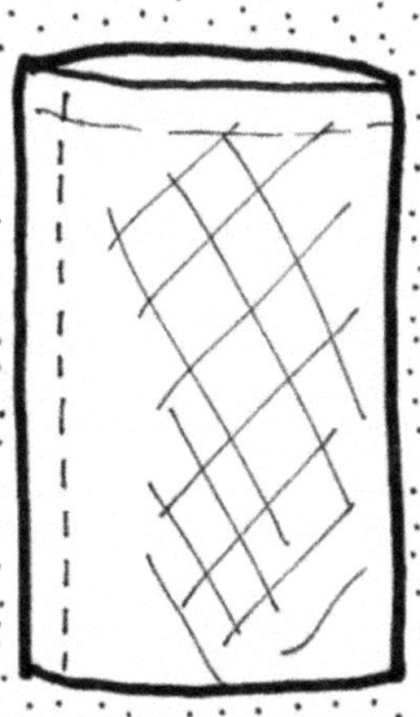

3 Iron the seam allowance open.

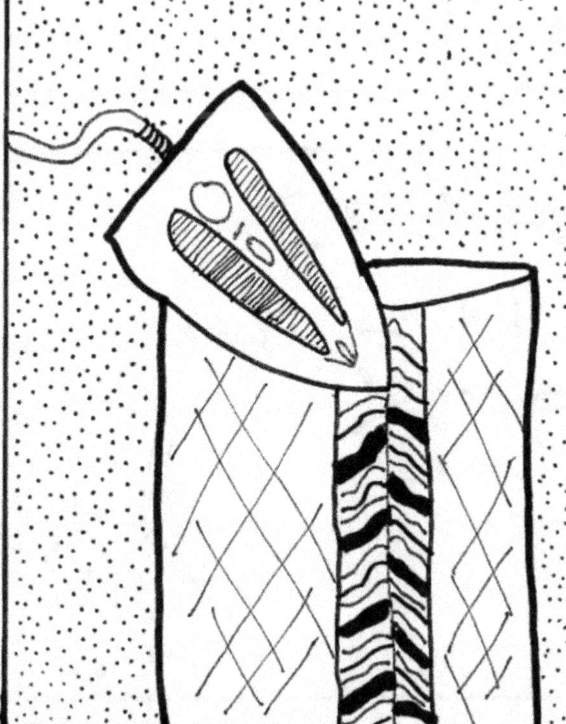

4 Sew down the seam on both sides using a zig zag stitch.

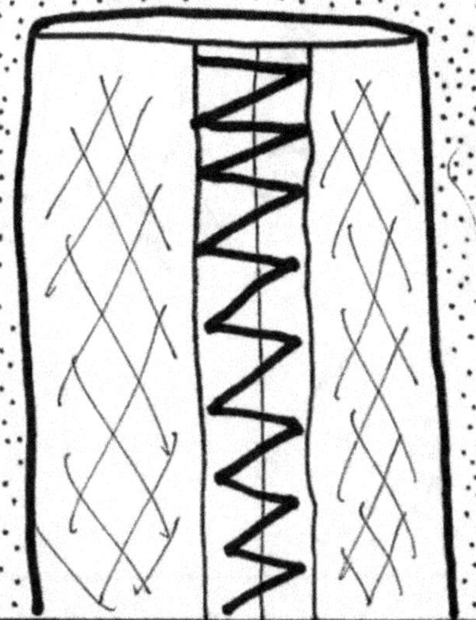

5 Fold over an inch at the unfinished edge. Iron flat or pin in place.

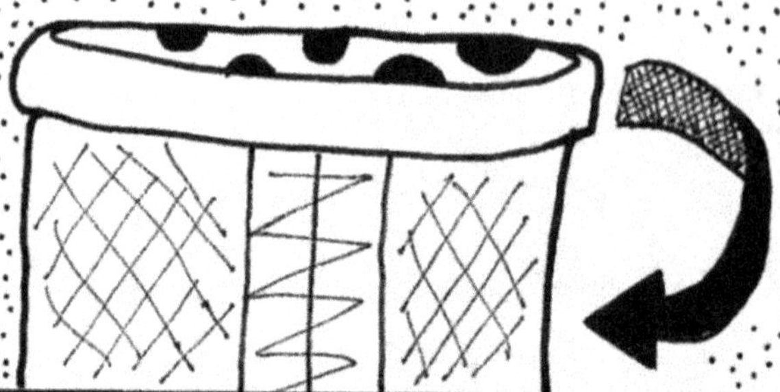

6 Sew in place using zig zag or straight stitch.
NOTE: If the other long edge is unfinished, fold over and sew down on that side, as well.

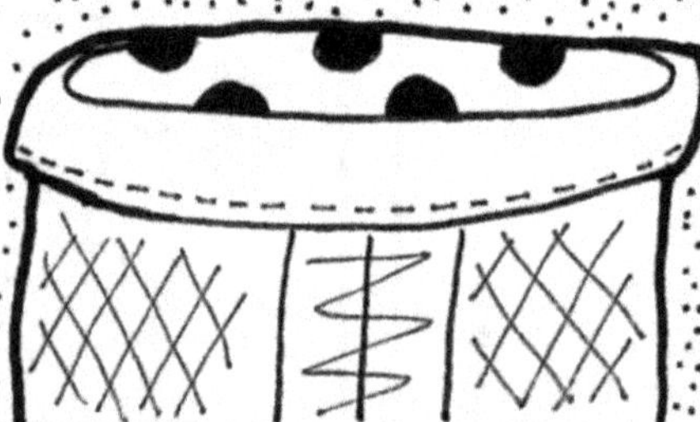

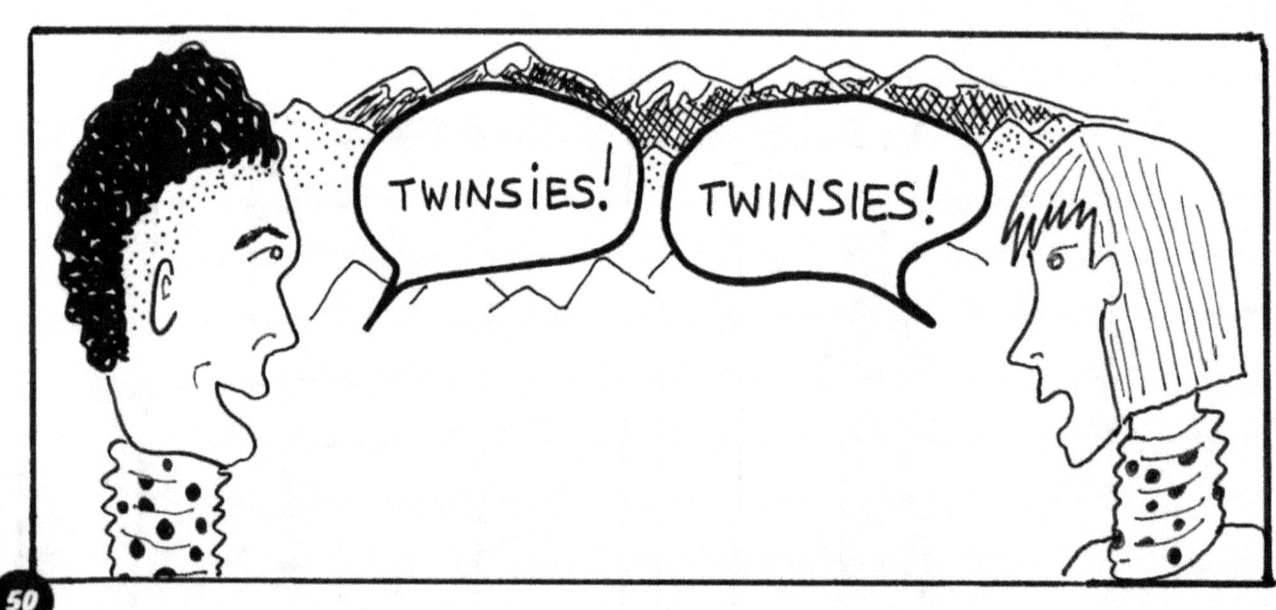

10 WAYS TO WEAR YOUR GAITER

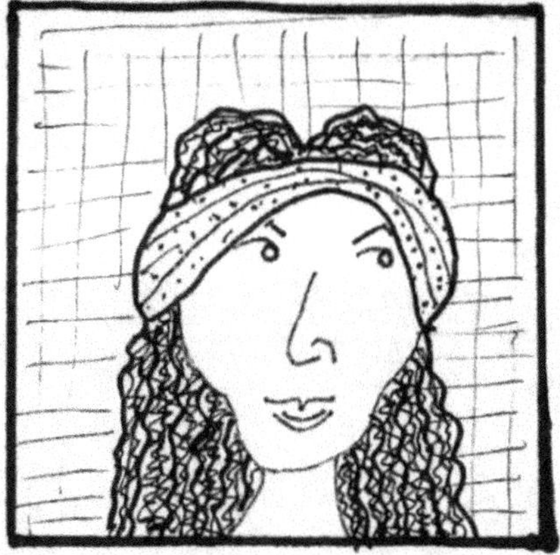

HEADBAND 1

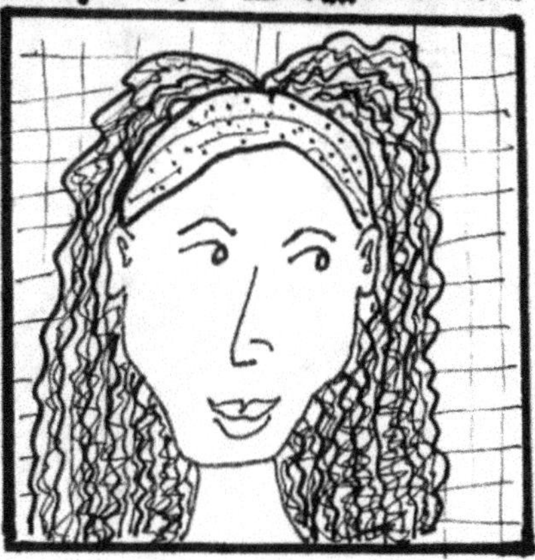

HEADBAND 2

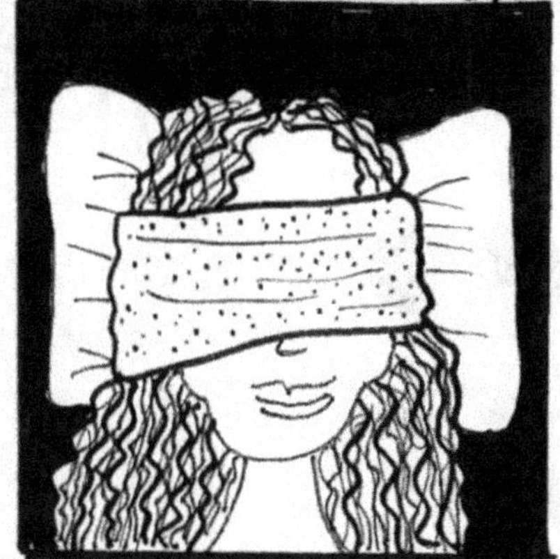

EYE MASK

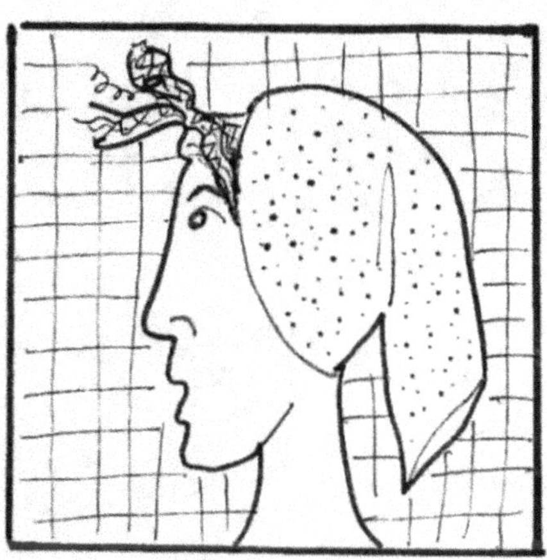

KERCHIEF

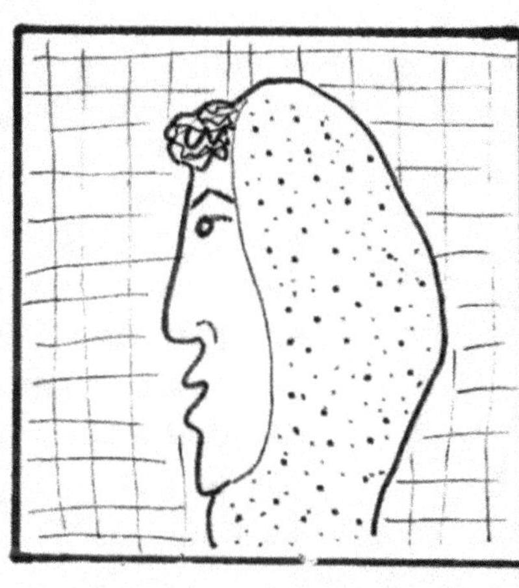

THE HALF BALACLAVA

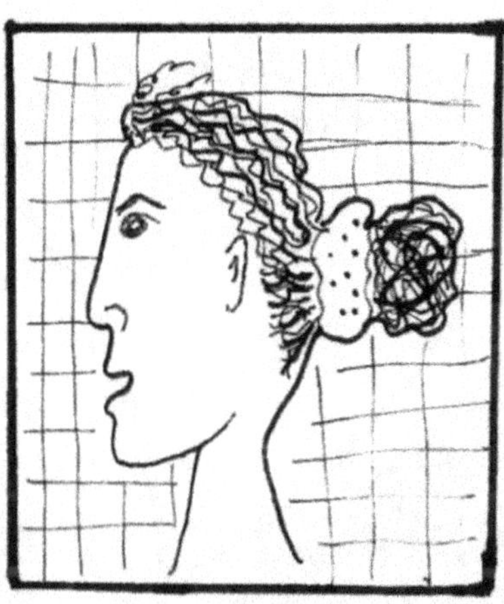

SCRUNCHIE

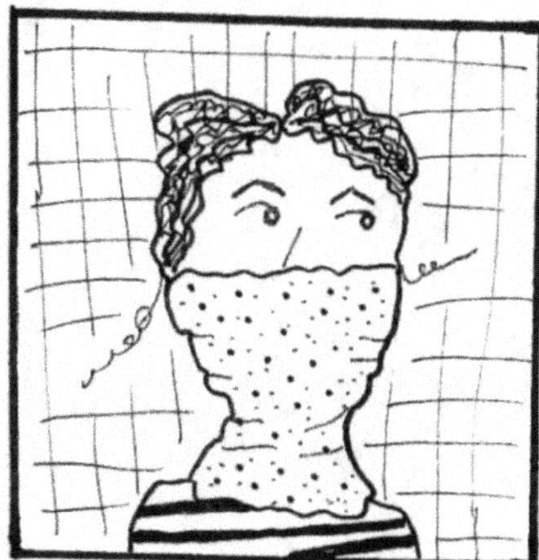

STORM FLAP

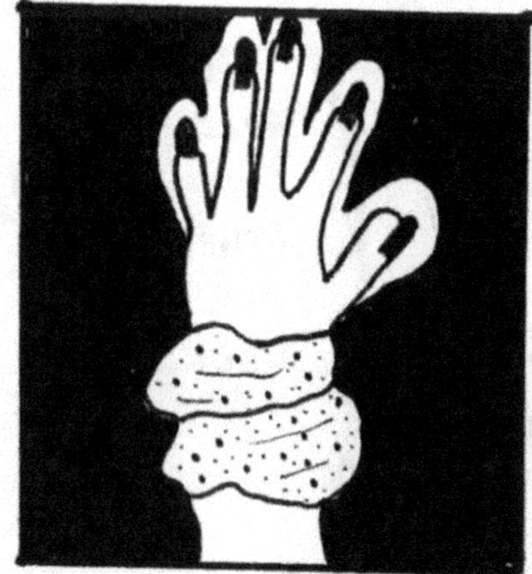

WRIST BAND

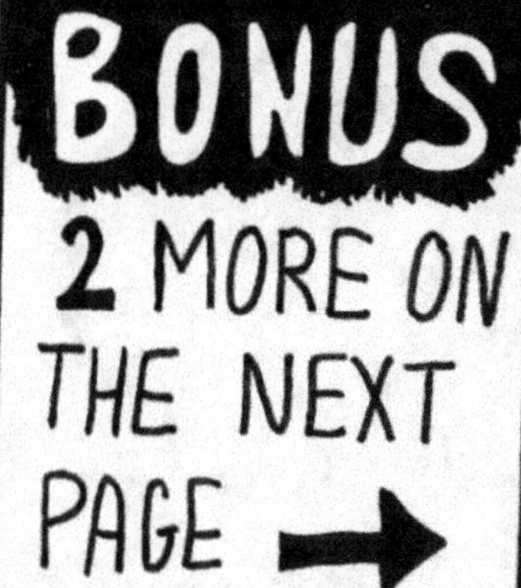

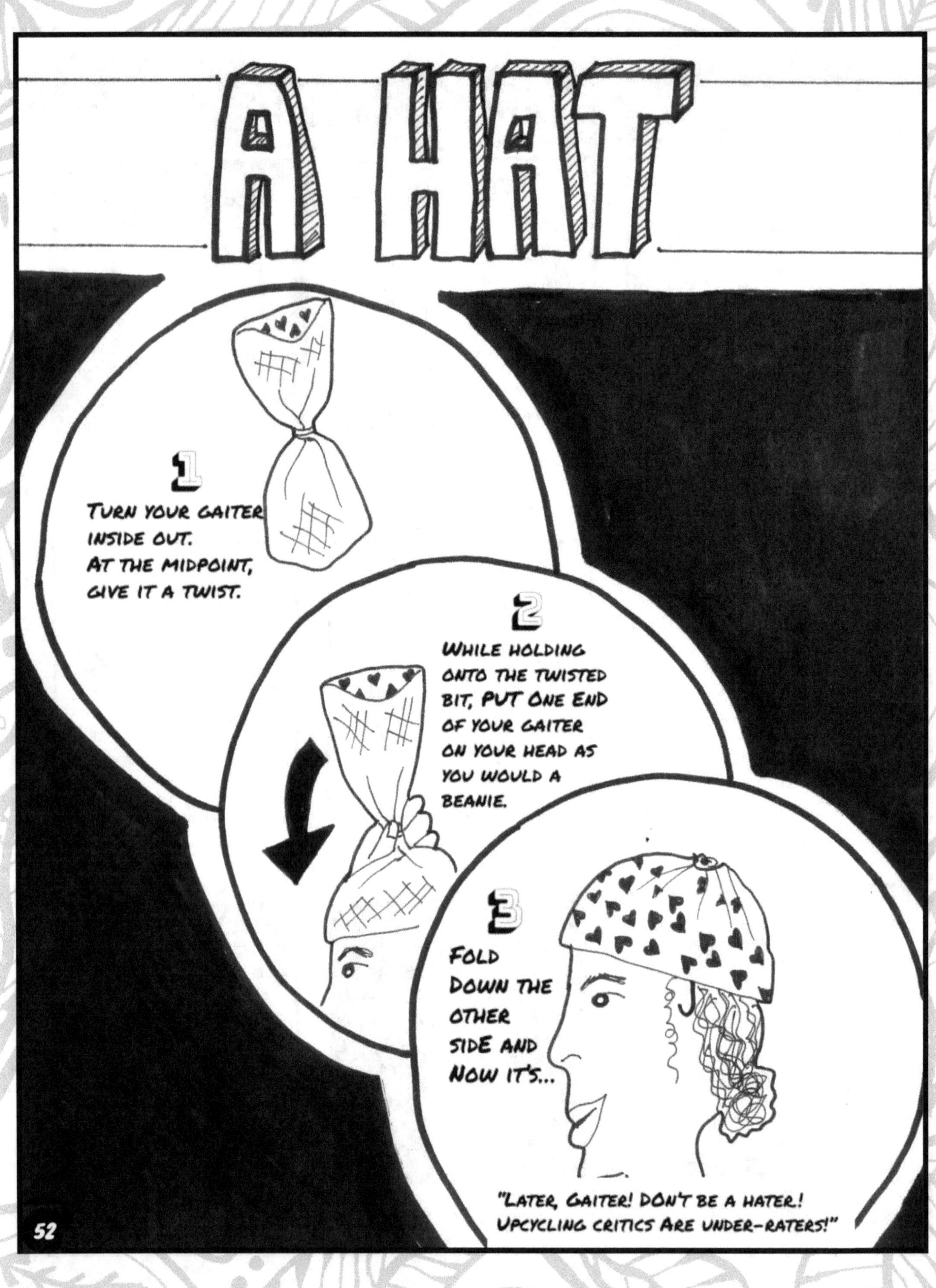
A HAT
1
TURN YOUR GAITER INSIDE OUT. AT THE MIDPOINT, GIVE IT A TWIST.
2
WHILE HOLDING ONTO THE TWISTED BIT, PUT ONE END OF YOUR GAITER ON YOUR HEAD AS YOU WOULD A BEANIE.
3
FOLD DOWN THE OTHER SIDE AND NOW IT'S...
"LATER, GAITER! DON'T BE A HATER! UPCYCLING CRITICS ARE UNDER-RATERS!"

THE PIRATE

*All instructions must be read out loud in your best pirate accent.

1

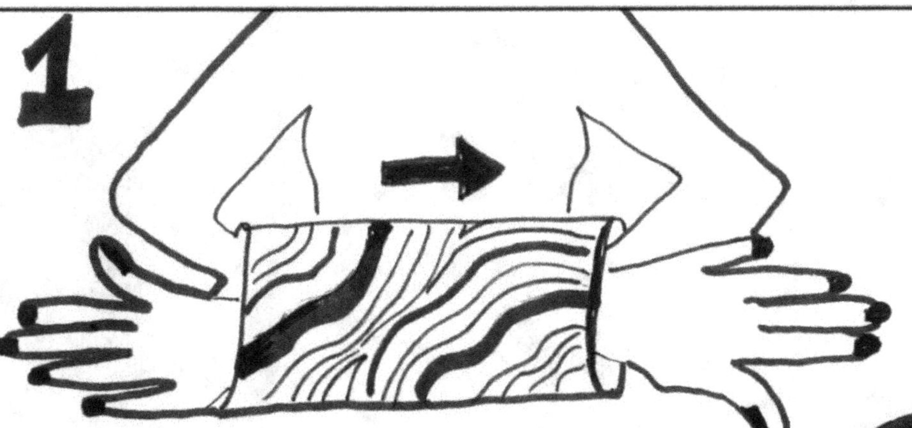

PLACE YOUR ARMS THROUGH THE GAITER. HOLDING ONTO THE GAITER WITH EACH HAND, PULL THROUGH, CREATING A KNOT.

2

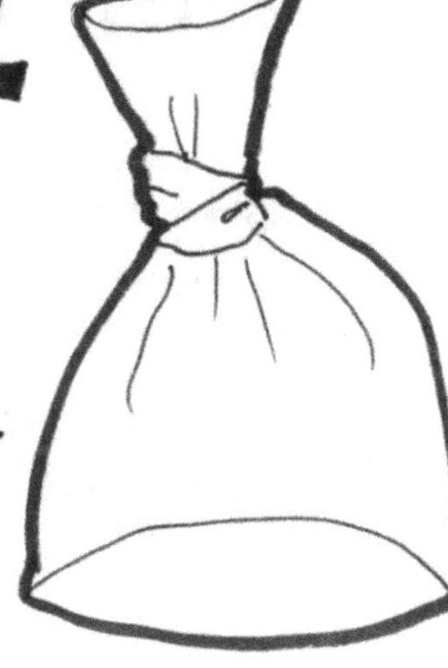

SCOOT THE KNOT UP IF NEEDED TO MAKE A BIGGER CAP.

3

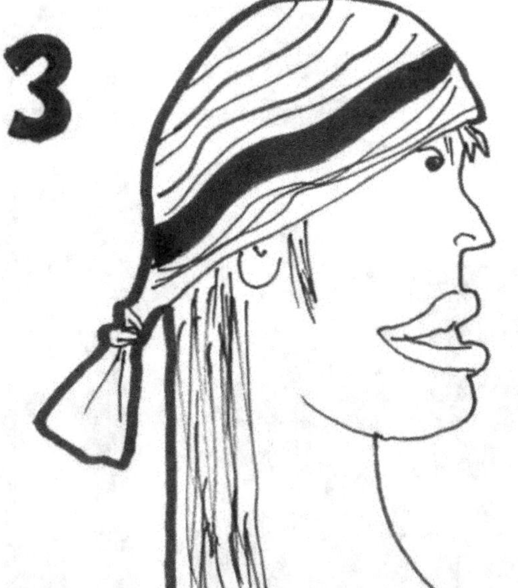

PLACE THE LARGER BIT ON YOUR HEAD.

WELL DONE, MATEY! ARRRRRR!

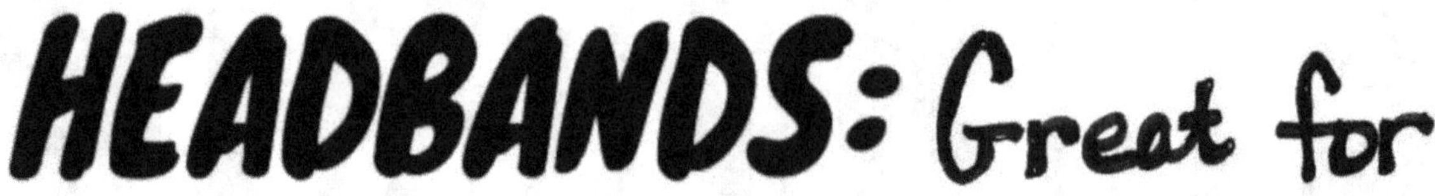

HIKING, CANOEING, SKATE-BOARDING, ULTIMATE FRISBEE, HORSE BACK RIDING and most importantly...

JAZZERCISE

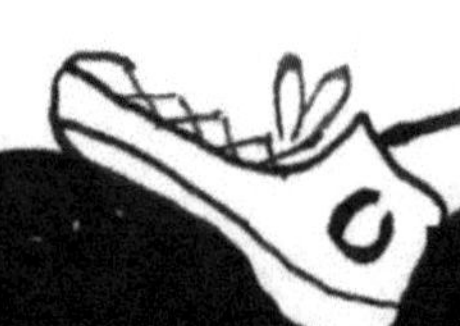

FOR ALL HEADBAND PROJECTS

You will need:

- An upcycled t-shirt

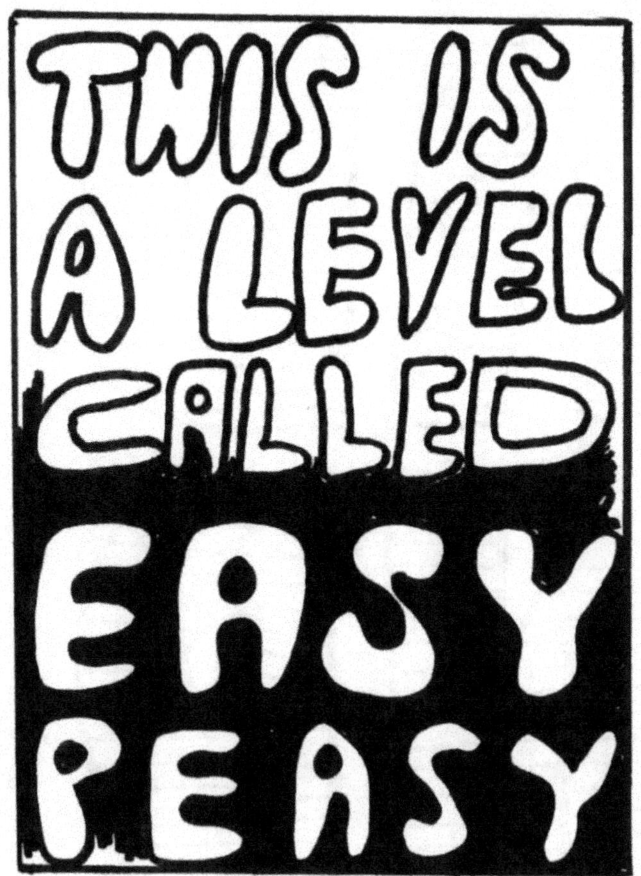
THIS IS
A LEVEL
CALLED
EASY
PEASY

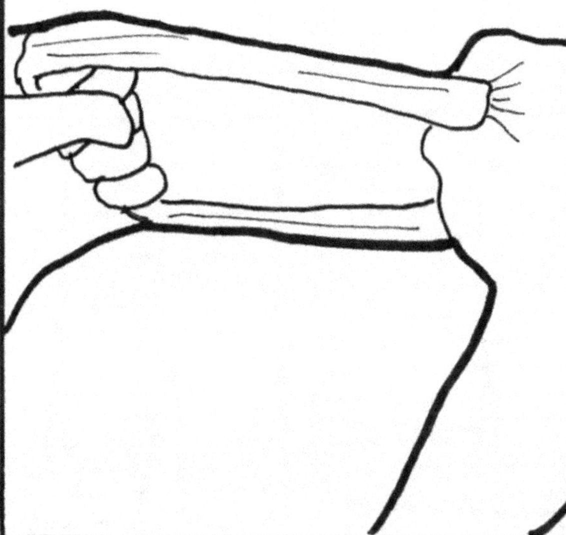
Cut about 4 inches off
the bottom of a small to
medium sized shirt.

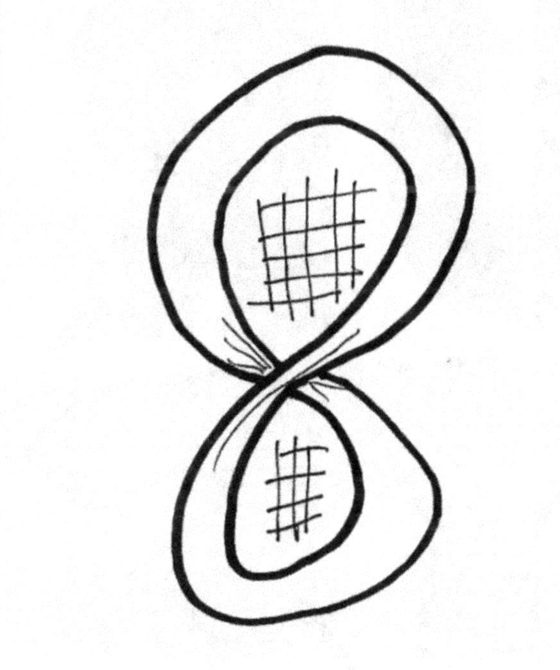
Twist at the midway point like so.

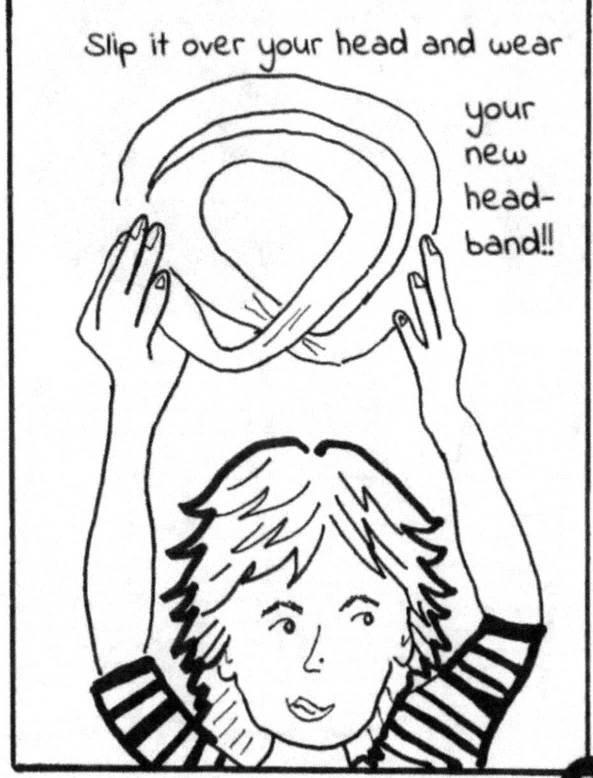
Slip it over your head and wear
your
new
head-
band!!

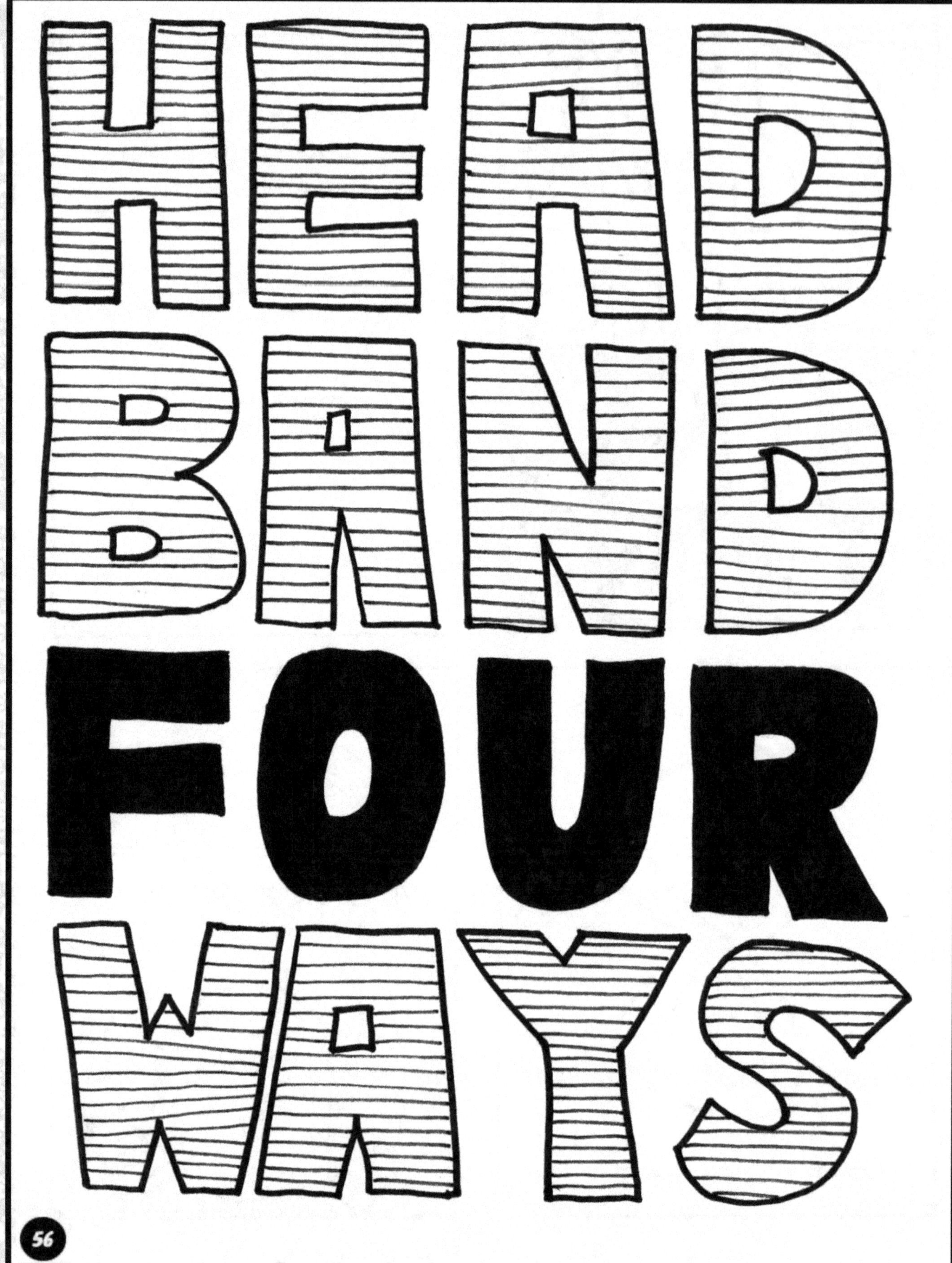
HEAD
BAND
FOUR
WAYS

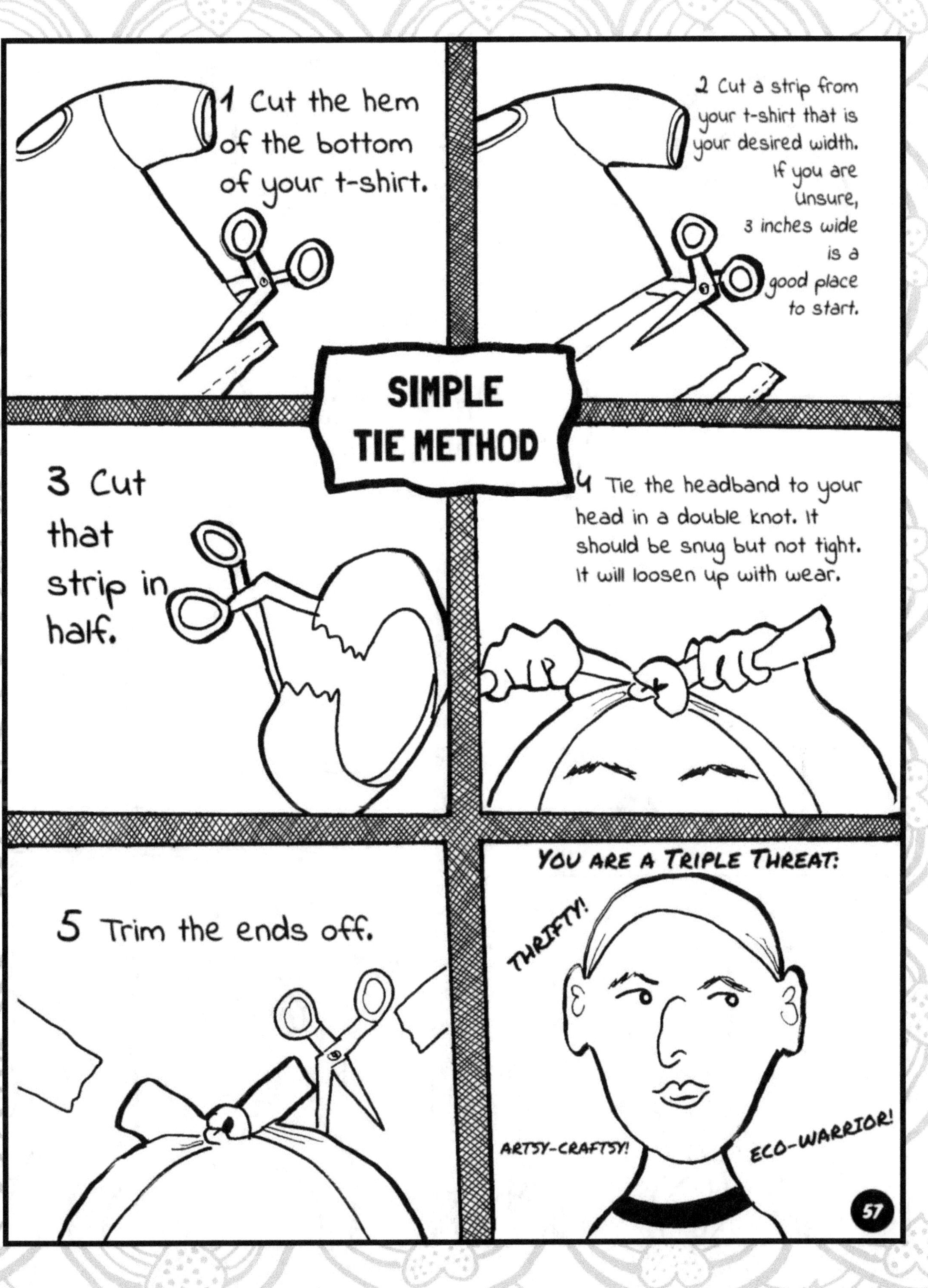
1 Cut the hem of the bottom of your t-shirt.
2 Cut a strip from your t-shirt that is your desired width. If you are unsure, 3 inches wide is a good place to start.
SIMPLE TIE METHOD
3 Cut that strip in half.
4 Tie the headband to your head in a double knot. It should be snug but not tight. It will loosen up with wear.
5 Trim the ends off.
YOU ARE A TRIPLE THREAT:
THRIFTY!
ARTSY-CRAFTSY!
ECO-WARRIOR!

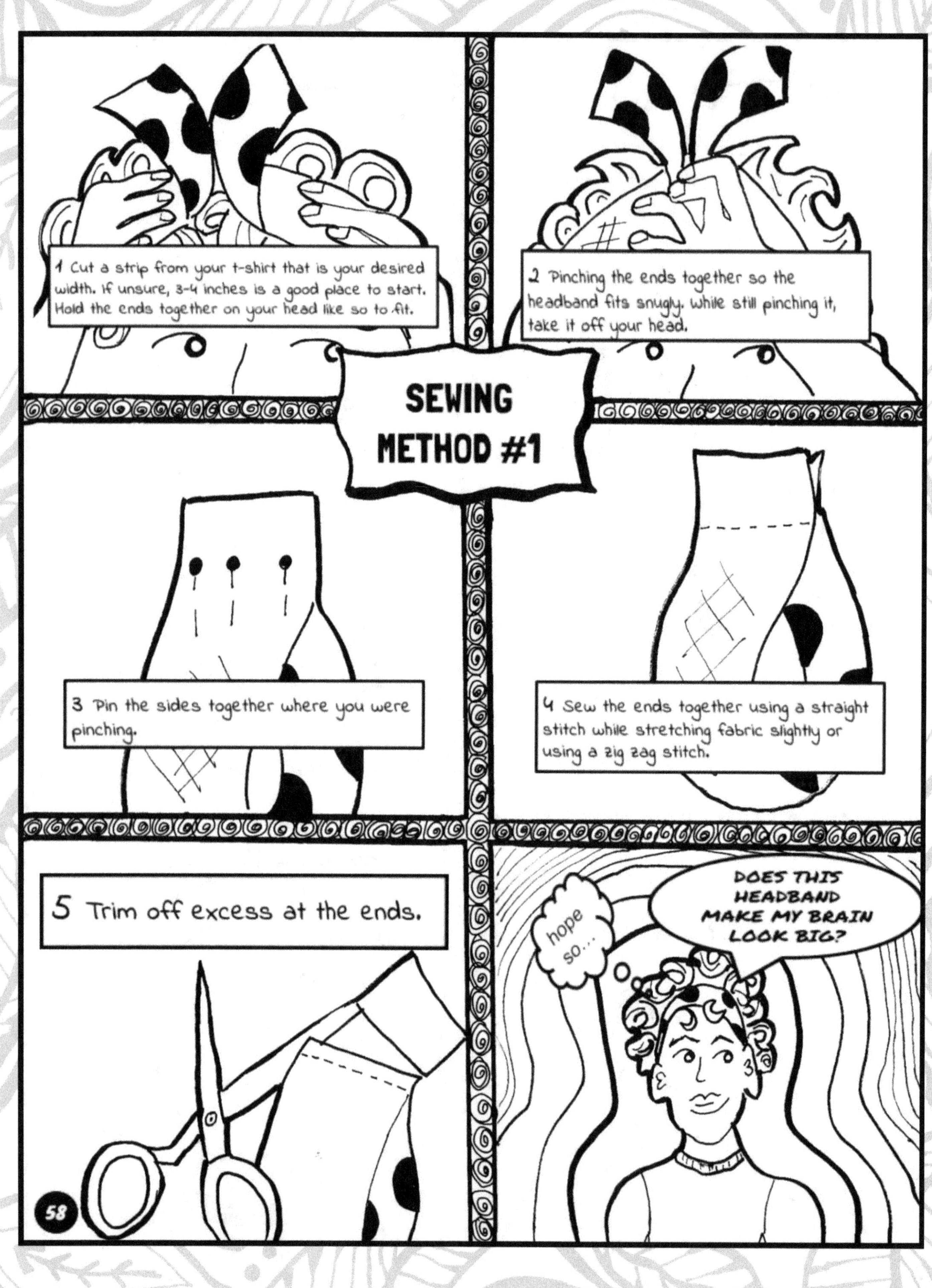
1 Cut a strip from your t-shirt that is your desired width. If unsure, 3-4 inches is a good place to start. Hold the ends together on your head like so to fit.
2 Pinching the ends together so the headband fits snugly. While still pinching it, take it off your head.
SEWING METHOD #1
3 Pin the sides together where you were pinching.
4 Sew the ends together using a straight stitch while stretching fabric slightly or using a zig zag stitch.
5 Trim off excess at the ends.
hope so...
DOES THIS HEADBAND MAKE MY BRAIN LOOK BIG?

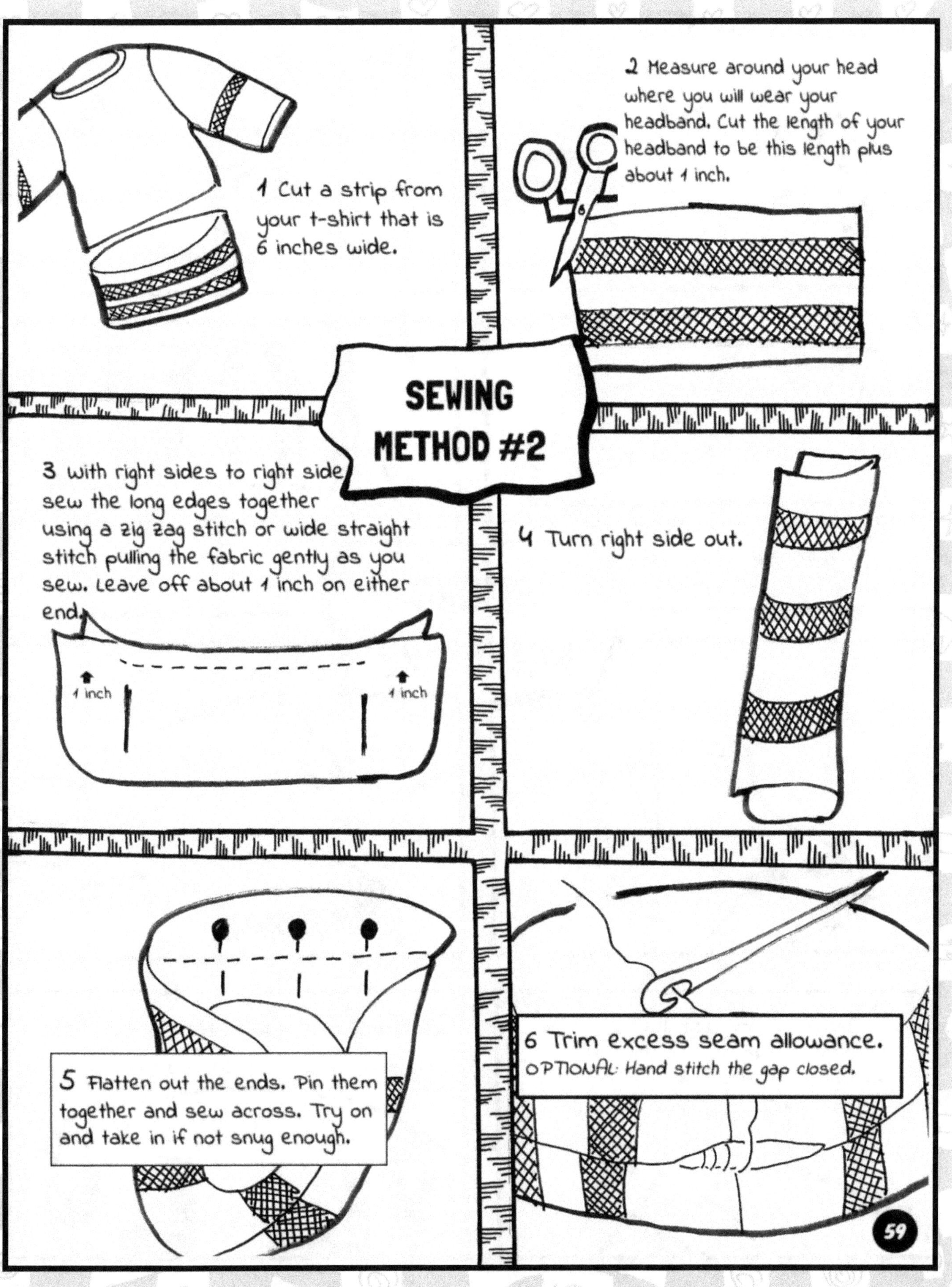
SEWING
METHOD #2
1 Cut a strip from your t-shirt that is 6 inches wide.
2 Measure around your head where you will wear your headband. Cut the length of your headband to be this length plus about 1 inch.
3 With right sides to right side sew the long edges together using a zig zag stitch or wide straight stitch pulling the fabric gently as you sew. Leave off about 1 inch on either end.
1 inch
1 inch
4 Turn right side out.
5 Flatten out the ends. Pin them together and sew across. Try on and take in if not snug enough.
6 Trim excess seam allowance.
OPTIONAL: Hand stitch the gap closed.

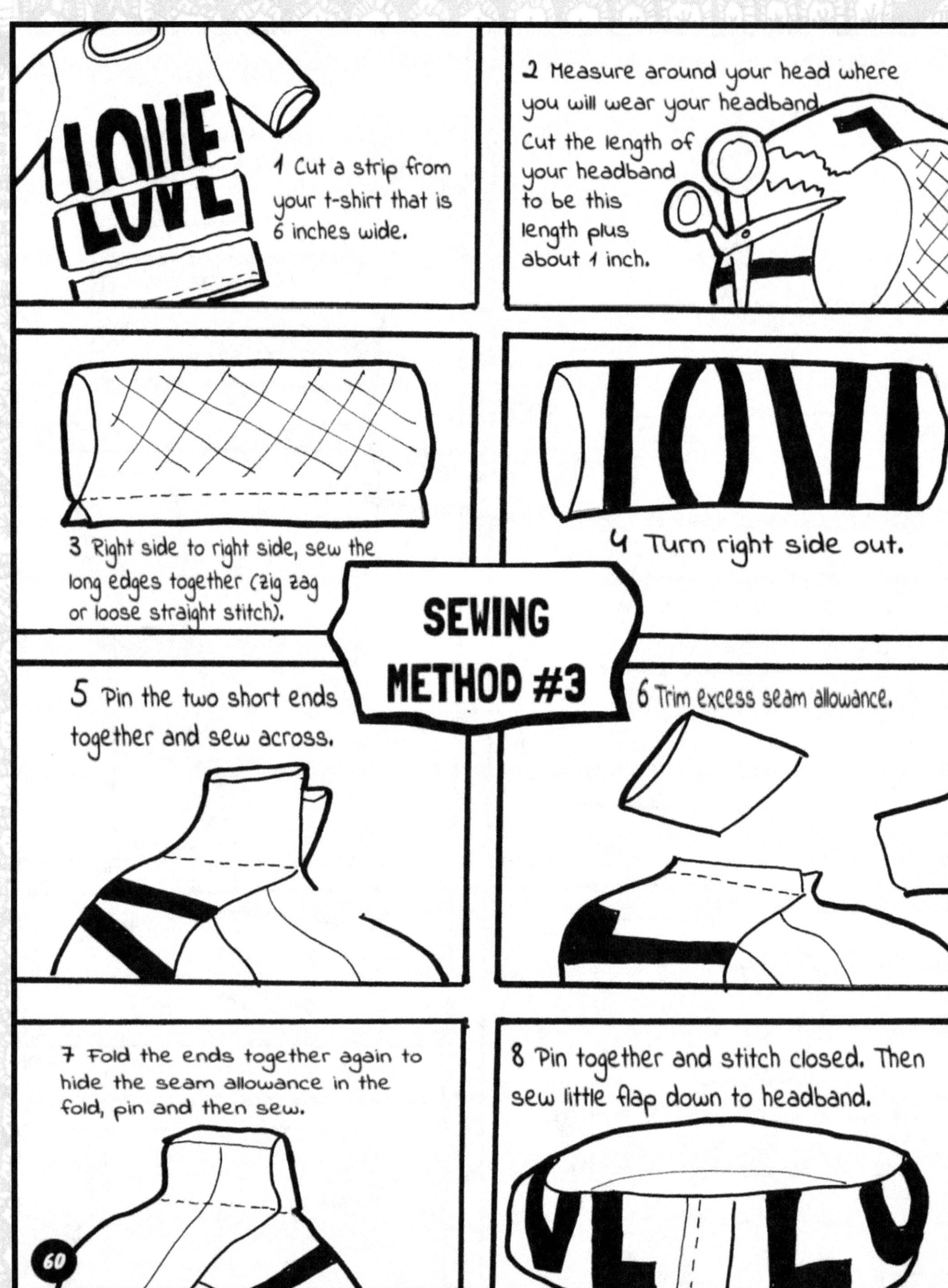
1 Cut a strip from your t-shirt that is 6 inches wide.
LOVE
2 Measure around your head where you will wear your headband.
Cut the length of your headband to be this length plus about 1 inch.
3 Right side to right side, sew the long edges together (zig zag or loose straight stitch).
4 Turn right side out.
SEWING METHOD #3
5 Pin the two short ends together and sew across.
6 Trim excess seam allowance.
7 Fold the ends together again to hide the seam allowance in the fold, pin and then sew.
8 Pin together and stitch closed. Then sew little flap down to headband.

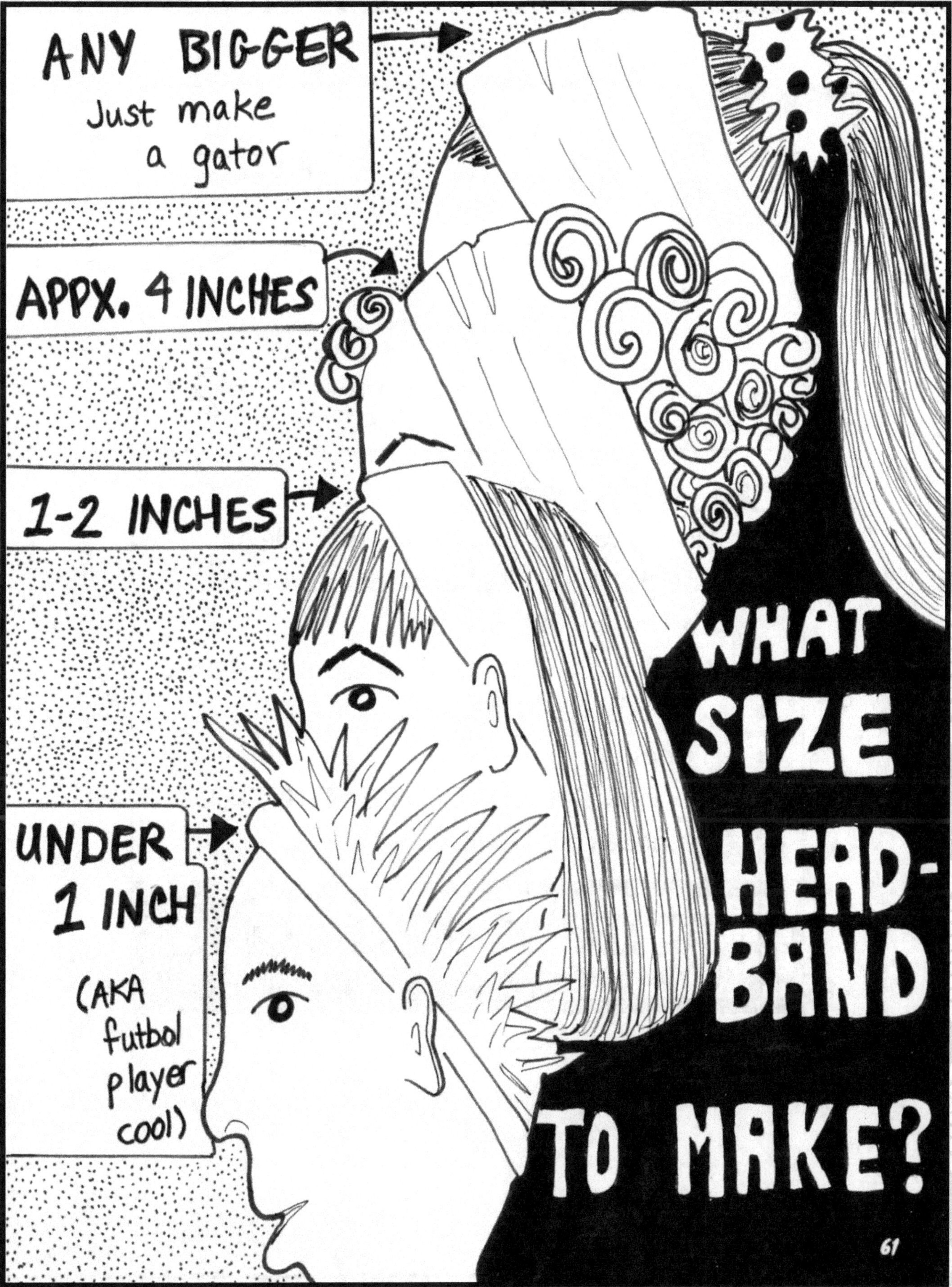

WHAT SIZE HEAD-BAND TO MAKE?
ANY BIGGER
Just make a gator
APPX. 4 INCHES
1-2 INCHES
UNDER 1 INCH
(AKA futbol player cool)

MITTENS

Single Layer

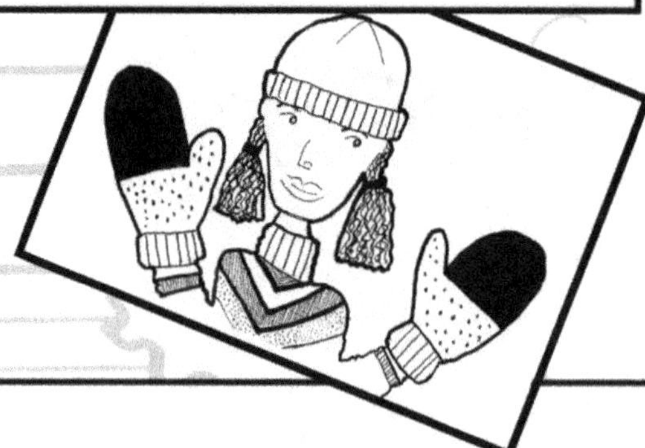

You will need:

- An upcycled wool sweater ideally one that you (ahem) or 'someone' shrunk in the dryer
- OPTIONAL: Contrasting wool sweater
- white scrap paper
- Pencil
- TO MAKE A WATERPROOF MITTEN: Raincoat

PAIRS NICELY WITH: BEANIE/ STOCKING CAP, EARWARMER.
FOR WATERPROOF MITTEN: DOG TREAT/ CHALK BAG, FANNY PACK Level 2

1 Find the mitten pattern pieces on page 68. Trace pieces A, B, and C in your size onto scrap paper.

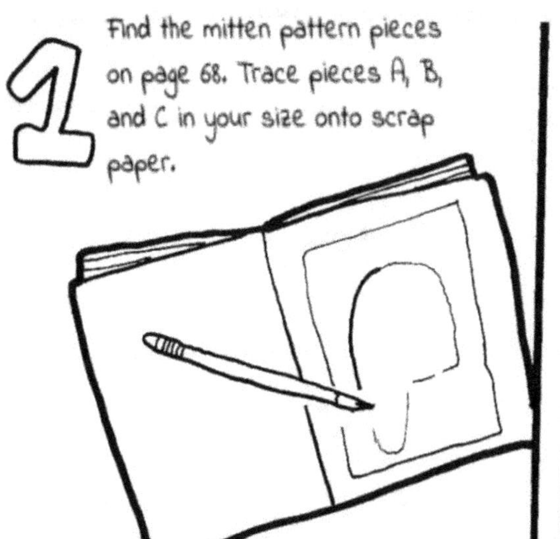

2 Cut out the pattern pieces that you just drew.

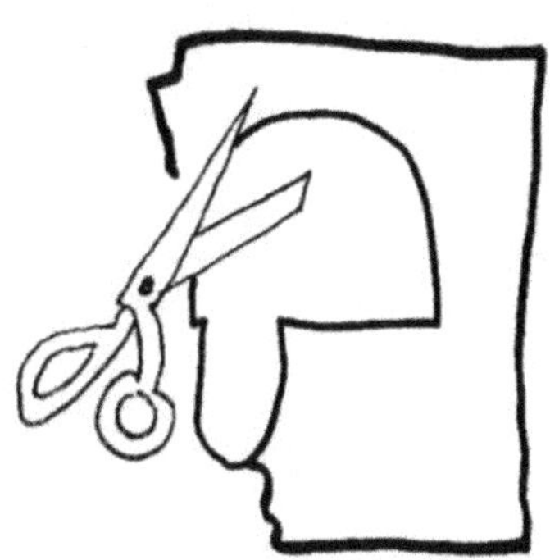

3 Cut the cuff off your recycled garment with about ½ inch seam allowance.

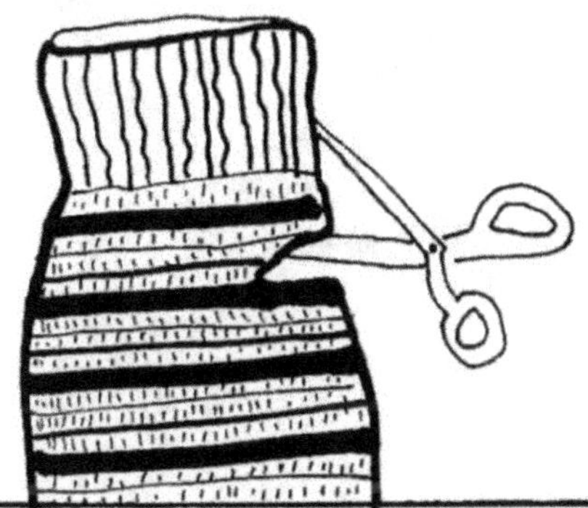

If you are making the mitten from a raincoat/waterproof garment, cut ½ below wrist closure.

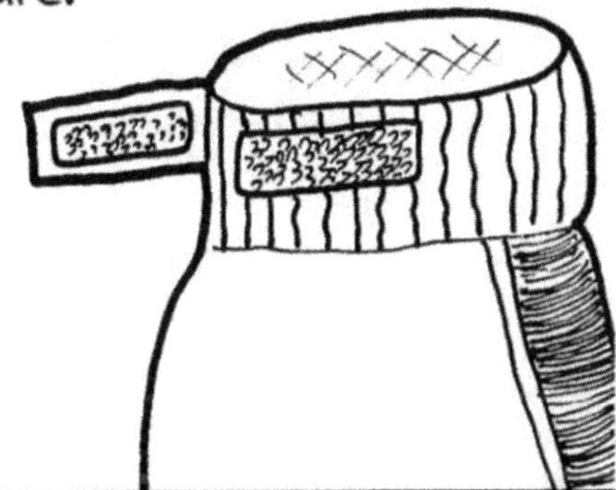

4 If cuff is too big, turn inside out and take in to fit your wrist.

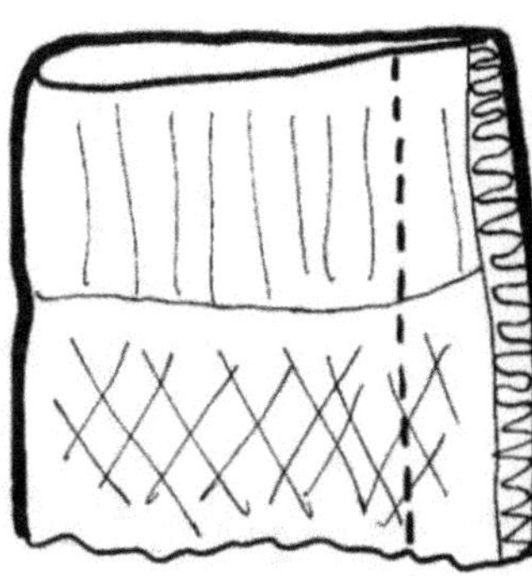

5 Place pattern pieces A and B onto fabric and cut one of each.

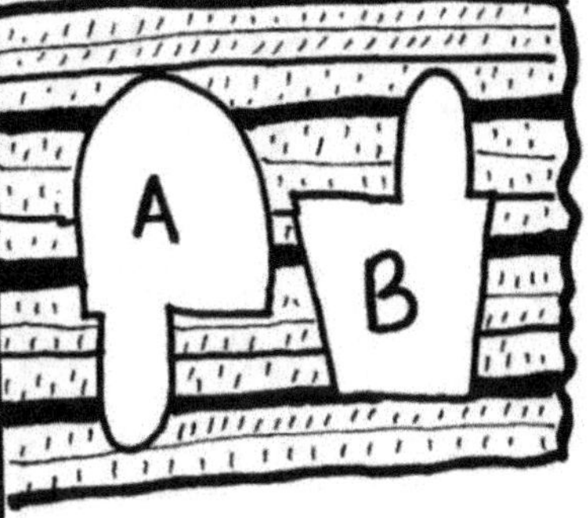

6 Turn over pattern pieces and cut one of each piece again.

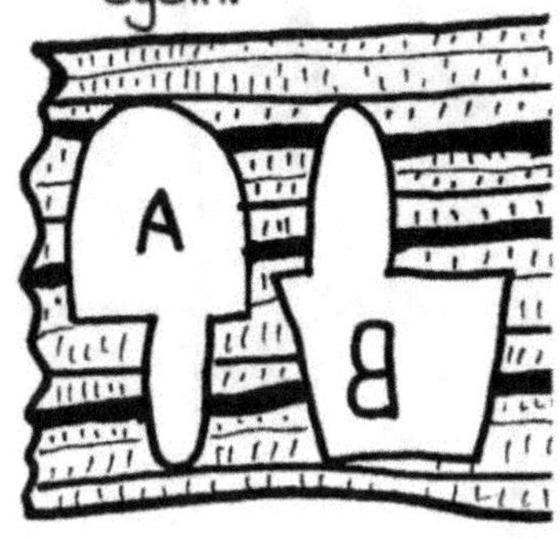

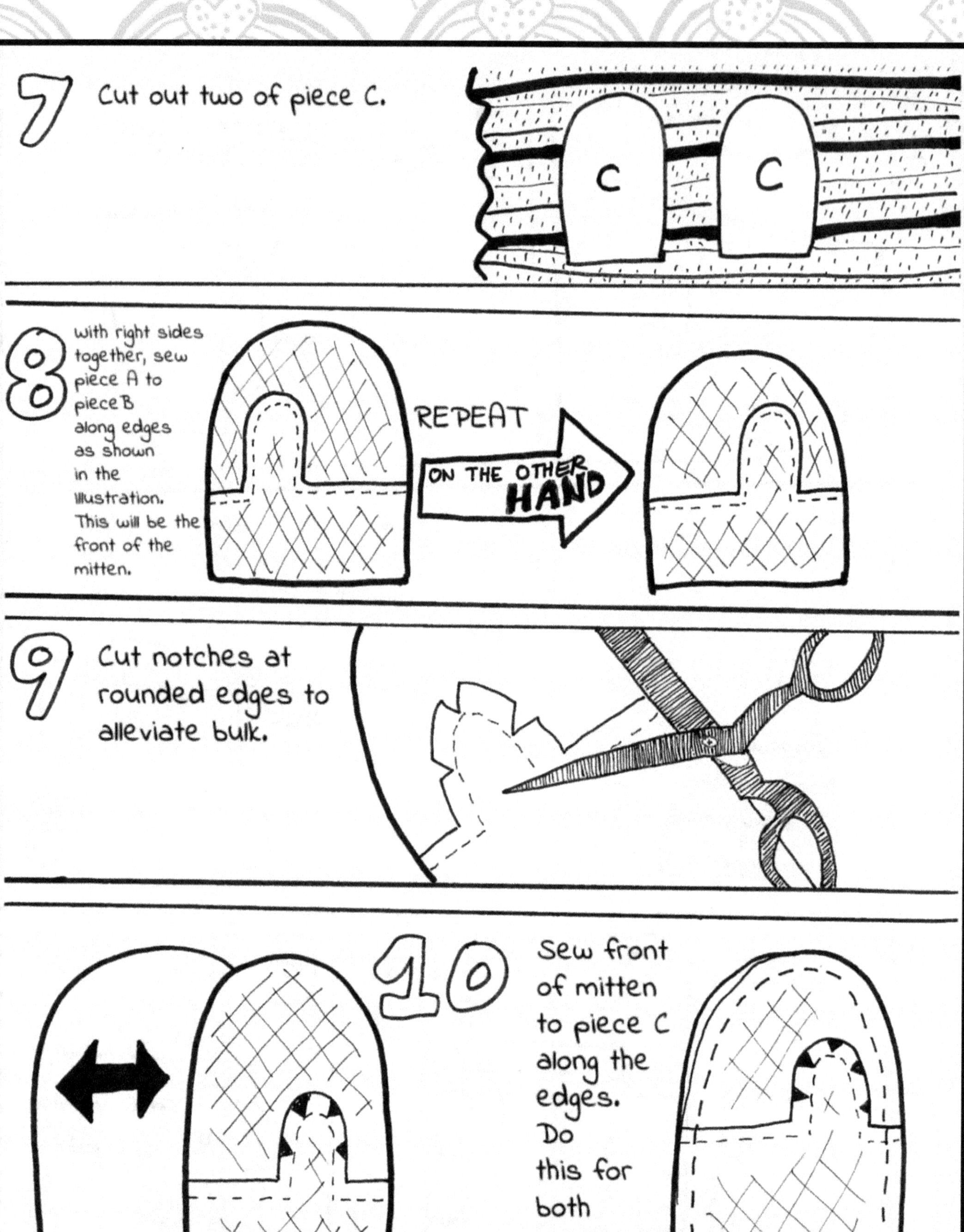
7
Cut out two of piece C.
C
C
8
with right sides together, sew piece A to piece B along edges as shown in the illustration. This will be the front of the mitten.
REPEAT
ON THE OTHER HAND
9
Cut notches at rounded edges to alleviate bulk.
10
Sew front of mitten to piece C along the edges. Do this for both mittens.

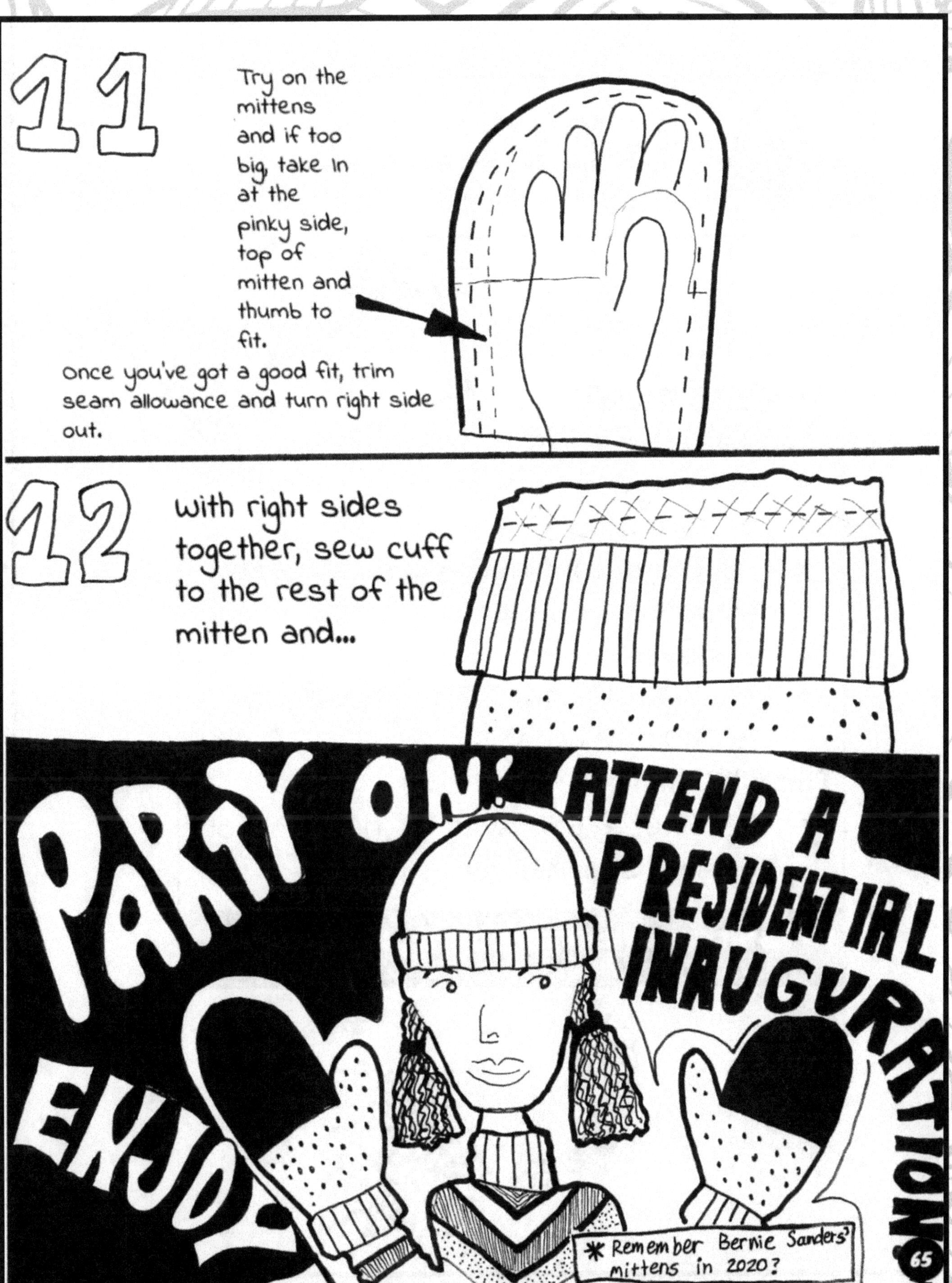
11
Try on the mittens and if too big, take in at the pinky side, top of mitten and thumb to fit.
once you've got a good fit, trim seam allowance and turn right side out.
12
with right sides together, sew cuff to the rest of the mitten and...
PARTY ON!
ATTEND A PRESIDENTIAL INAUGURATION!
ENJOY!
* Remember Bernie Sanders' mittens in 2020?

MITTENS

Lined

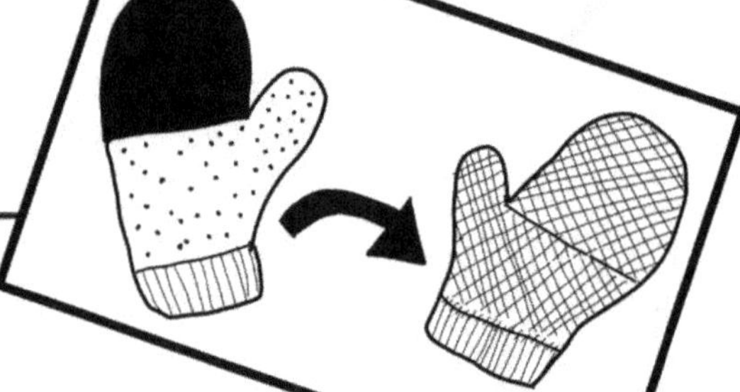

You will need:

FOR YOUR OUTER GLOVE:

- An upcycled wool sweater (shrunk or normal)
- OPTIONal: contrasting wool sweater
- white scrap paper
- Pencil
- TO MAKE AN OUTER WATERPROOF MITTEN: Raincoat

FOR YOUR LINING:

- A softer fabric such as Merino wool or soft spandex jersey

PAIRS NICELY WITH: BEANIE, GATOR, HEADBANDS

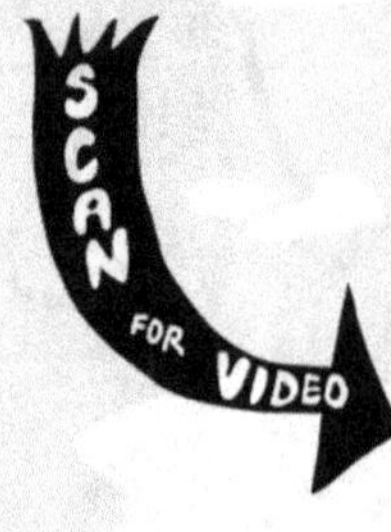

LINED MITTENS

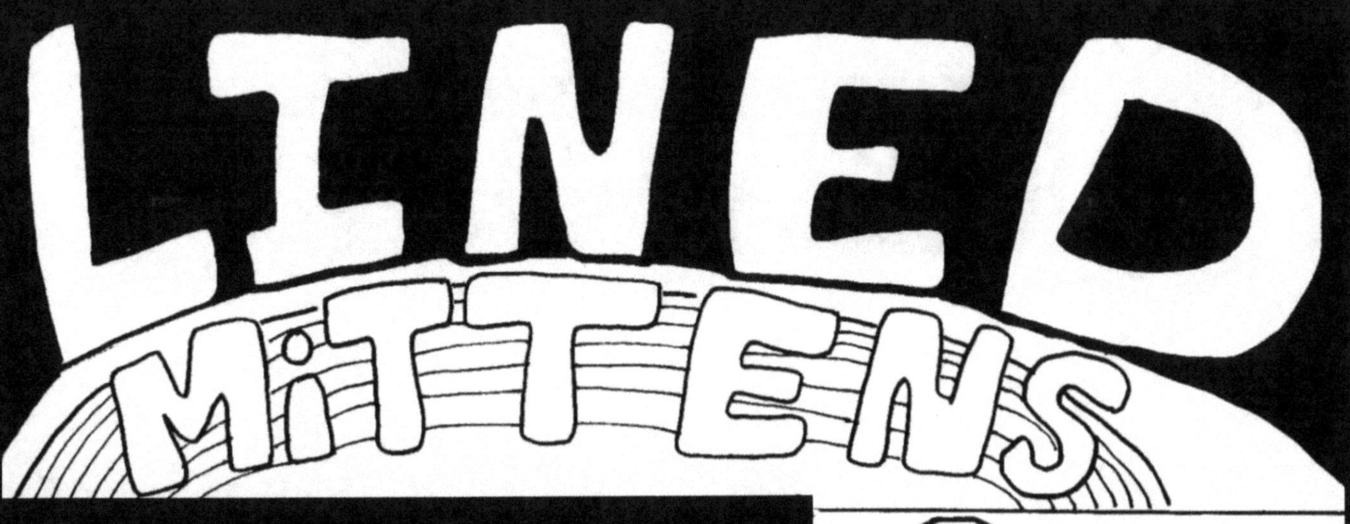

FOR YOUR OUTER MITTENS:
FOLLOW INSTRUCTIONS FOR THE MITTENS PROJECT

FOR YOUR INNER MITTENS:
FOLLOW STEPS 1–11 WITH THE SOFTER FABRIC,
making sure to cut pattern pieces on line that says 'cut here for lining.'

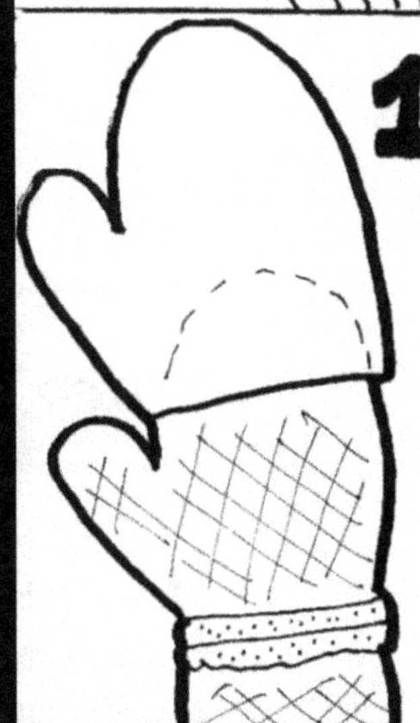

1 Turn outer layer inside out and place liner over it (wrong sides together).

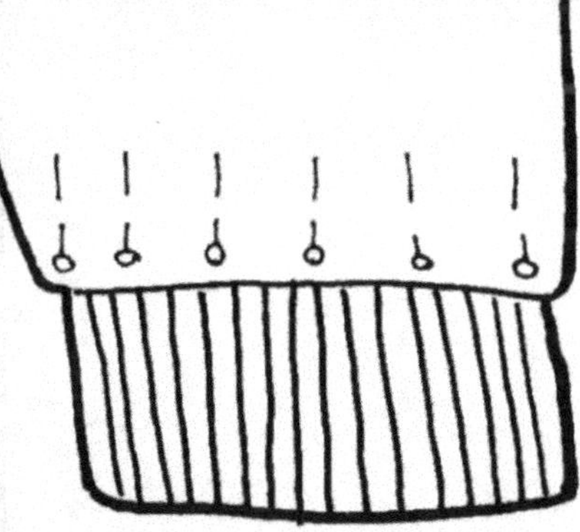

2 Turn raw edges of liner in and pin to outer layer slightly below seam.

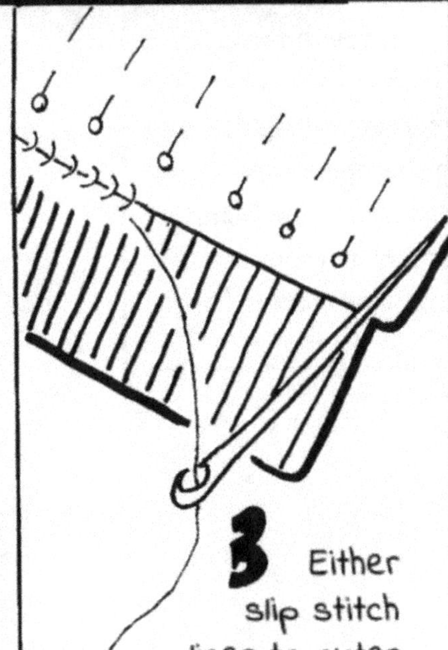

3 Either slip stitch liner to outer layer by hand or...

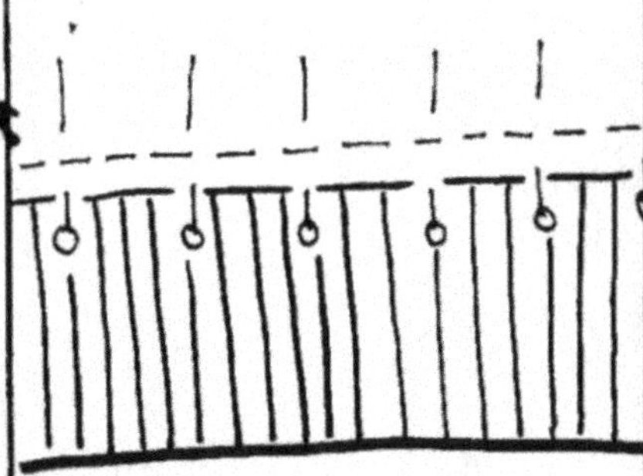

4 Sew lining to outer layer at seam with a machine.

MITTEN PATTERN PIECES

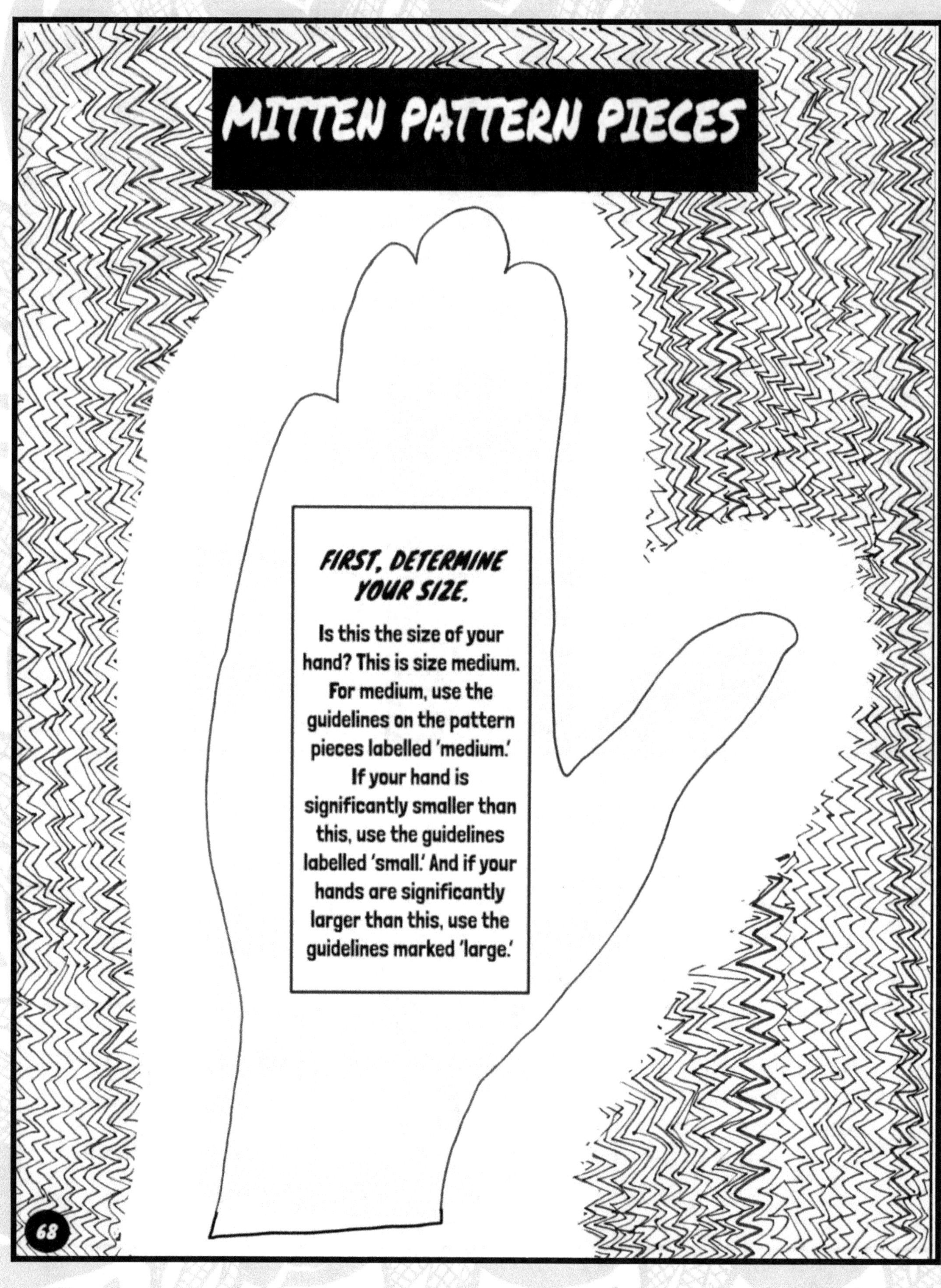

FIRST, DETERMINE YOUR SIZE.

Is this the size of your hand? This is size medium. For medium, use the guidelines on the pattern pieces labelled 'medium.' If your hand is significantly smaller than this, use the guidelines labelled 'small.' And if your hands are significantly larger than this, use the guidelines marked 'large.'

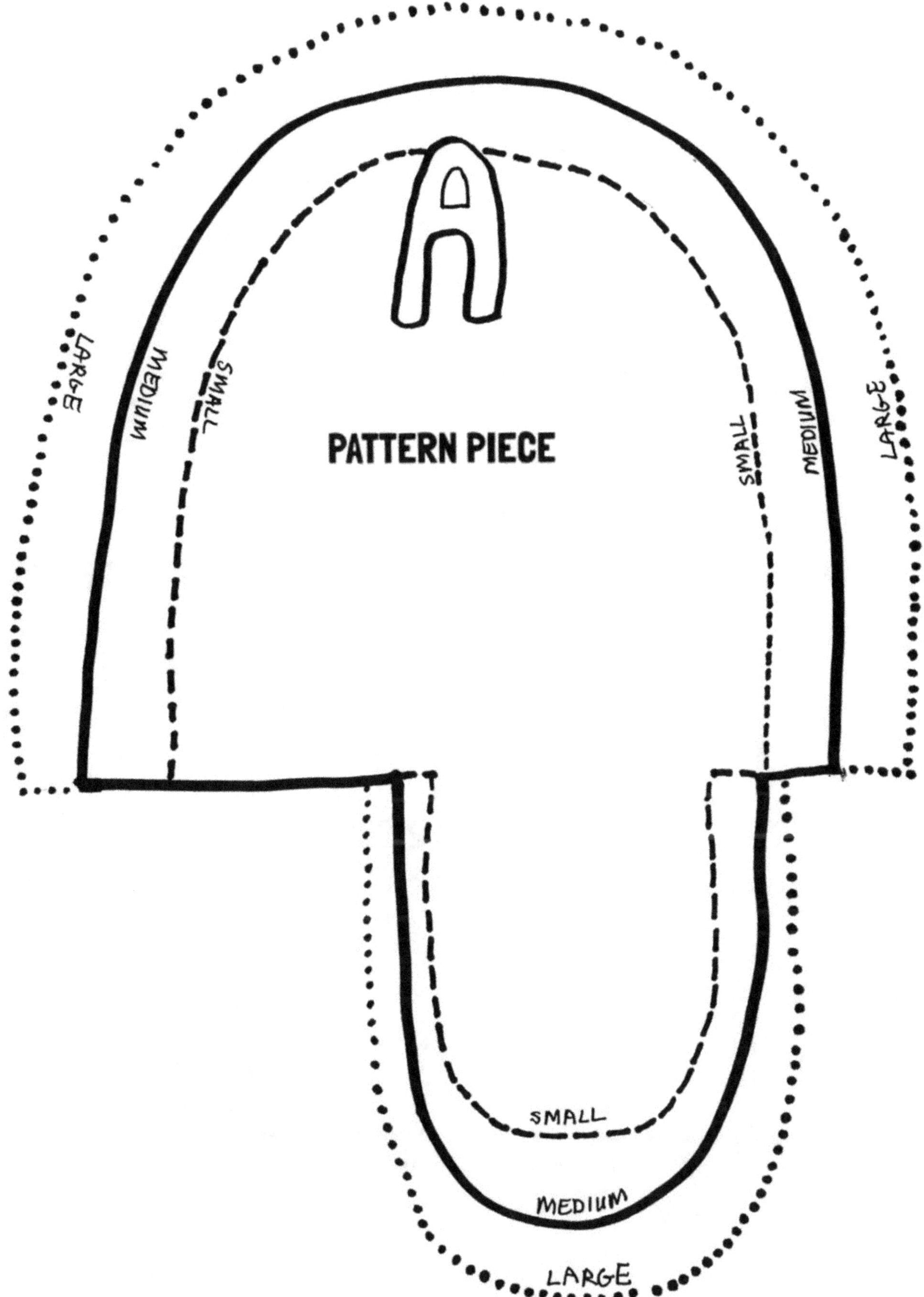
A
PATTERN PIECE
LARGE
MEDIUM
SMALL
SMALL
MEDIUM
LARGE
SMALL
MEDIUM
LARGE

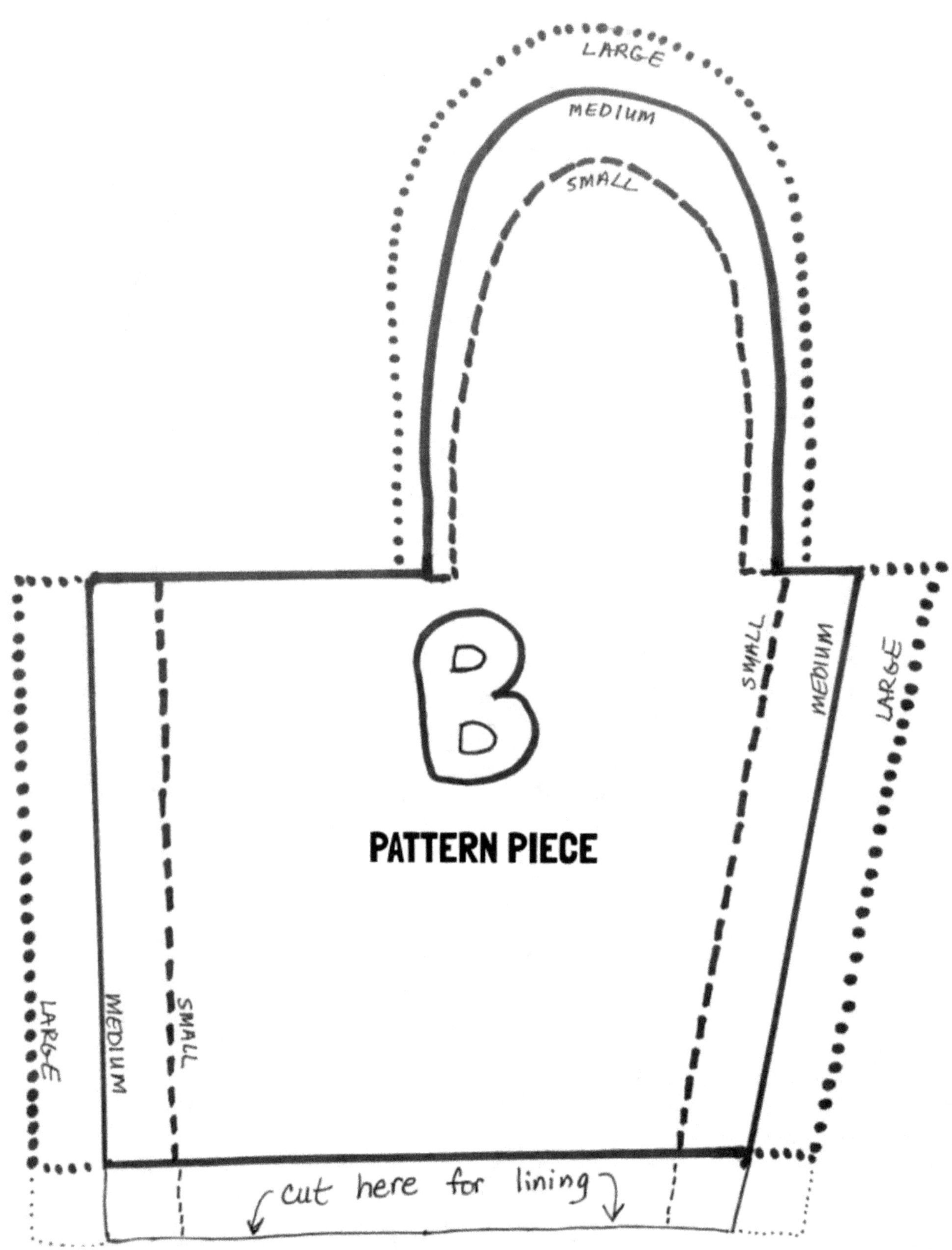
LARGE
MEDIUM
SMALL
B
PATTERN PIECE
SMALL
MEDIUM
LARGE
LARGE
MEDIUM
SMALL
cut here for lining

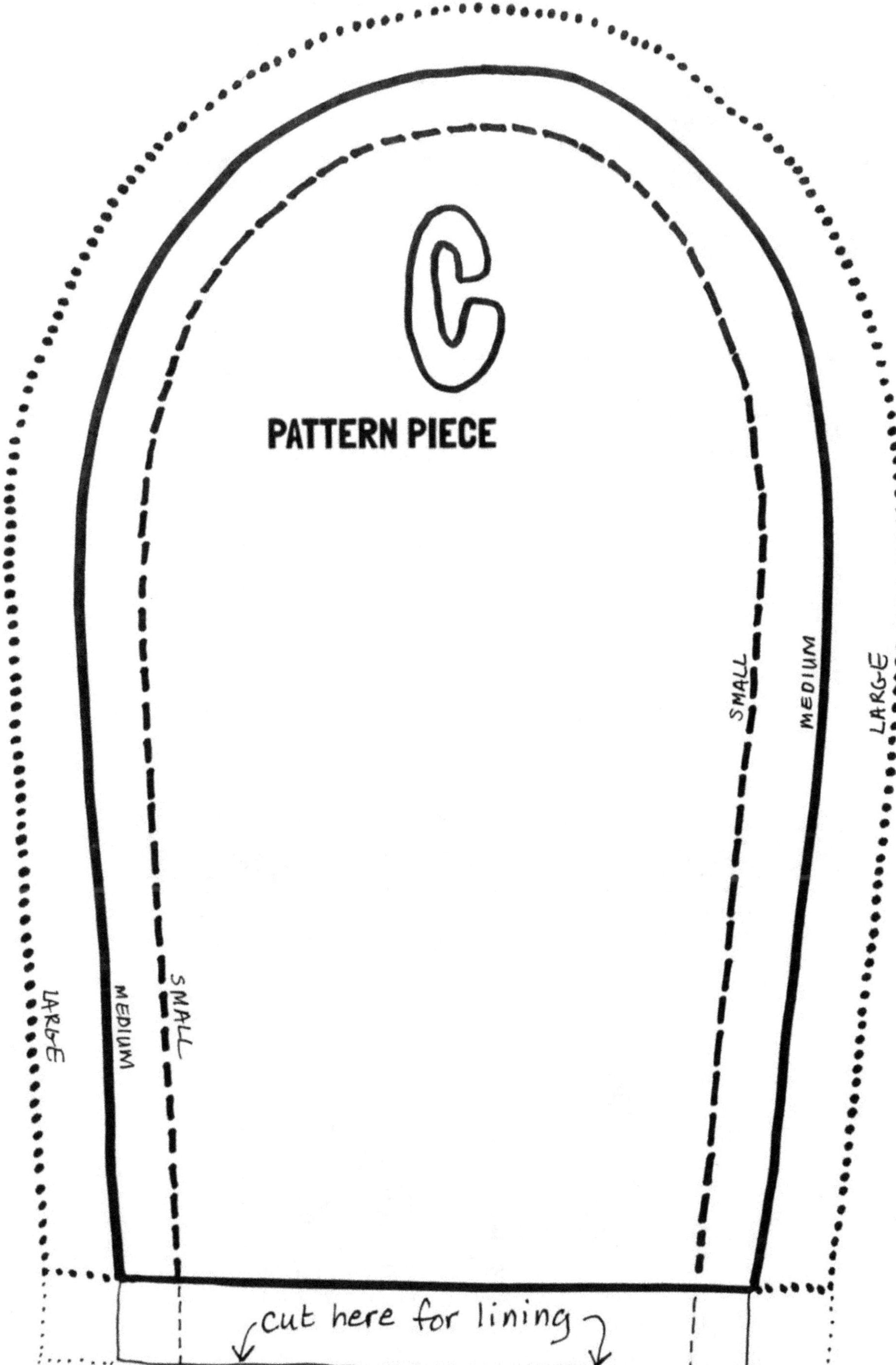

C
PATTERN PIECE
SMALL
MEDIUM
LARGE
LARGE
MEDIUM
SMALL
cut here for lining

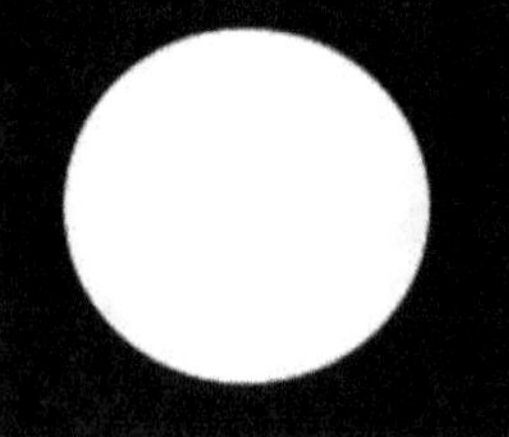

*BEANIE

Single Layer

You will need:

- A garment made of spandex and cotton
- A beanie that fits your well to use as a guide)

NOTE: You can also use something synthetic like polyester to make your beanie less water absorbent and more quick-drying. However, synthetic fabrics can make hair staticky.

PAIRS NICELY WITH: *FANNY PACK Level 1* and *TOWEL*

* These instructions work for both stocking caps and beanies; the only difference is the fabric (e.g., a sweater for a stocking cap, a T-shirt for a beanie).

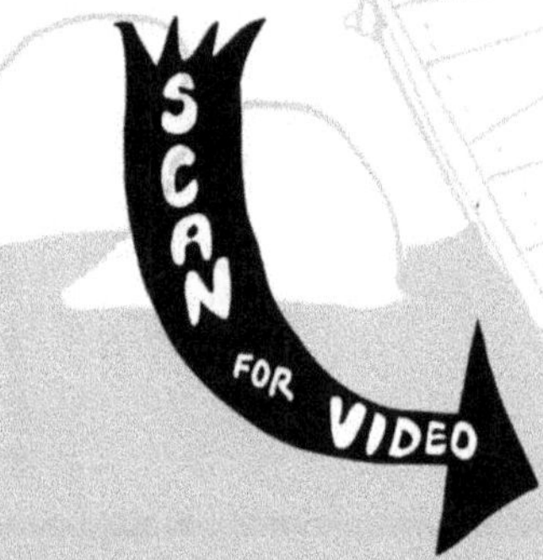

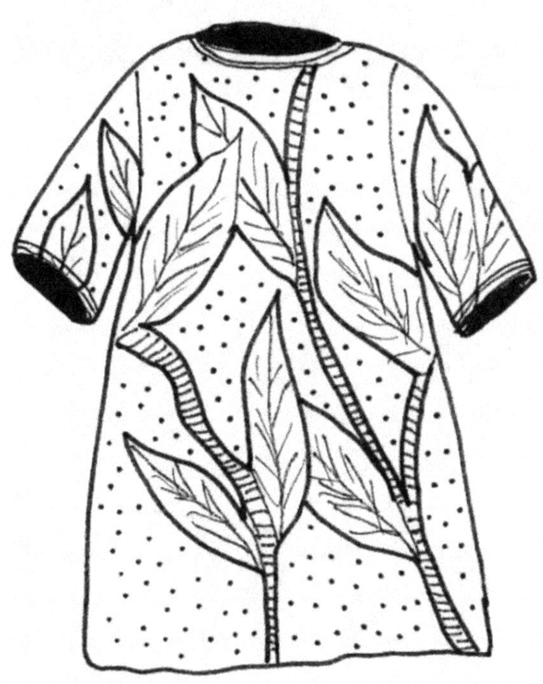

1 Lay down your stocking cap with the bottom lined up with the hem of your garment. If there is only raw edge, leave a gap between the bottom of the cap and the raw edge to create a brim (about 1-2 inches).

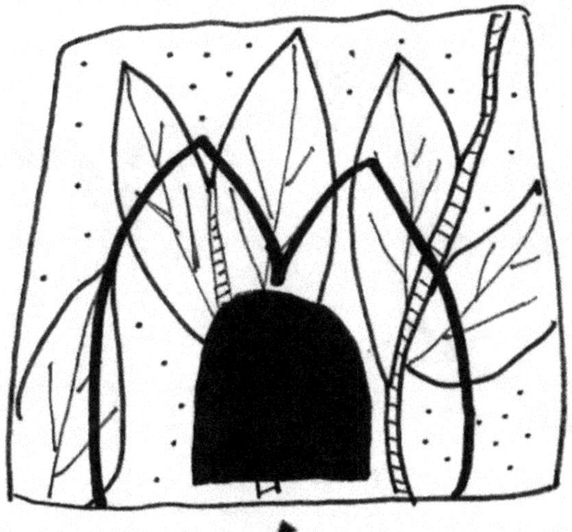

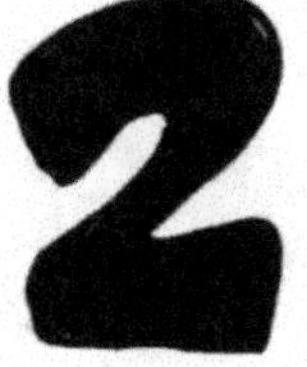

2 With right sides to right sides, sew the sides together like so.

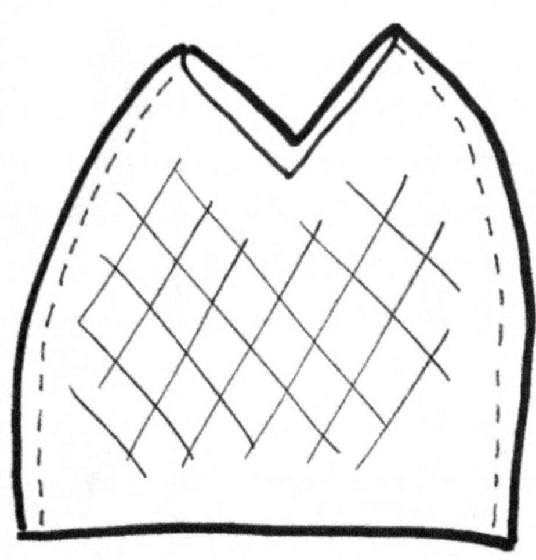

3 Open up the cap and realign so that the two seams are lined up together down the center. Trim the top to make the cap round.

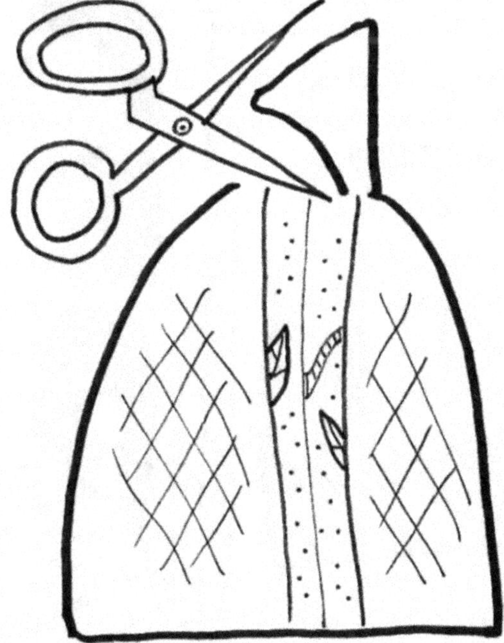

BEANIE

4 Sew the open edges of the cap together, tapering (see vocabulary section) on both sides. Use a straight stitch while pulling gently on the fabric or a zig zag stitch.

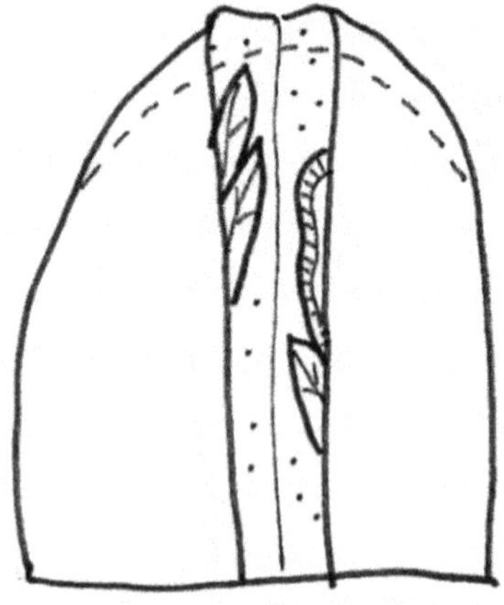

5 If needed, fold up the extra fabric at the bottom (from step 1). Zig zag into place, pulling gently as you sew.

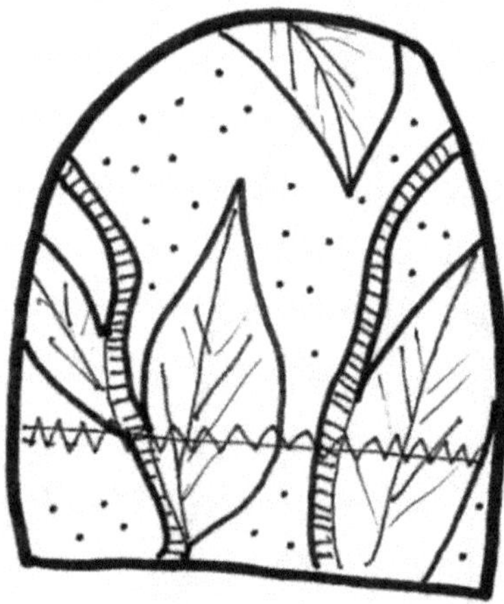

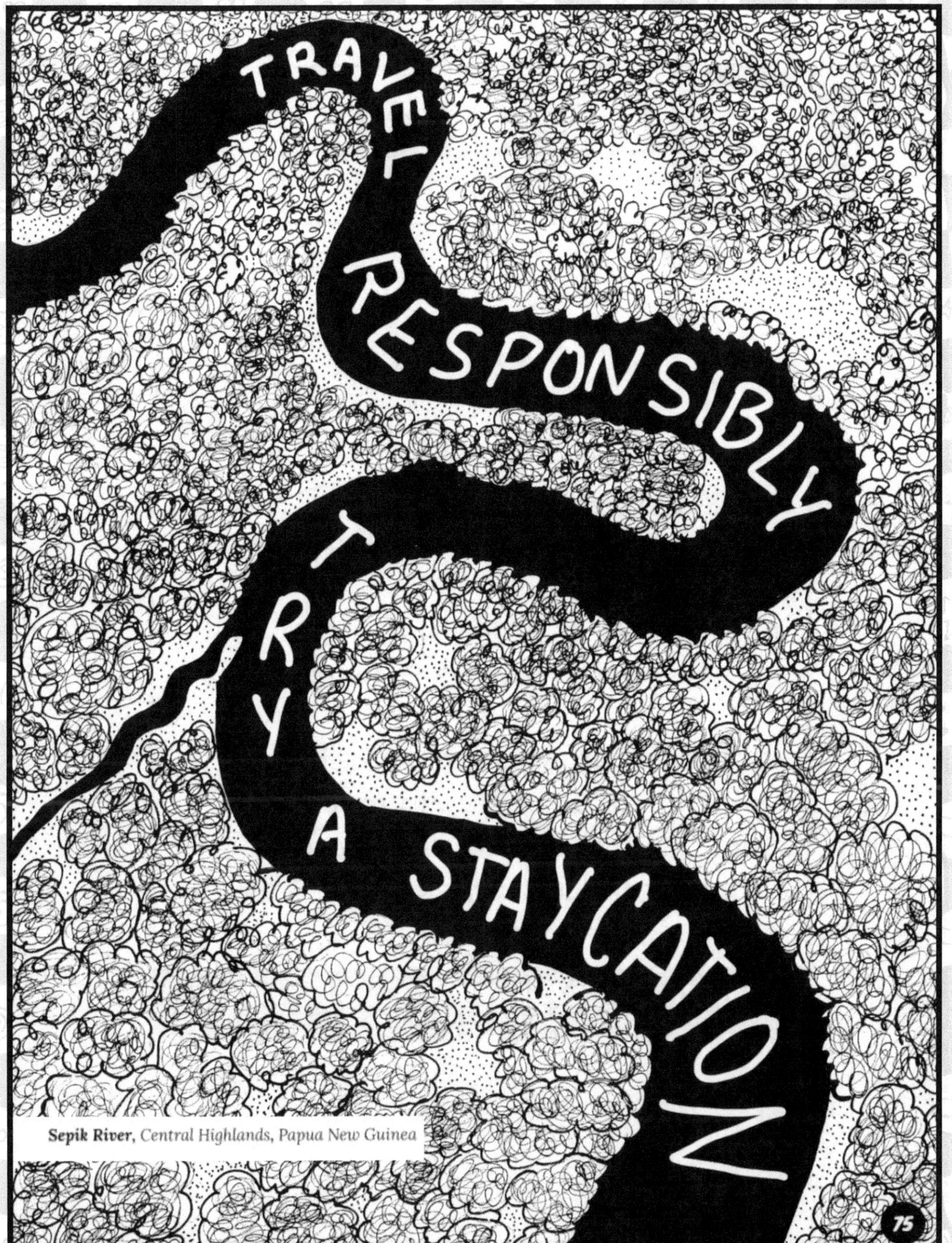

Sepik River, *Central Highlands, Papua New Guinea*

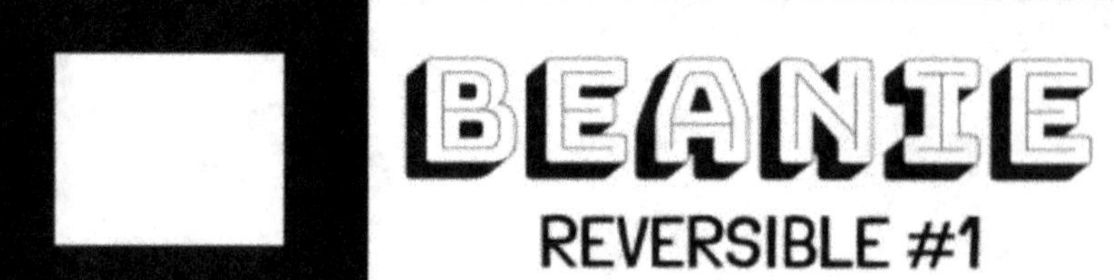

You will need:

- A garment made of spandex and cotton
- A beanie or stocking cap that fits your well to use as a guide)

NOTE: You can also use something synthetic like polyester to make your beanie less absorbent and more quick-drying. However, synthetic fabrics can make hair staticky.

PAIRS NICELY WITH: *FANNY PACK Level 1* and *TOWEL*

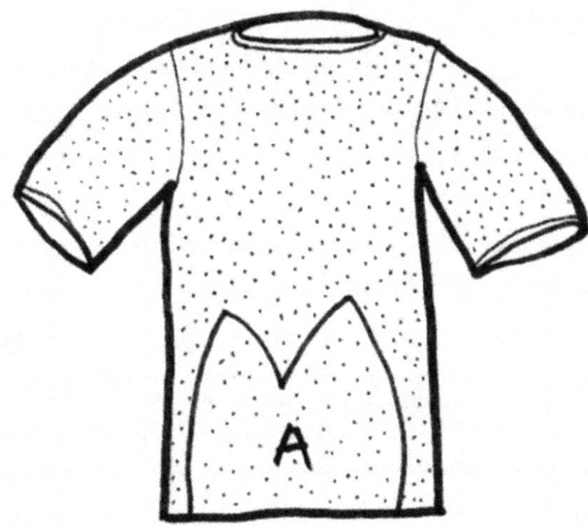

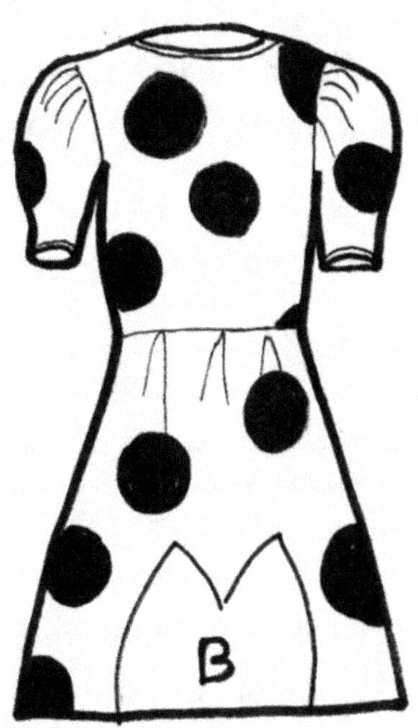

NOTE: For clarity of instruction, I have labelled my two fictional garments A and B. Because this is a reversible beanie, which garments you call A and which you call B does not matter.

1

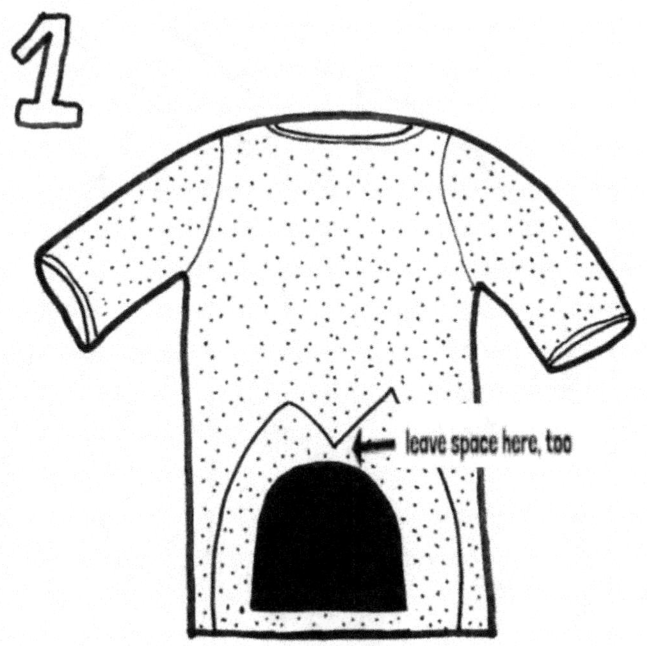

Using a beanie you like as a pattern, trace this shape. Leave about ½" seam allowance on all sides and the little valley of the M.

2

Sew the two pieces together, right side to right side. Use a zig-zag stitch or a wide straight stitch while stretching fabric slightly.

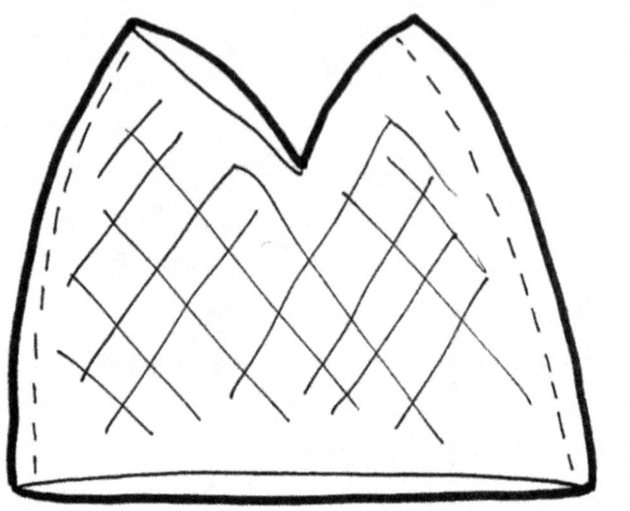

3

Open up the cap and realign so that the two seams are lined up together down the center.

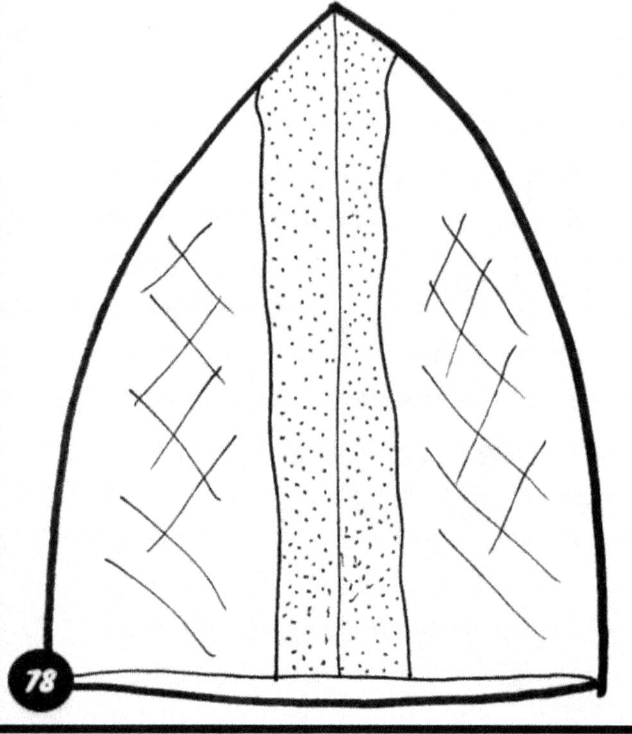

4

Trim the top to make the cap round.

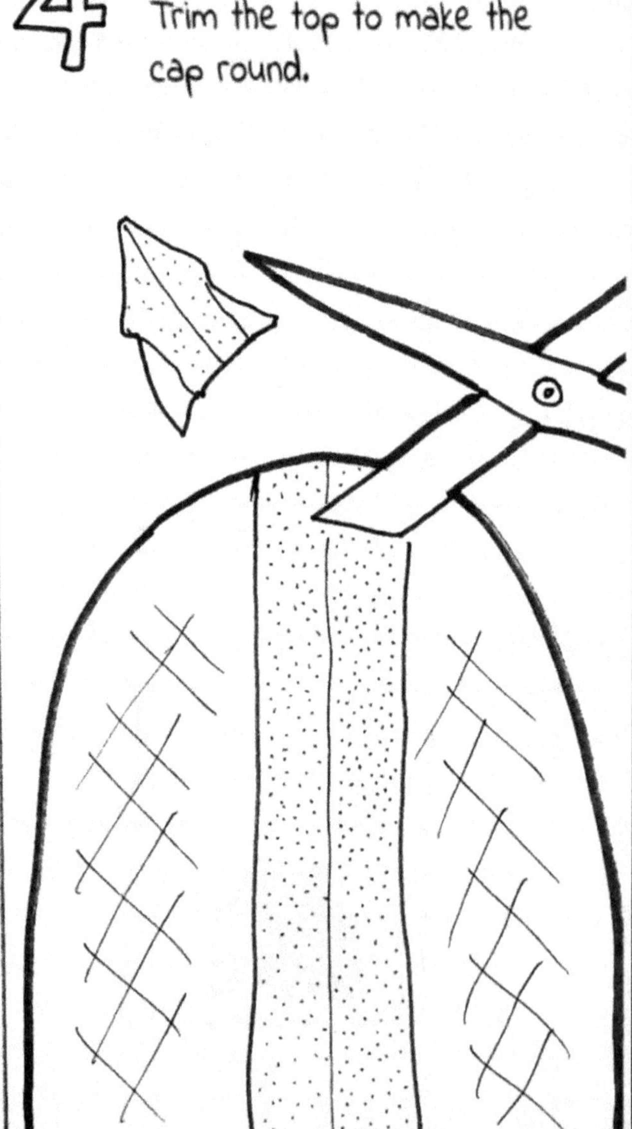

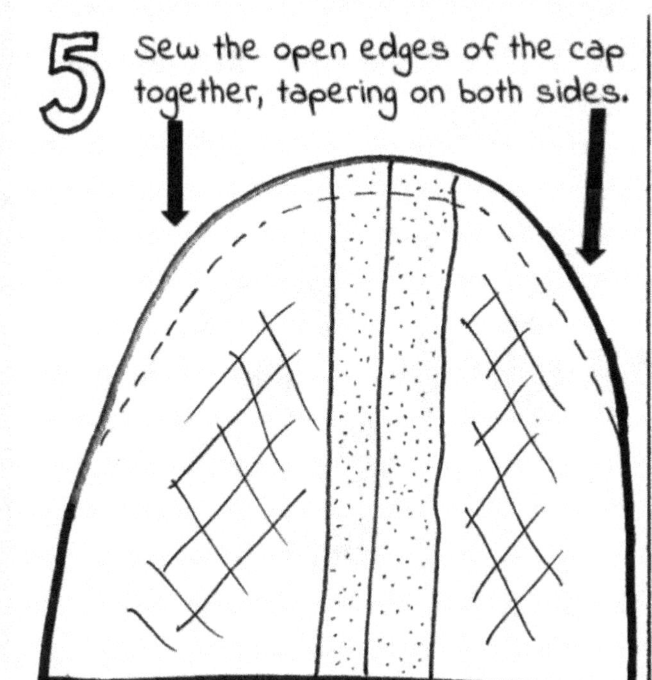
5
Sew the open edges of the cap together, tapering on both sides.

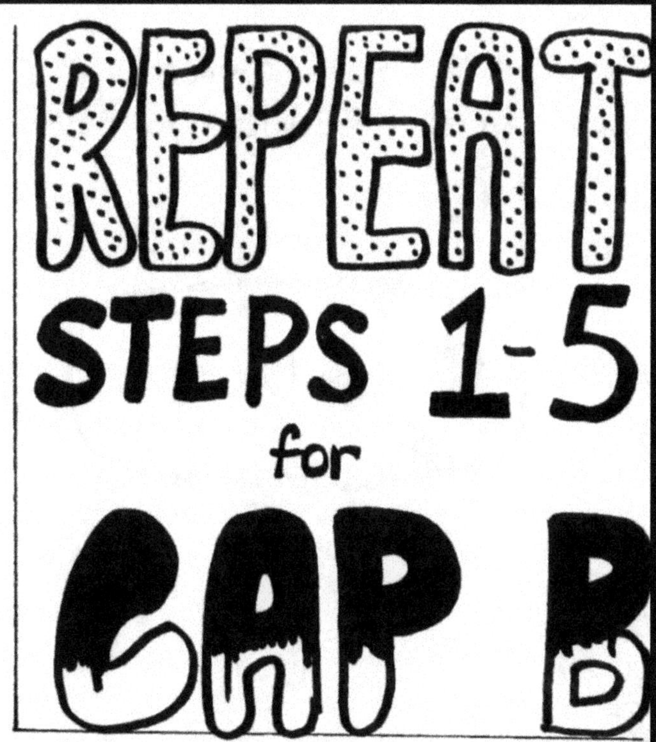
REPEAT
STEPS 1-5
for
CAP B

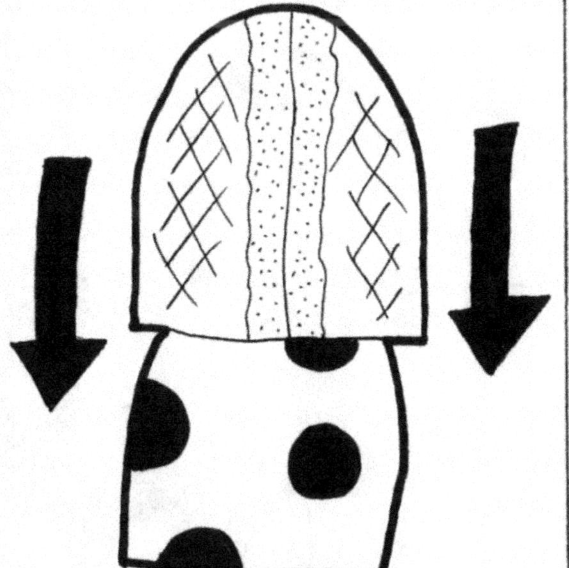
6
with right sides together, slip one cap inside the other.

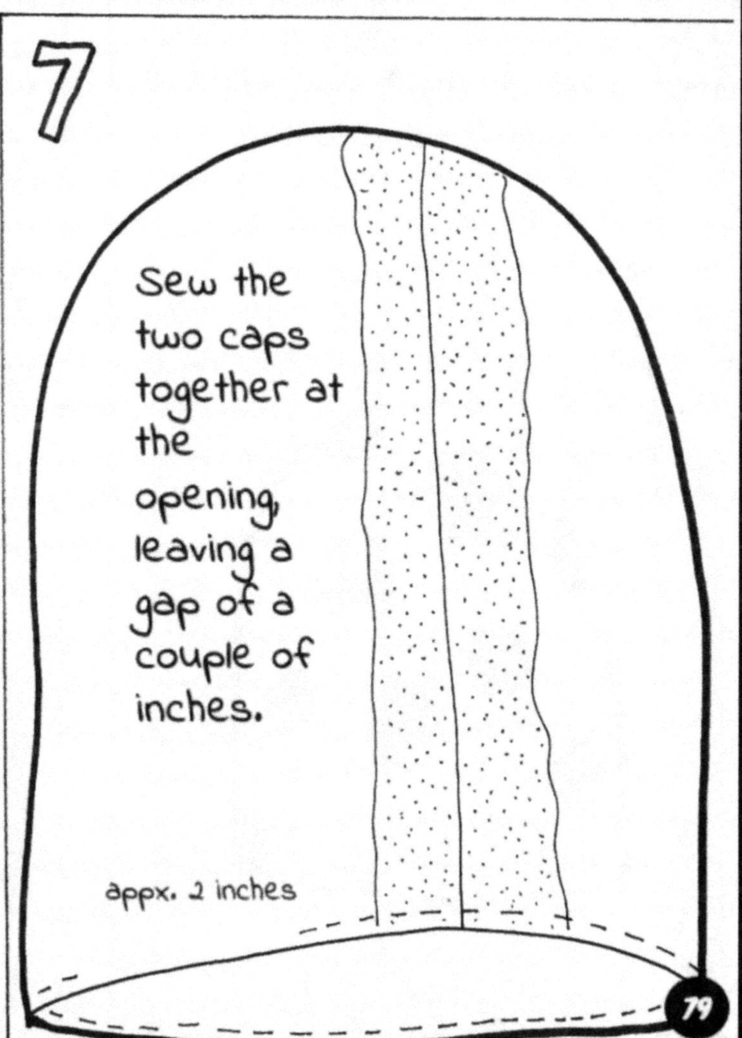
7
Sew the two caps together at the opening, leaving a gap of a couple of inches.
appx. 2 inches

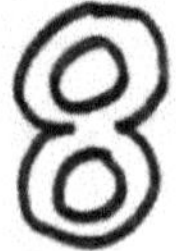

Turn both beanies right side out by stuffing through the gap. Insert BEANIE A into BEANIE B as shown.

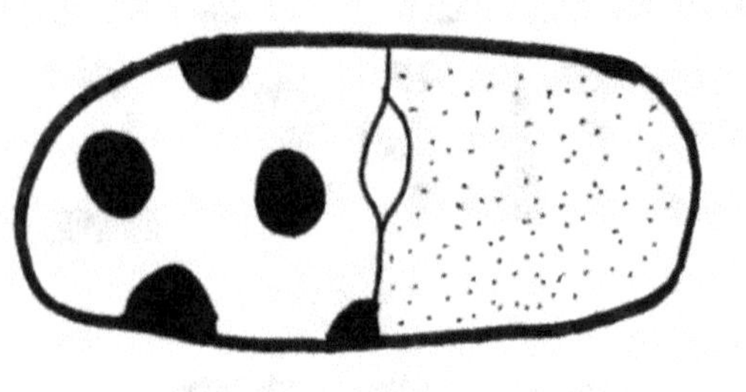

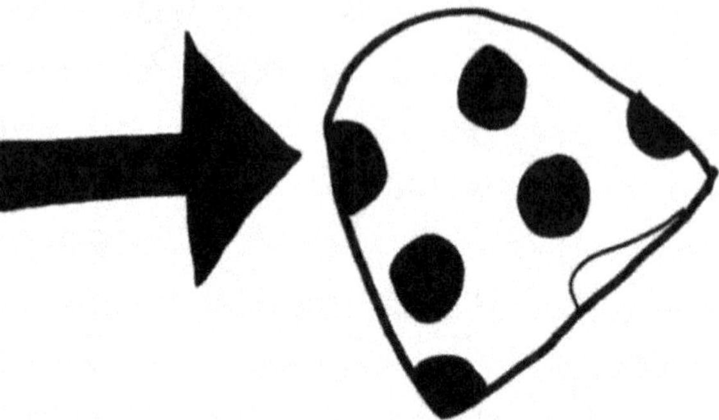

9 Hand stitch opening shut using a whip stitch.

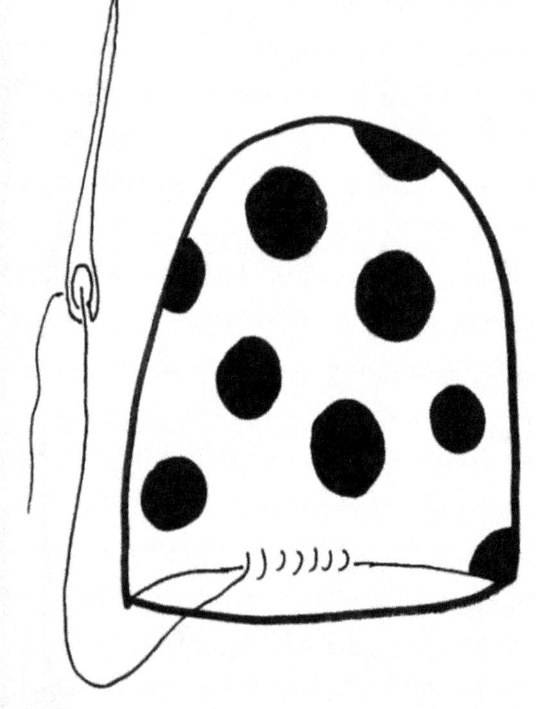

LOOKS SO GOOD!
GREAT GIFTS
FOR ALL YOUR PALS!

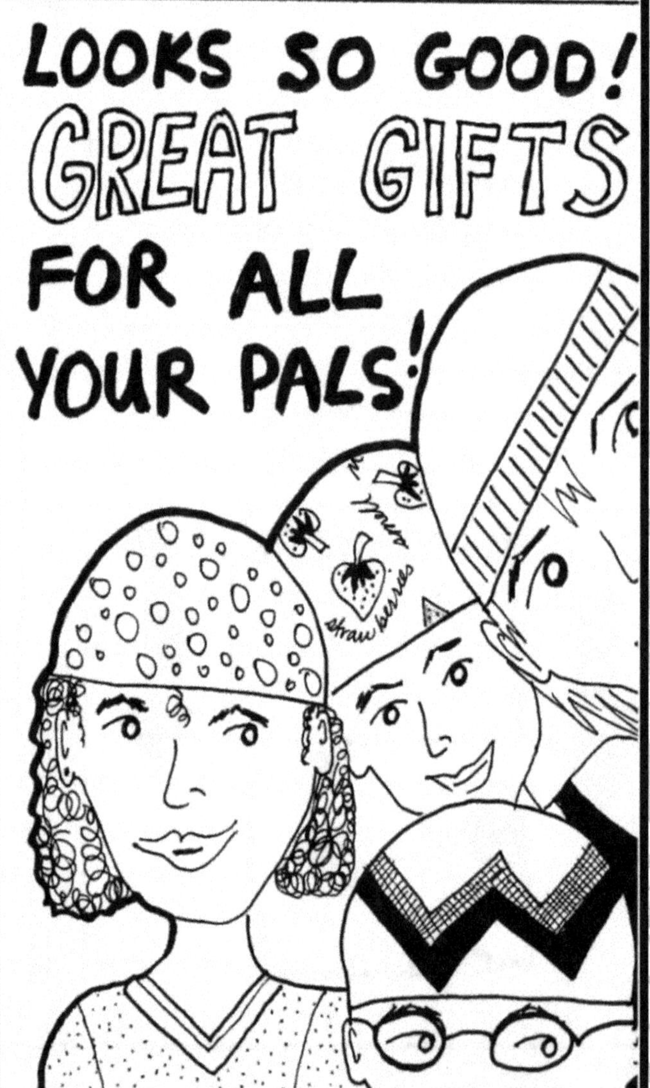

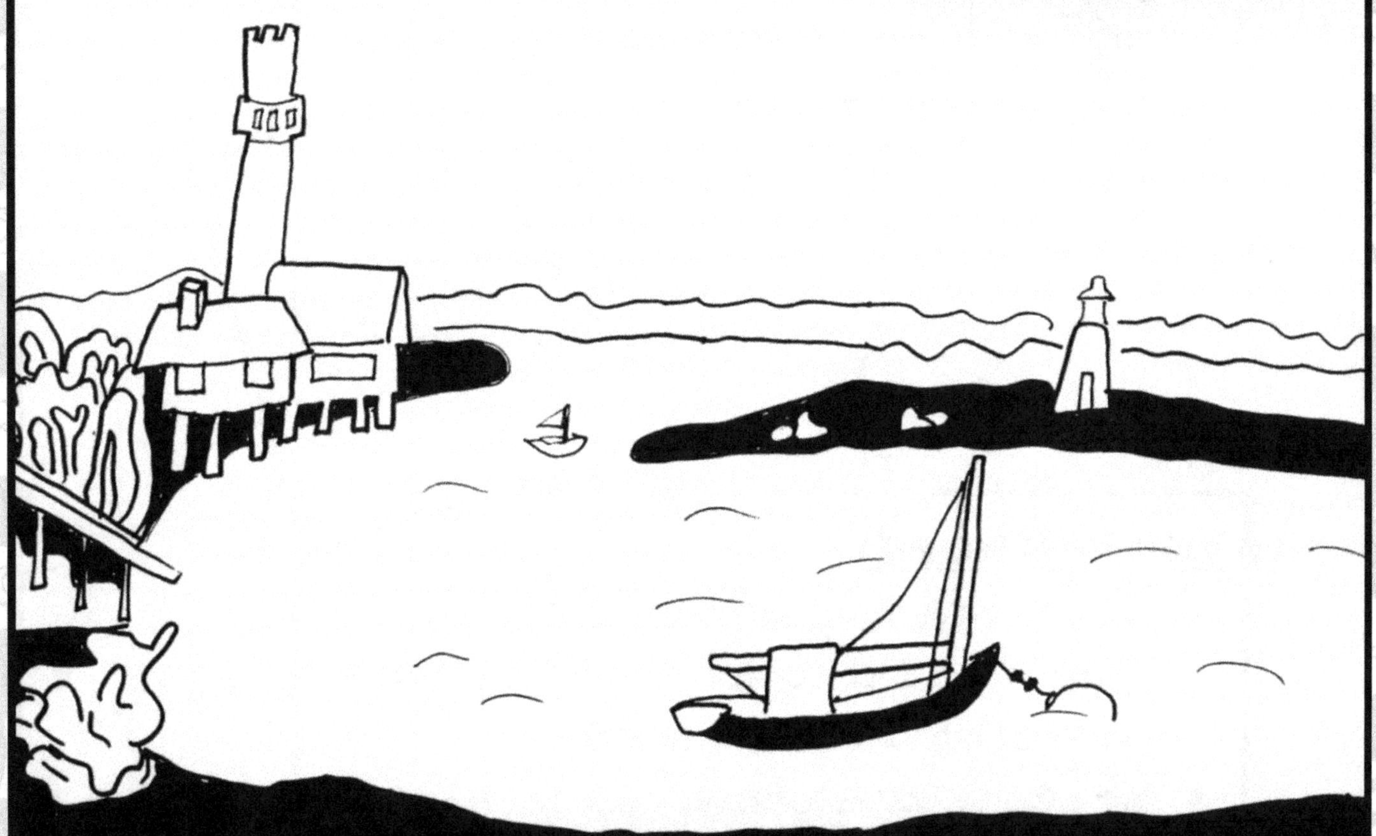

GO LOCAL

Yes, support local business, charities and people.
And also, get involved in local government.
Find out what all your neighbors' lawn signs are about,
go to a town meeting.

Be the change you want to see!

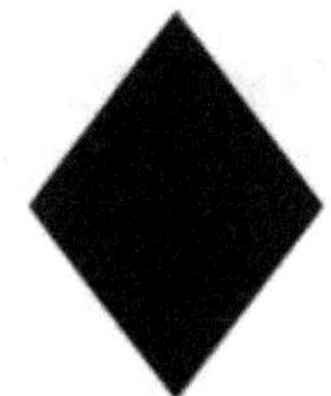

BEANIE

Reversible #2

You will need:

- An *extra long garment made of spandex and cotton (think an extra long shirt, dress or skirt)
- A beanie or stocking cap that fits your well to use as a guide)

*If your garment is not long enough, you can use another garment of similar fabric (see page 85).

PAIRS NICELY WITH: *FANNY PACK Level 1 and TOWEL*

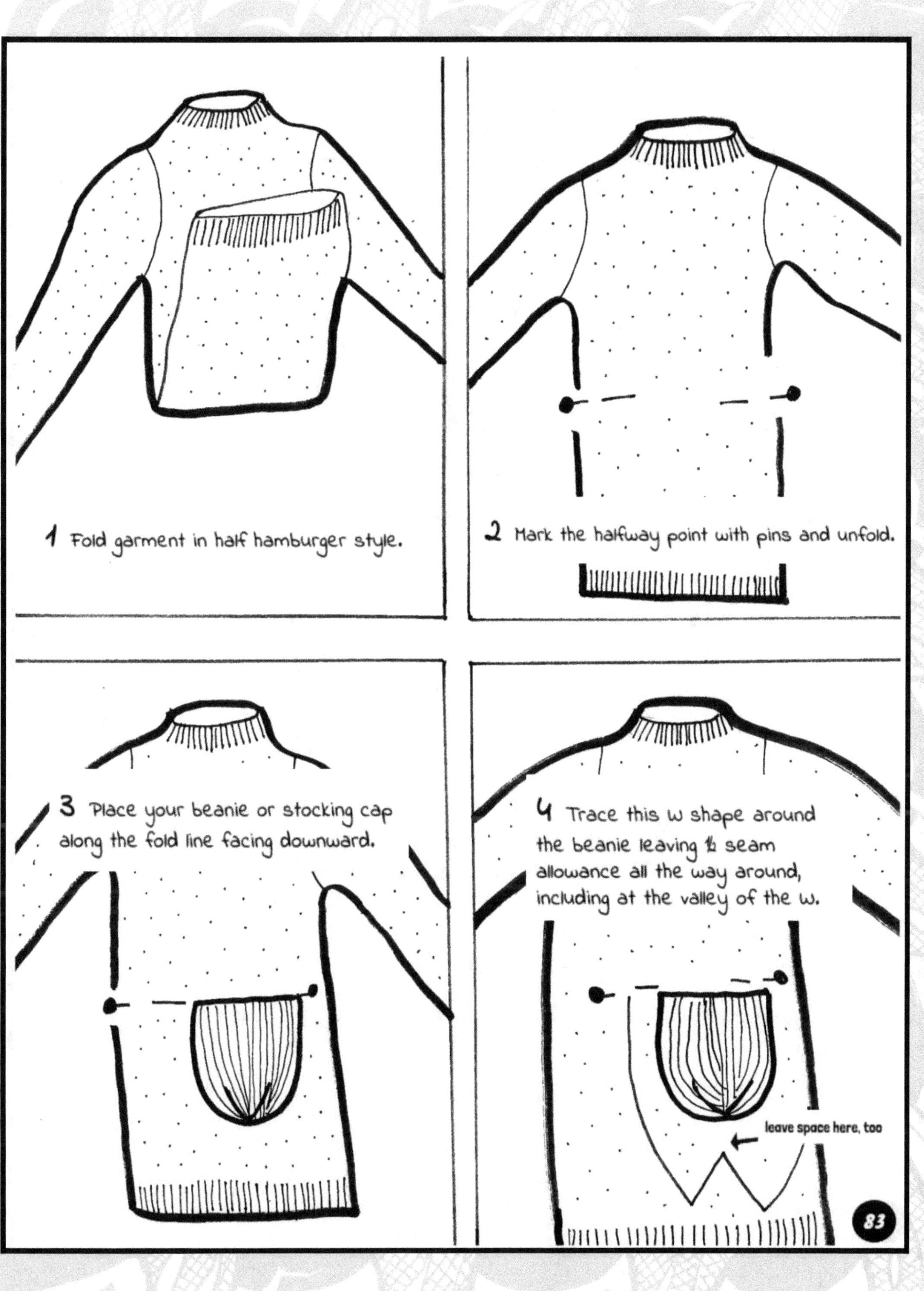
1 Fold garment in half hamburger style.
2 Mark the halfway point with pins and unfold.
3 Place your beanie or stocking cap along the fold line facing downward.
4 Trace this w shape around the beanie leaving ½ seam allowance all the way around, including at the valley of the w.
leave space here, too

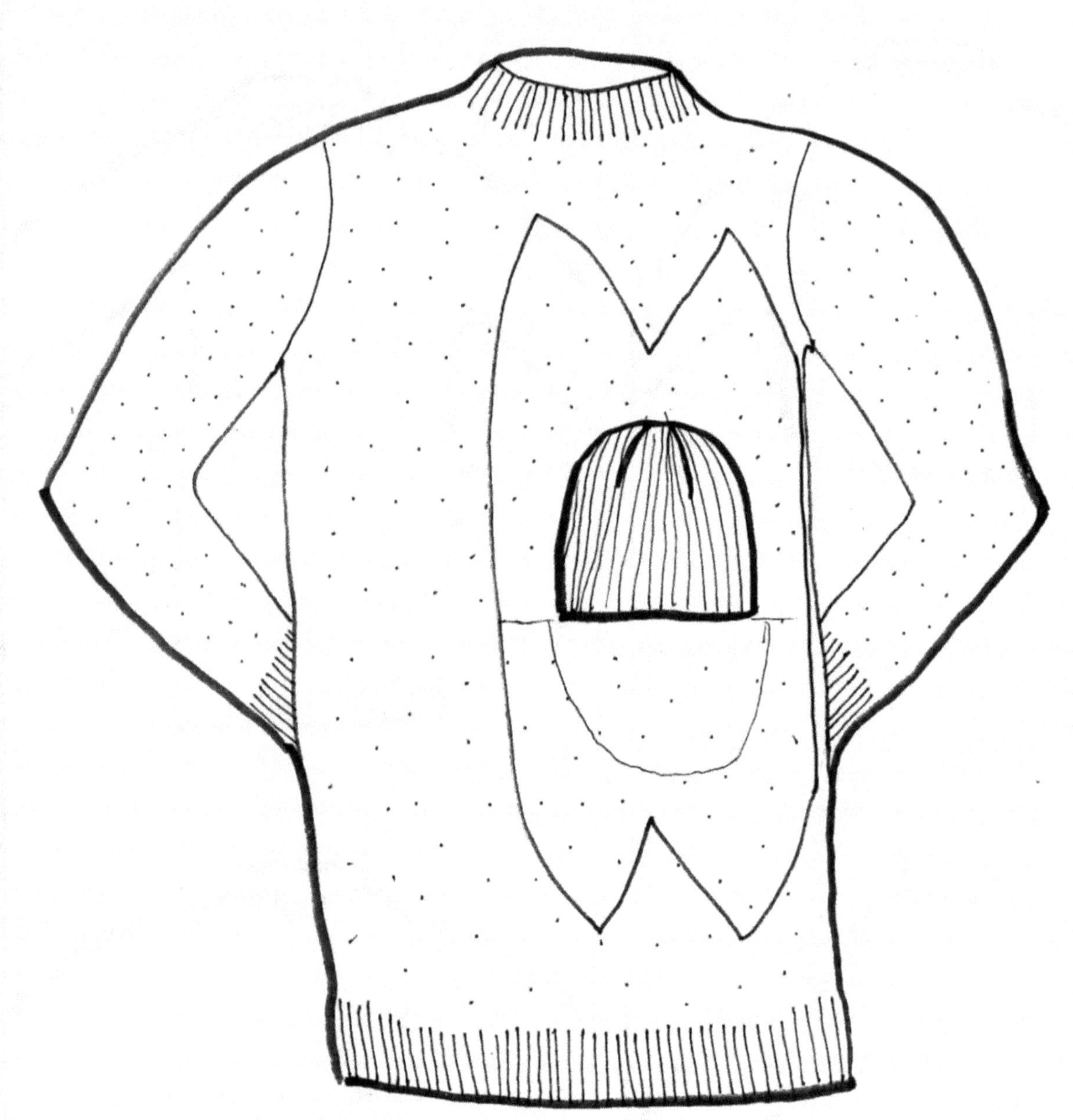

5 Flip the hat up along the fold line and repeat. Cut out your shape through both layers along all edges.

In the event that the garment you are upcycling is not long enough…

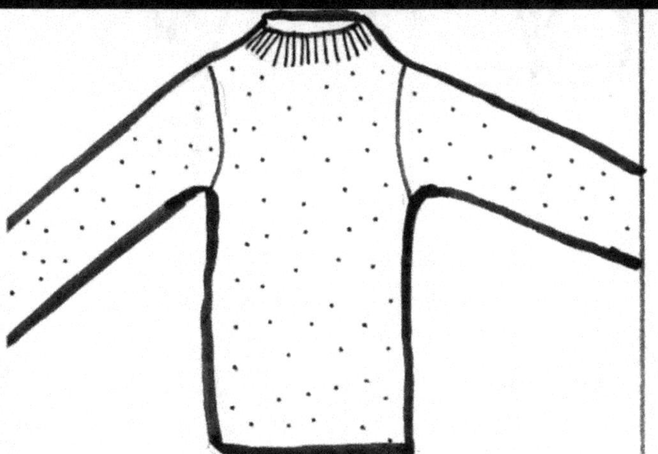

Lay Shirt A out flat so that the bottom edges are even.

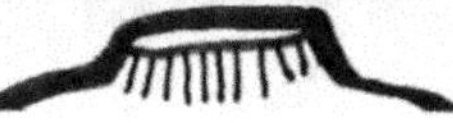

Cut off the sleeves of shirt B, turn it inside out and position right sides together.

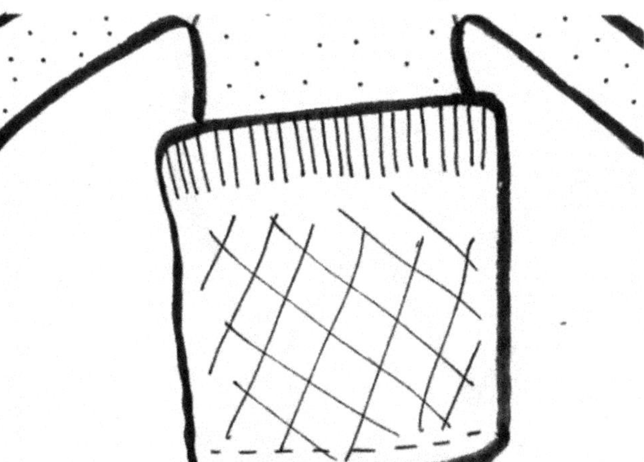

Line up the hems and sew together all the way around.

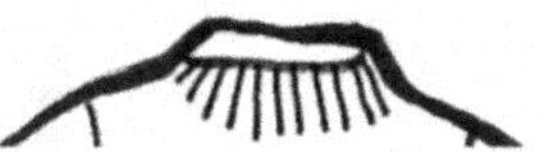

Open up the garments.

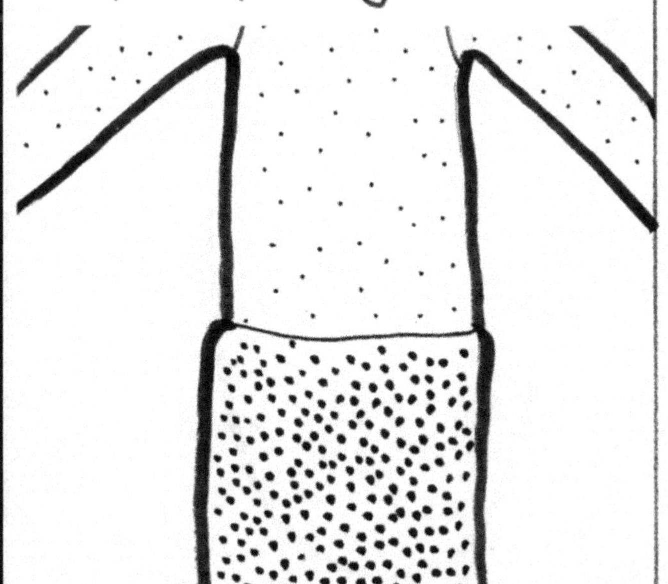

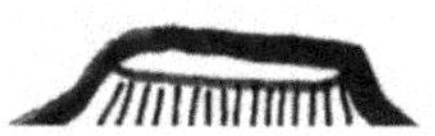

Complete steps 1-5.

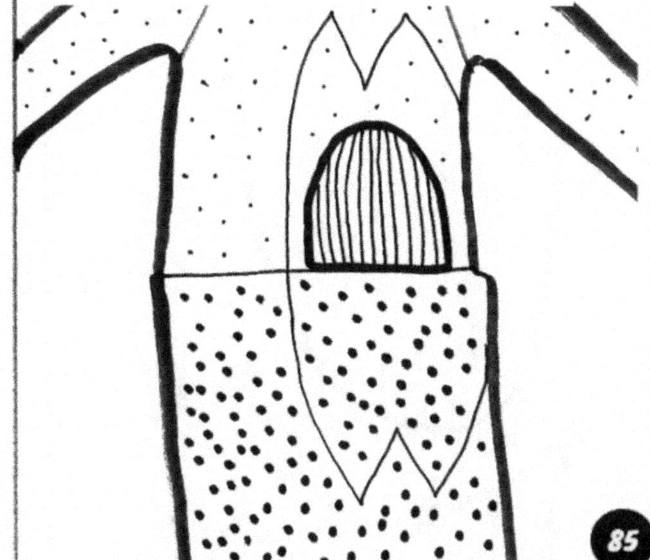

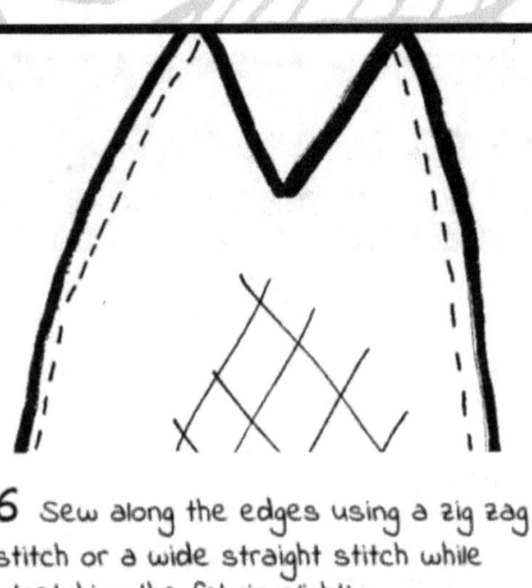

6 Sew along the edges using a zig zag stitch or a wide straight stitch while stretching the fabric slightly.

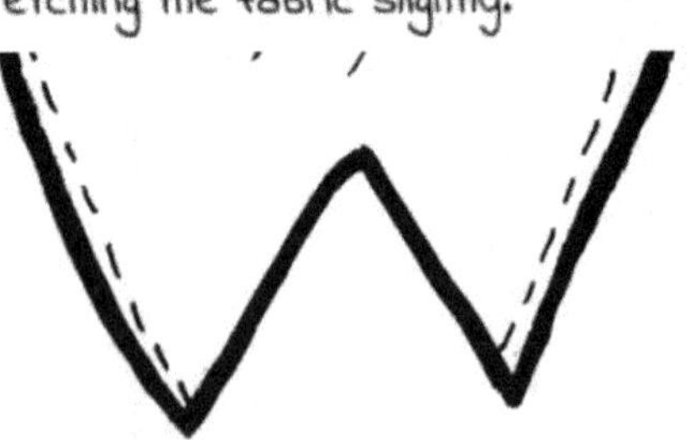

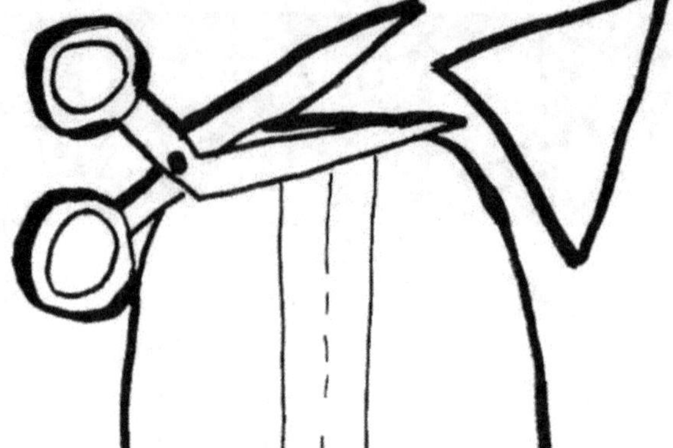

7 Reposition so that the seams are lined up in the middle. Trim the top to make it round.

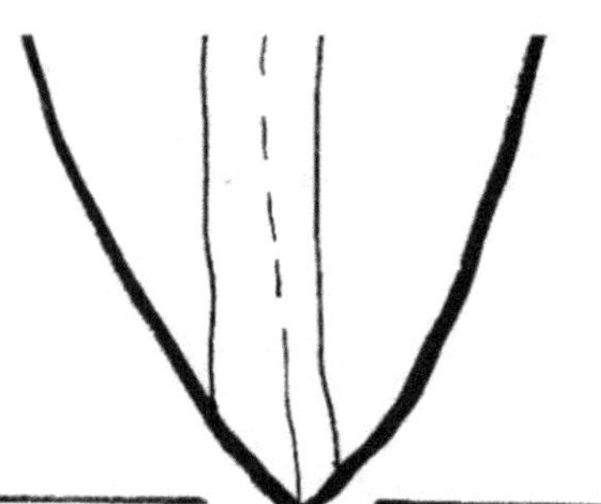

8 Trim the bottom to make it round.

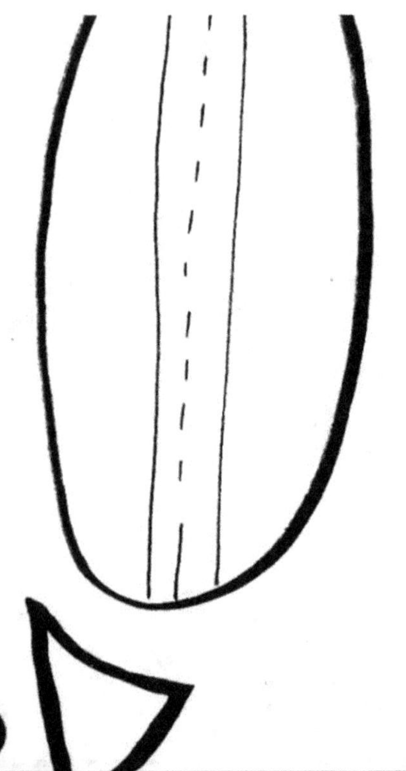

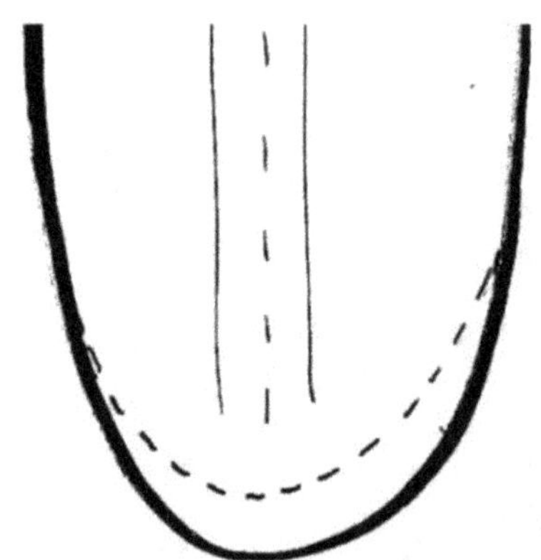

9 Leaving a gap of a couple inches on one side, sew the rounded edges closed. Taper on the sides as shown.

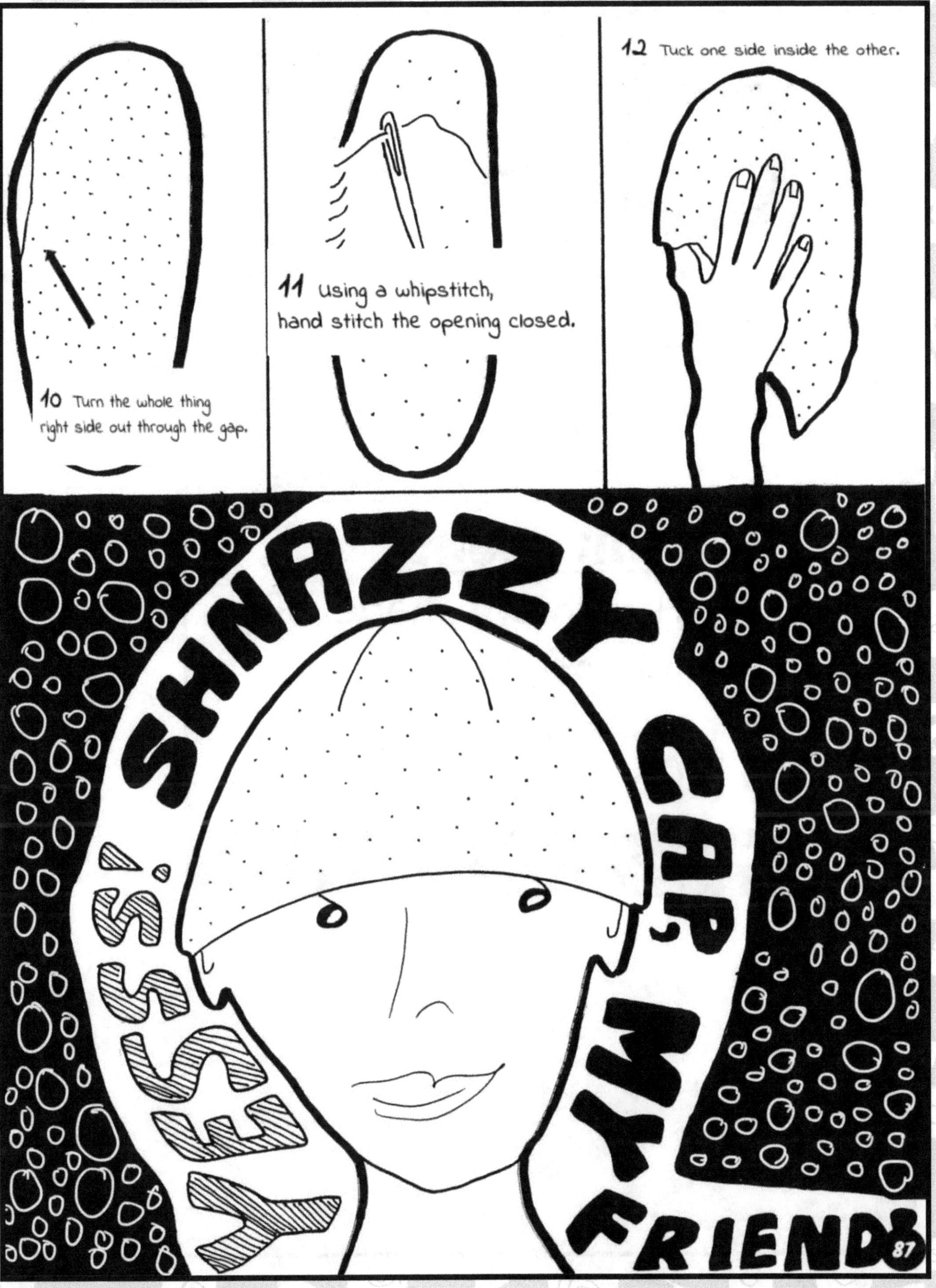

10 Turn the whole thing right side out through the gap.
11 Using a whipstitch, hand stitch the opening closed.
12 Tuck one side inside the other.
YES! SHNAZZY CAP, MY FRIENDS

TOWEL

No Sew

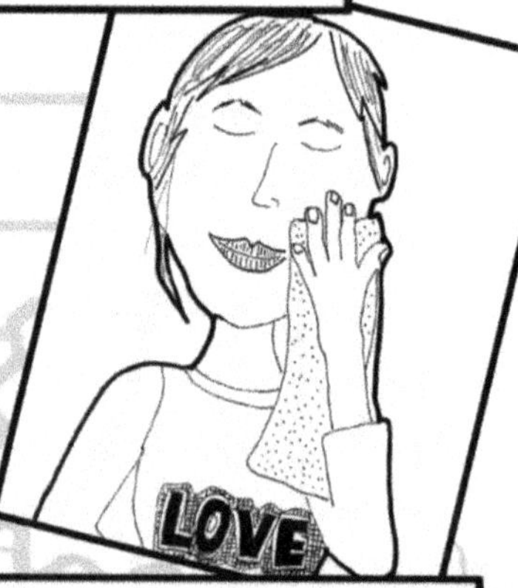

You will need:

- A garment made of microfiber or wickaway
- A measuring device

PAIRS NICELY WITH: *FANNY PACK Level 1 and TOWEL*

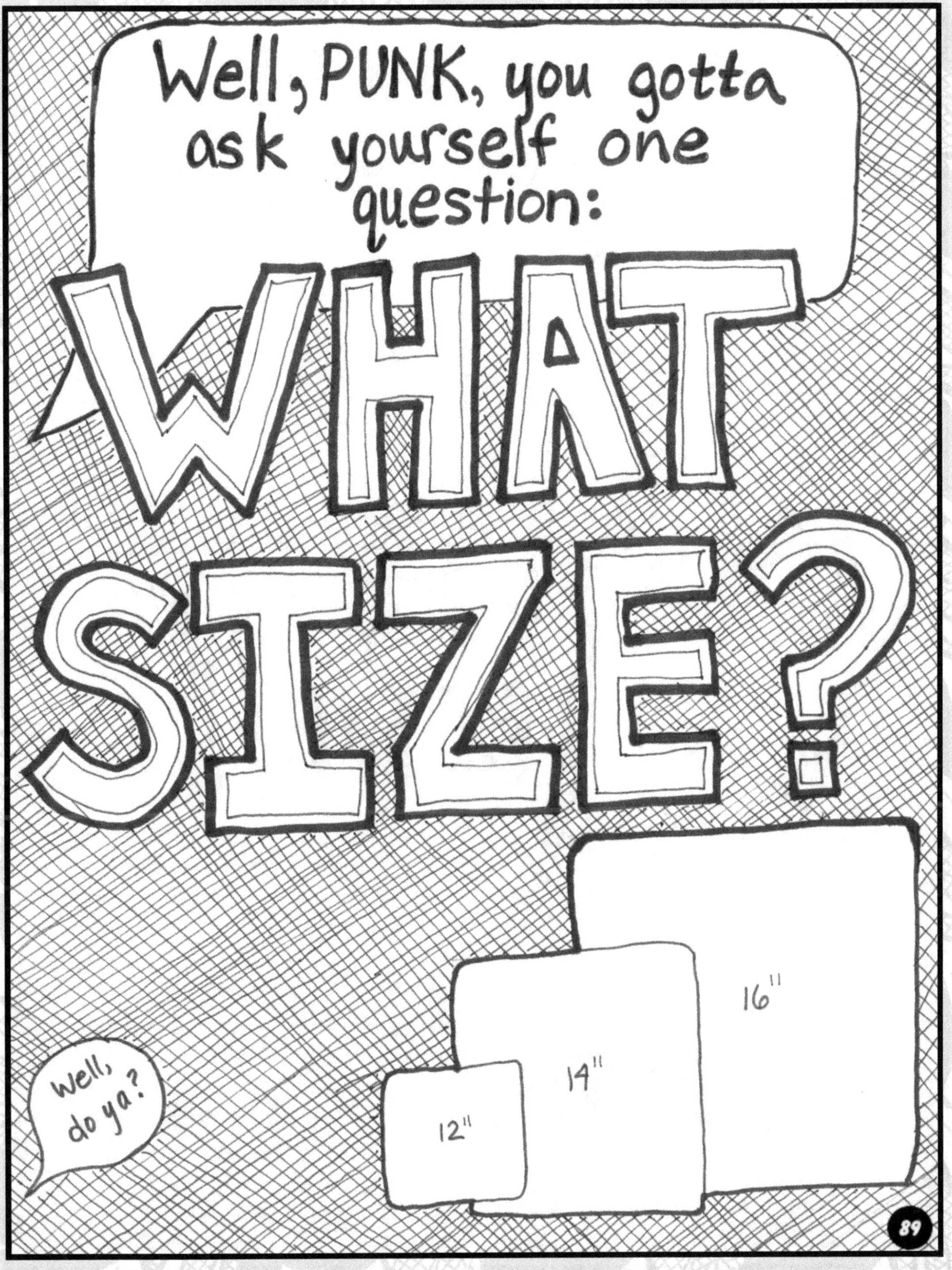
Well, PUNK, you gotta ask yourself one question:
WHAT SIZE?
16"
14"
12"
Well, do ya?

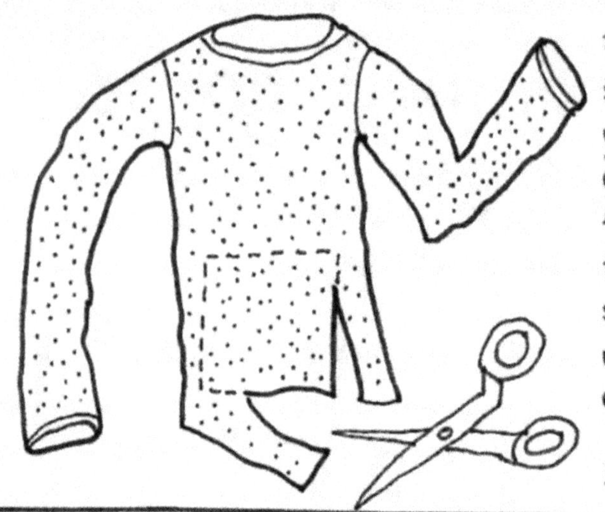

From your garment cut a square slightly larger all around than you want your finished towel to be; the edges will curl a bit. For example, for a finished 14x14 inch towel, cut a piece that is 14.5 x 14.5 inch square. Make sure you are cutting where there are no seams for a more enjoyable experience!

←

Now, start using your towel!

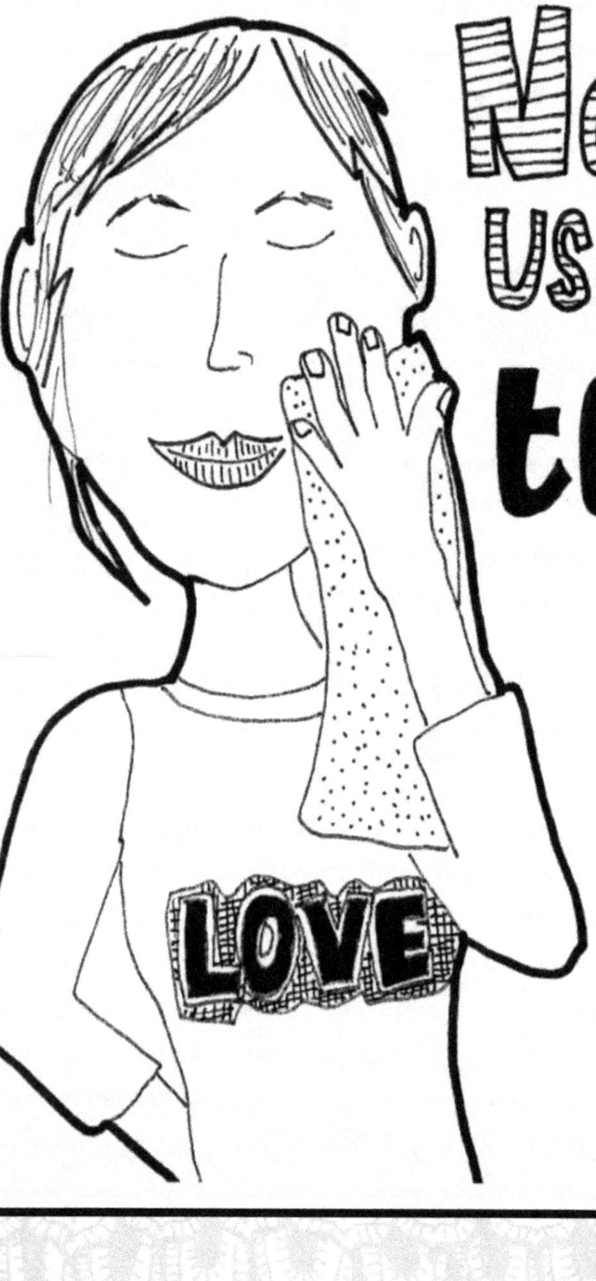

LOVE

LIVE YOUR VALUES

Support individuals and companies that advocate for the environment.

Be one of those individuals!

Make sustainable lifestyle choices: ride your bike more, order online less, grow a pollinator garden!

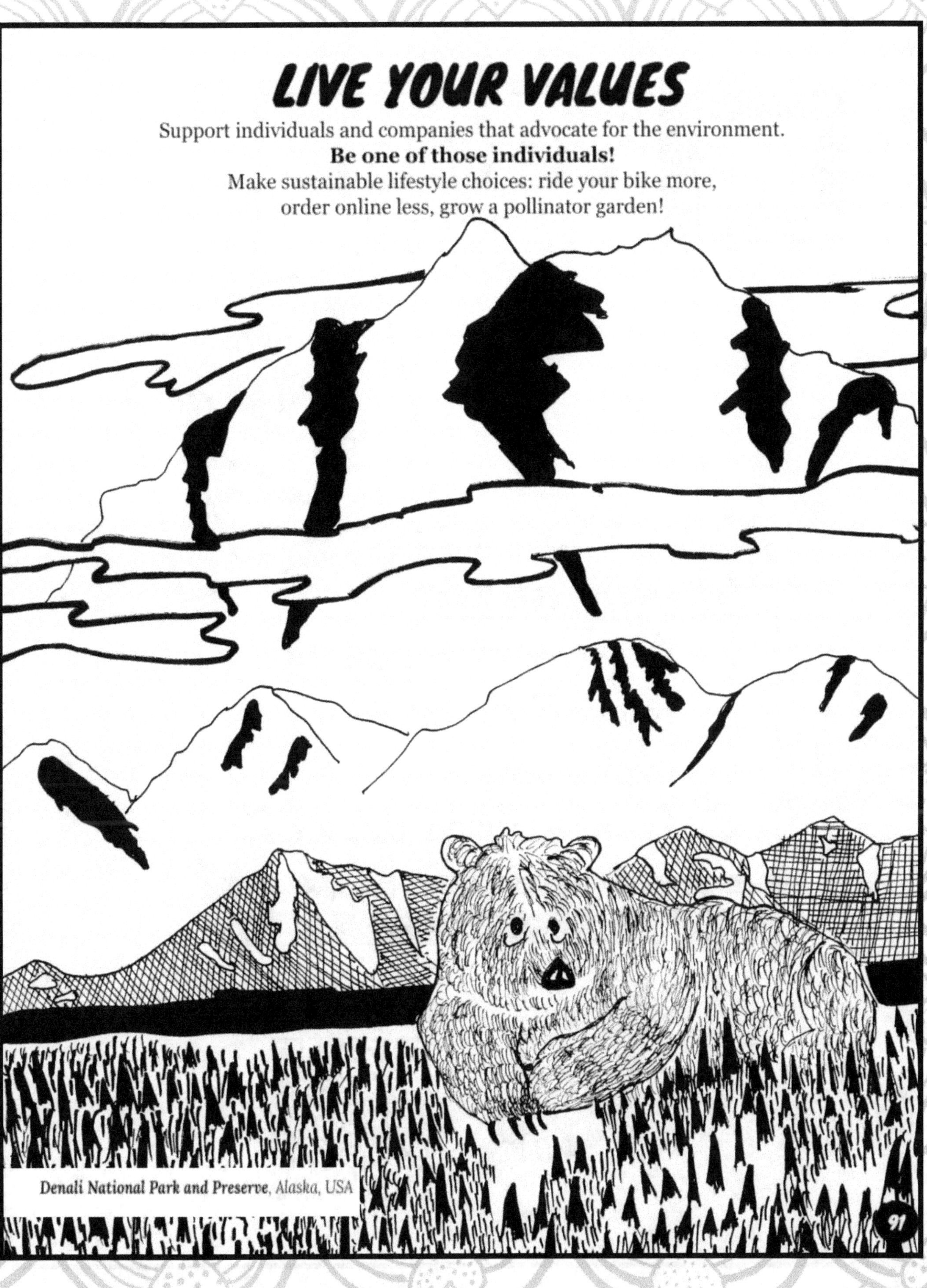

***Denali National Park and Preserve**, Alaska, USA*

TOWEL

Single Layer

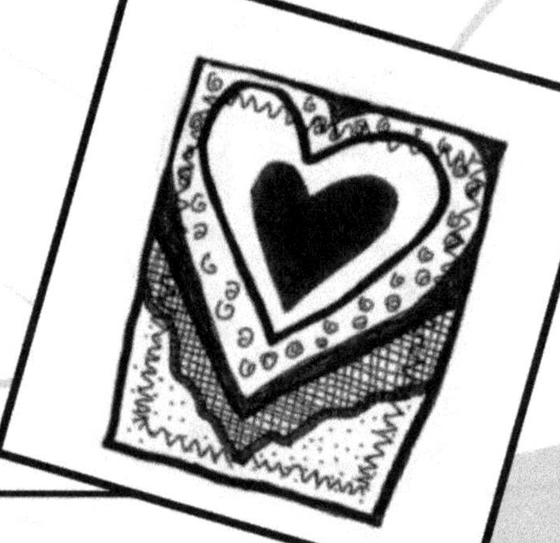

You will need:

- A garment made of microfiber or wickaway
- A measuring device

PAIRS NICELY WITH: *FANNY PACK Level 1 and TOWEL*

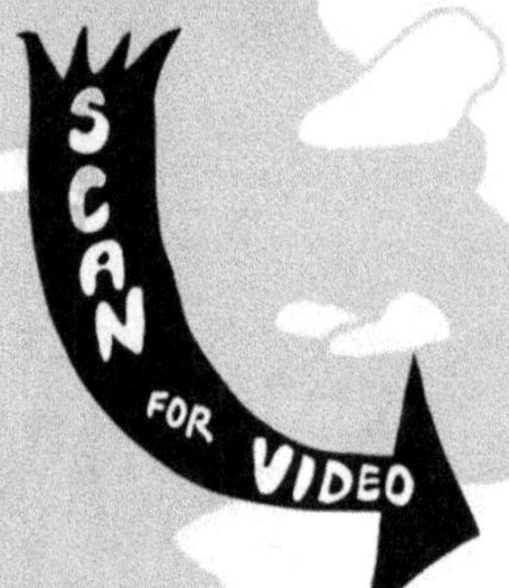

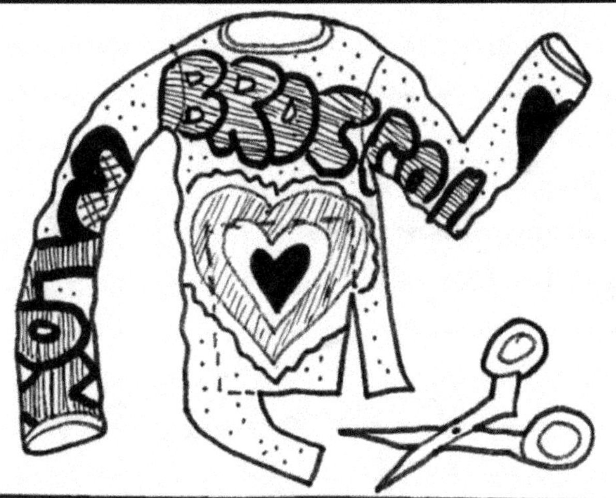

1

Cut a square 1 inch bigger than you want your finished towel to be. For example for a 14 x 14 inch towel, cut a 15 x 15 inch square. Use a portion of the garment without any seams.

2

Next, fold over ½ inch on one side, pin and zig zag stitch. Stretch the material SLIGHTLy as you sew.

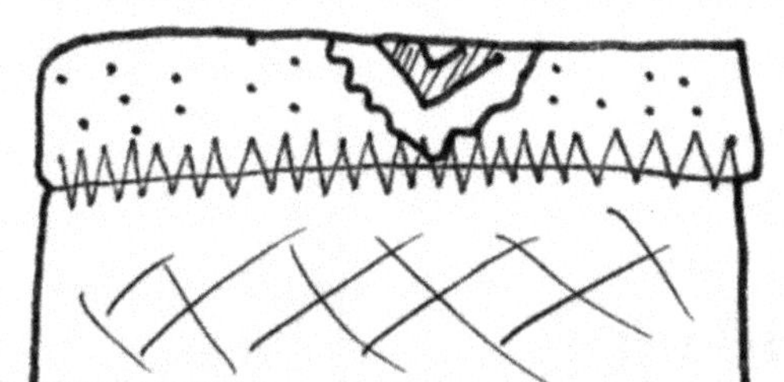

3

Do the same to the opposite side.

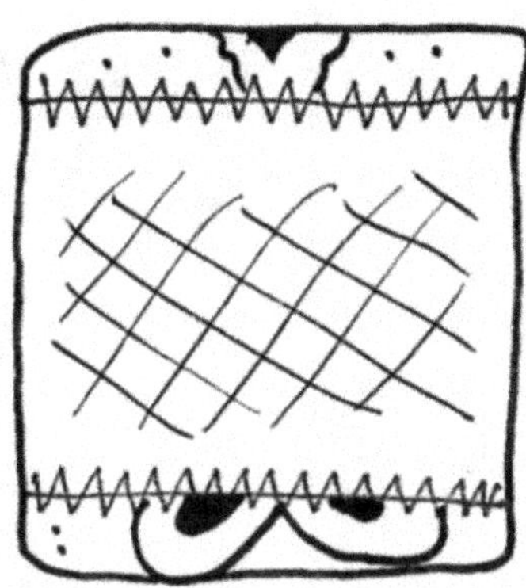

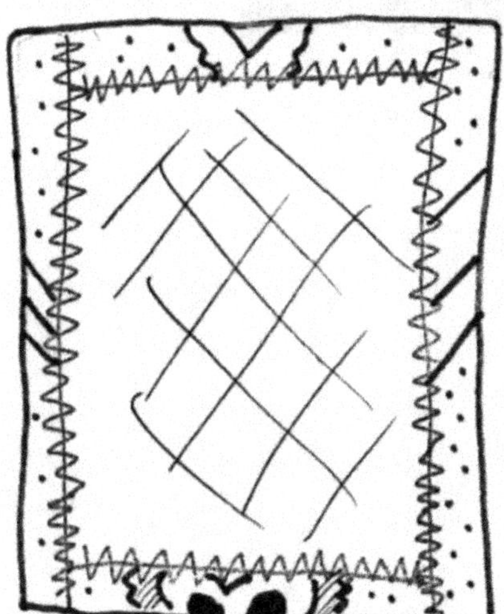

4

Repeat on remaining two sides, making sure to sew all the way to the edge.

VOILA! YOUR TOWEL AWAITS

TOWEL

Double Ply

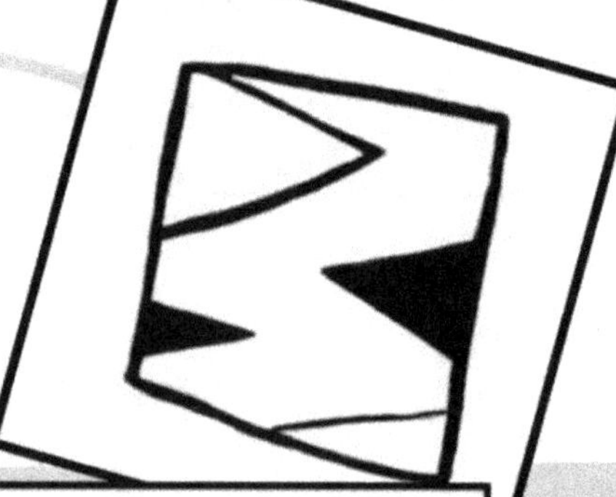

You will need:

- A garment made of microfiber or wickaway
- A measuring device

PAIRS NICELY WITH: *FANNY PACK Level 1 and TOWEL*

1 Cut a square 1 inch bigger than you want your finished towel to be. For example for a 14 x 14 inch towel, cut a 15 x 15 inch square. Do this with both fabrics.

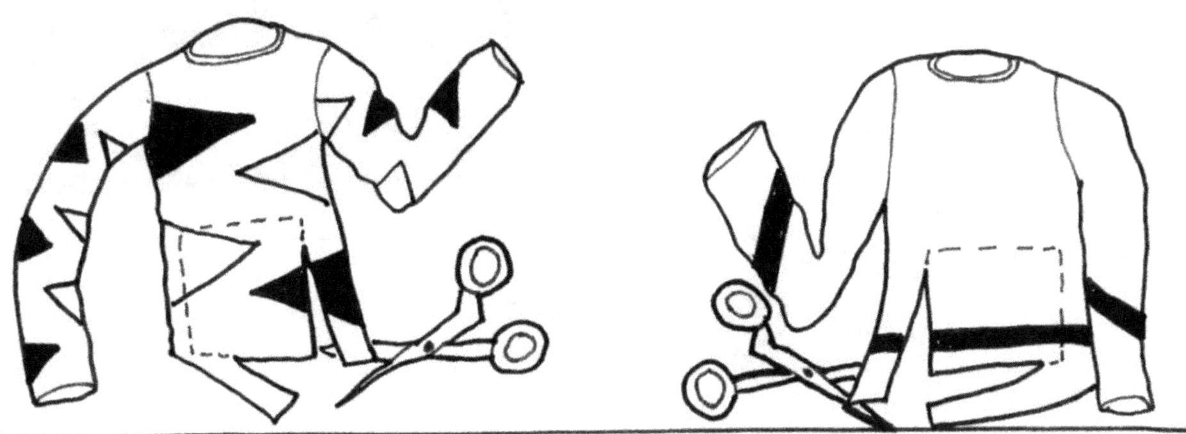

2

With right sides together, sew both pieces together, stretching SLIGHTLY as you go. Use a ½ inch seam allowance. Leave a couple inch gap so you can turn everything right side out.

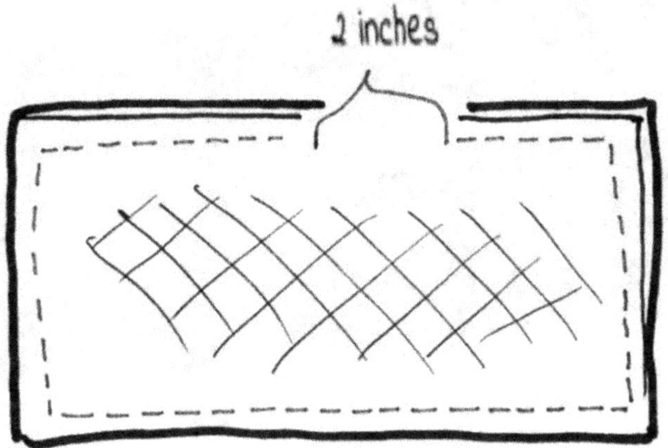

3

Trim close to stitching at corners then turn rightside out. Use a chopstick or dull pencil to push corners out. Pin sides together and zigzag stitch opening shut.

Did you work up a sweat sewing? Wipe your brow with your new towel!

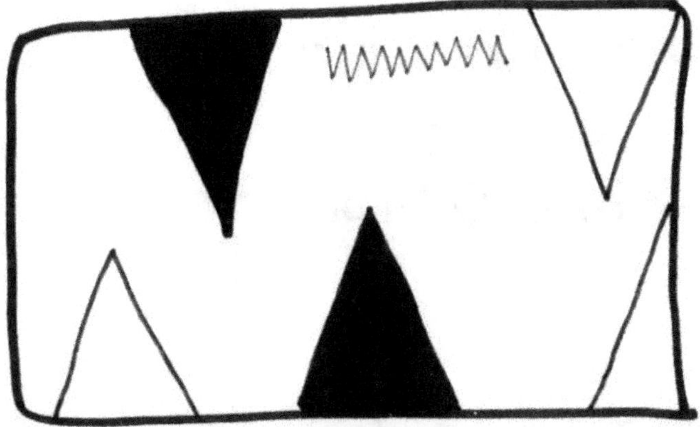

In the end we will preserve only what we love. We love only what we understand. We will understand only what we are taught.

–Baba Dioum

TELL ME, WHAT IS IT YOU PLAN TO DO WITH YOUR ONE WILD AND PRECIOUS LIFE?

–MARY OLIVER

There are two ways to be rich: Acquire More or Desire Less

Trees are the poems that the earth writes upon the sky.

–Khalil Gibran

Jesus, it's beautiful!
Great Mother of Big
Apples is it a pretty
world!
I don't know how the
rest of you feel but
mostly I feel drunk all
of the time!

–Kenneth Patchen

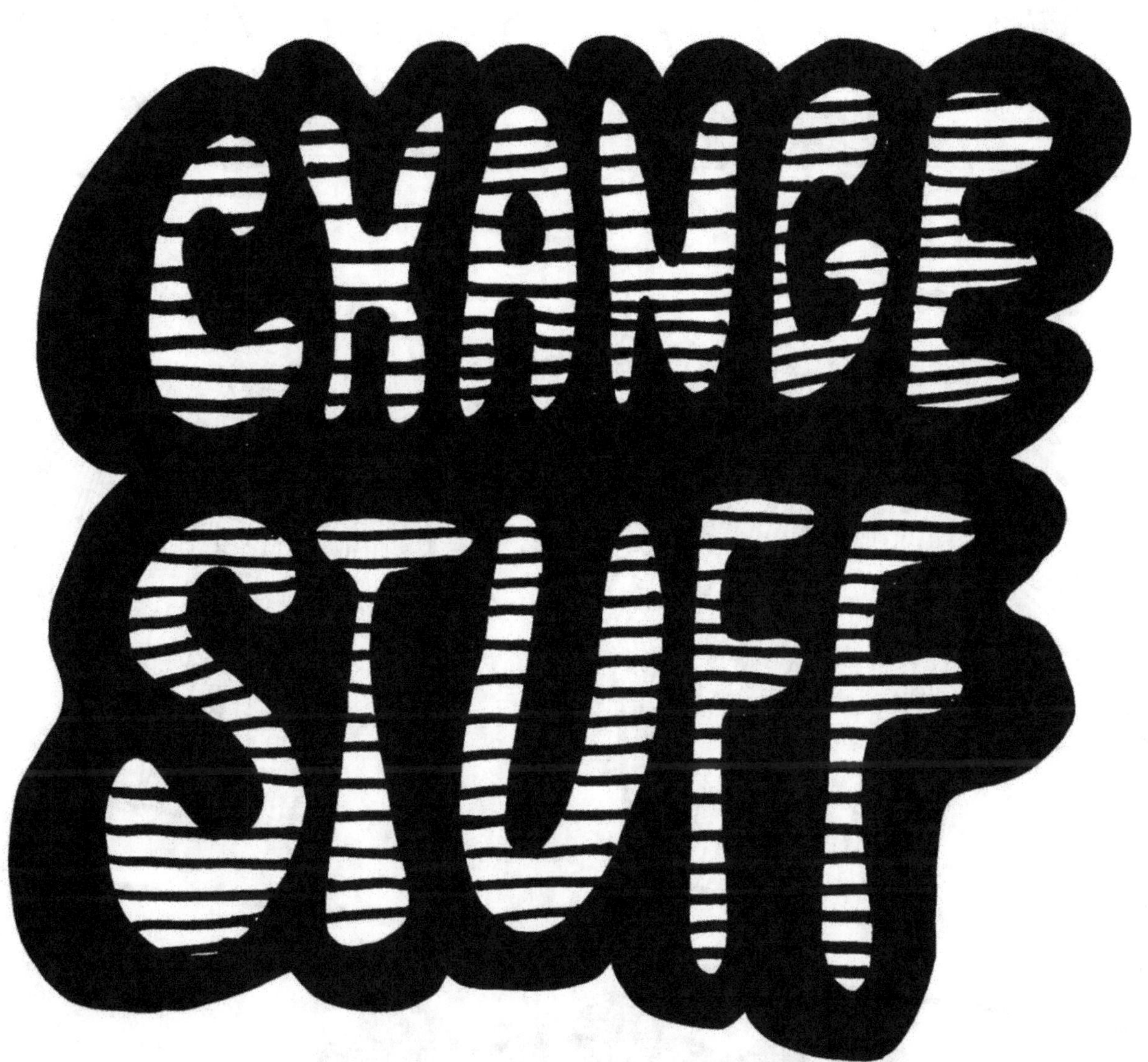
CHANGE
STUFF

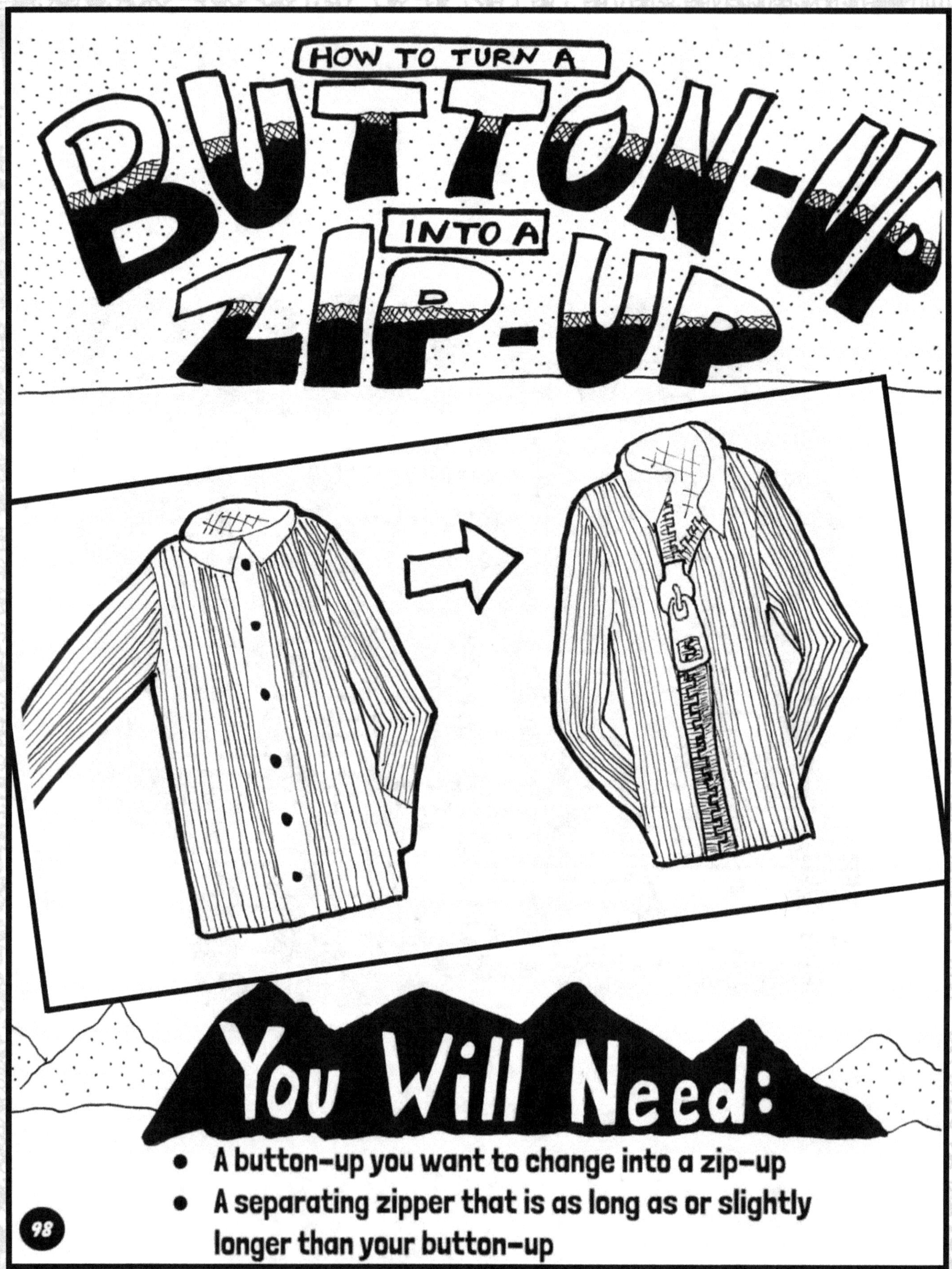

You Will Need:

- A button-up you want to change into a zip-up
- A separating zipper that is as long as or slightly longer than your button-up

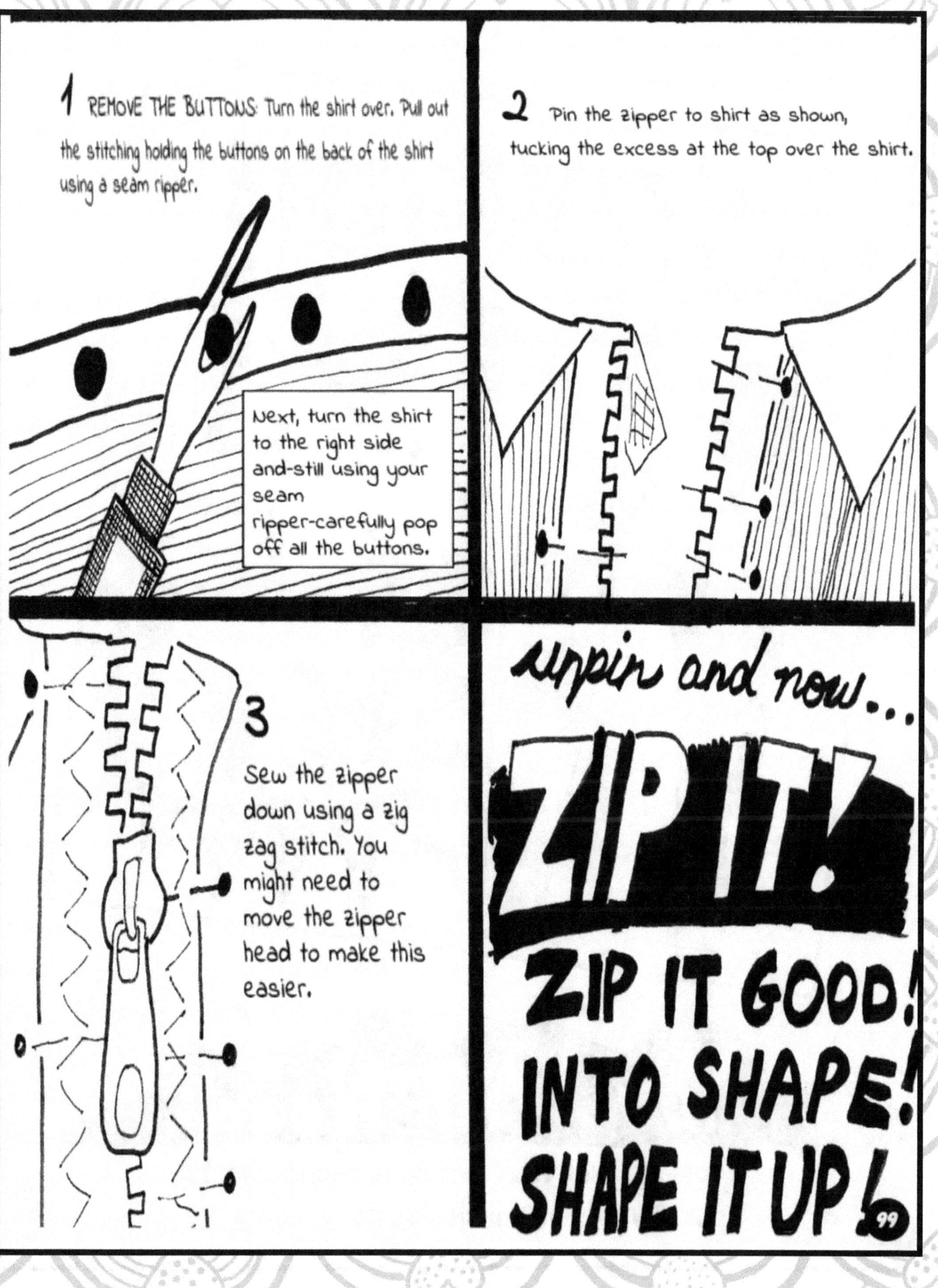

1 REMOVE THE BUTTONS: Turn the shirt over. Pull out the stitching holding the buttons on the back of the shirt using a seam ripper.
Next, turn the shirt to the right side and-still using your seam ripper-carefully pop off all the buttons.
2 Pin the zipper to shirt as shown, tucking the excess at the top over the shirt.
3
Sew the zipper down using a zig zag stitch. You might need to move the zipper head to make this easier.
zippin and now...
ZIP IT!
ZIP IT GOOD!
INTO SHAPE!
SHAPE IT UP!

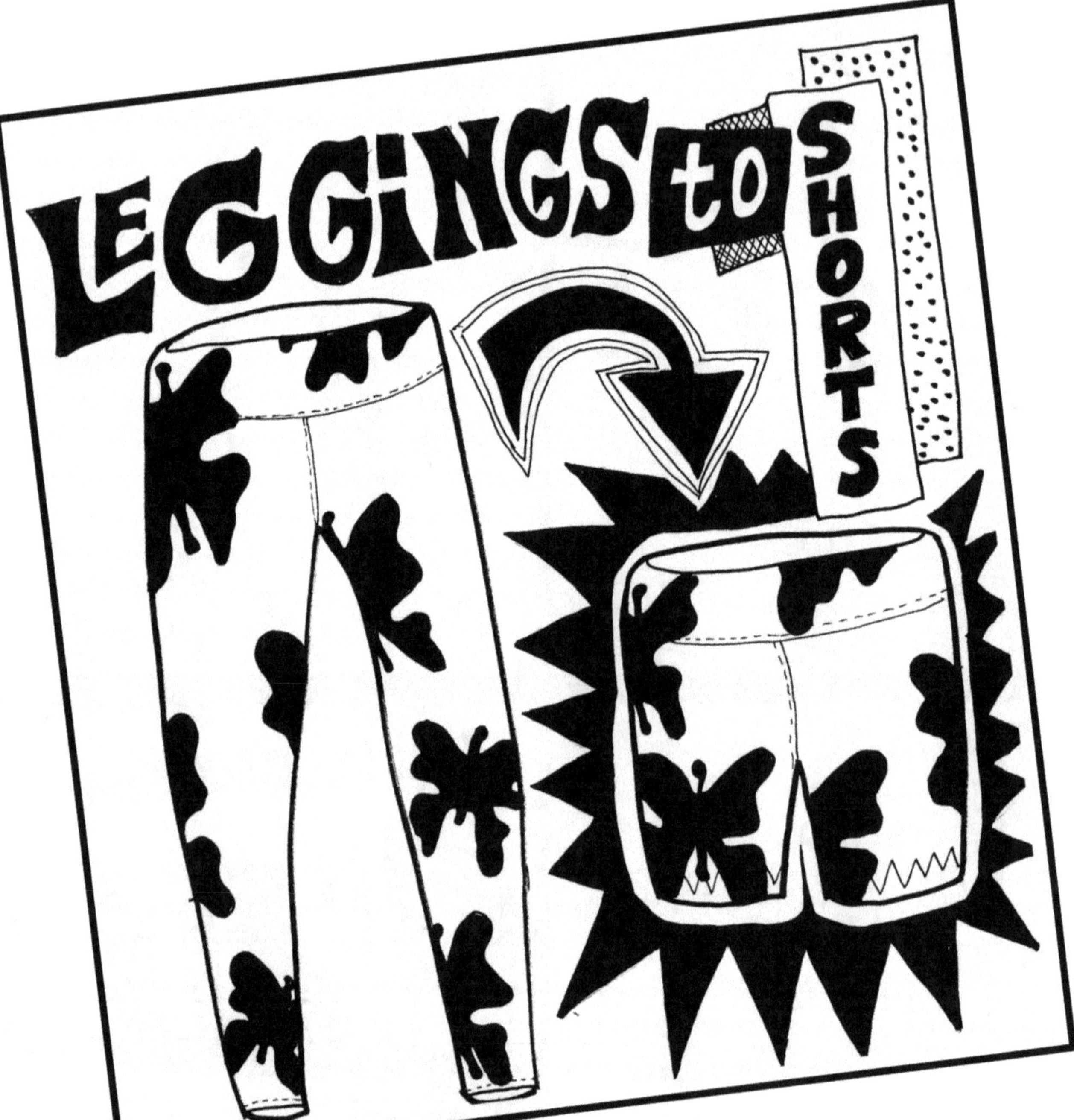

You Will Need:

- **Leggings that you want to turn into shorts**
- **Appx. 3 yards of ½ inch elastic**

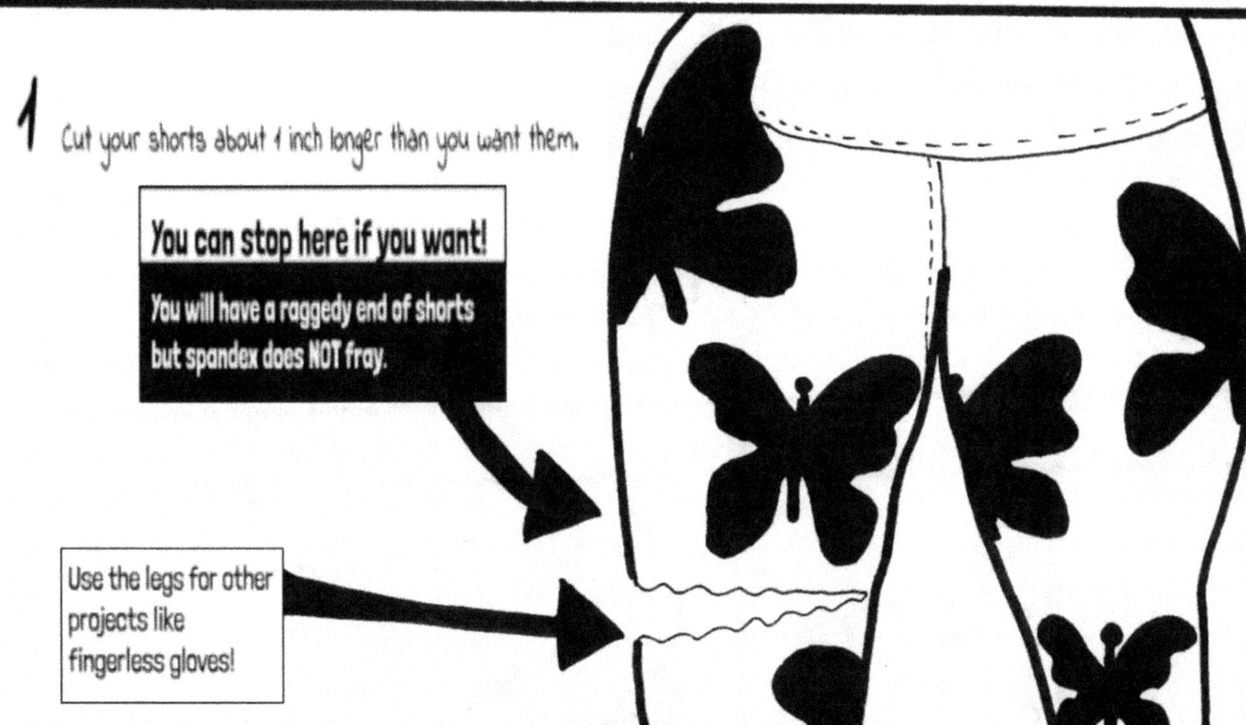

1 Cut your shorts about 1 inch longer than you want them.

You can stop here if you want!

You will have a raggedy end of shorts but spandex does NOT fray.

Use the legs for other projects like fingerless gloves!

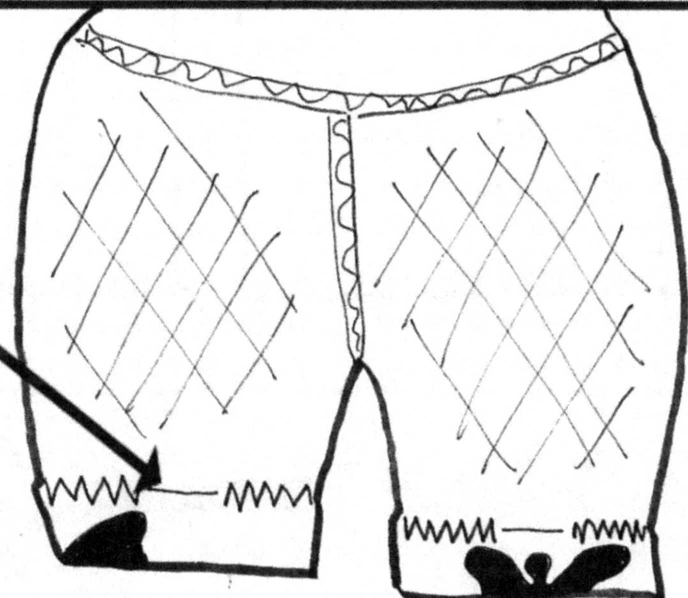

2 Turn the shorts inside out.

On each leg, turn up 1 inch and zig zag stitch in place along the raw edge.

NOTE: If planning on adding elastic, leave a couple inch gap in your stitching.

You can stop here if you want!

If your shorts are tight enough and/or you are not worried about them riding up.

3 Use your elastic to measure where your shorts will end. Add 1/2 inch. Now cut two pieces of elastic this length.

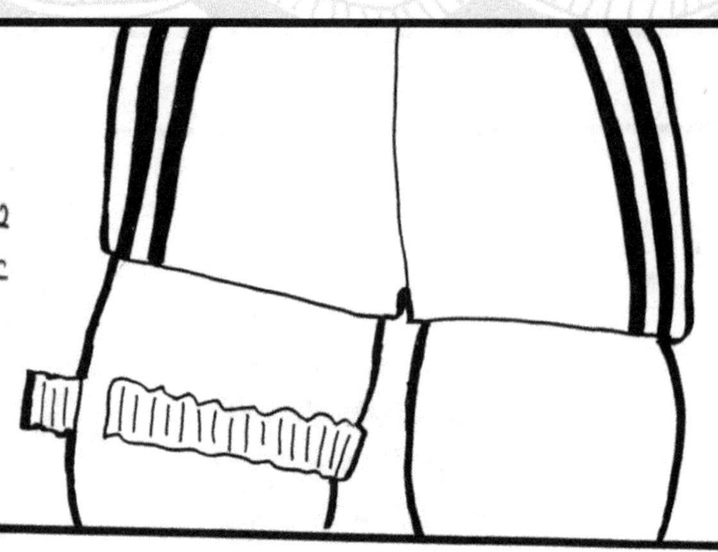

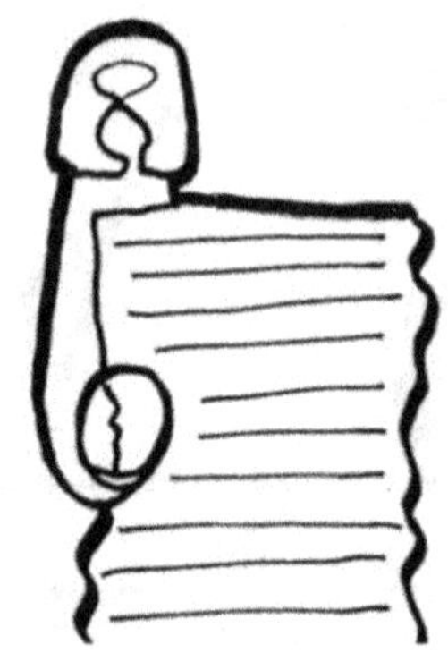

4 Attach a large safety pin at one end of the elastic.

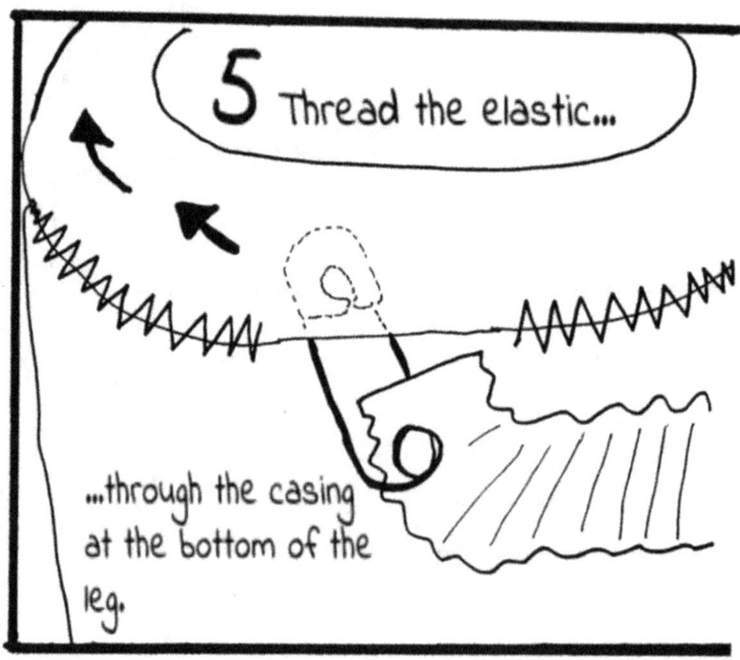

6 Sew the ends of the elastic together. Do this for both legs. Try shorts on.

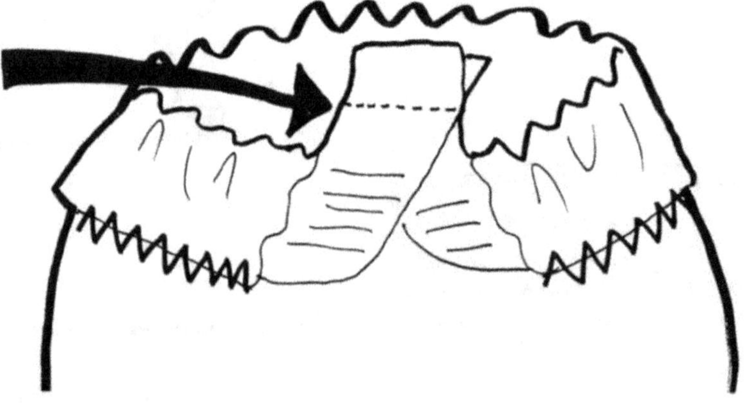

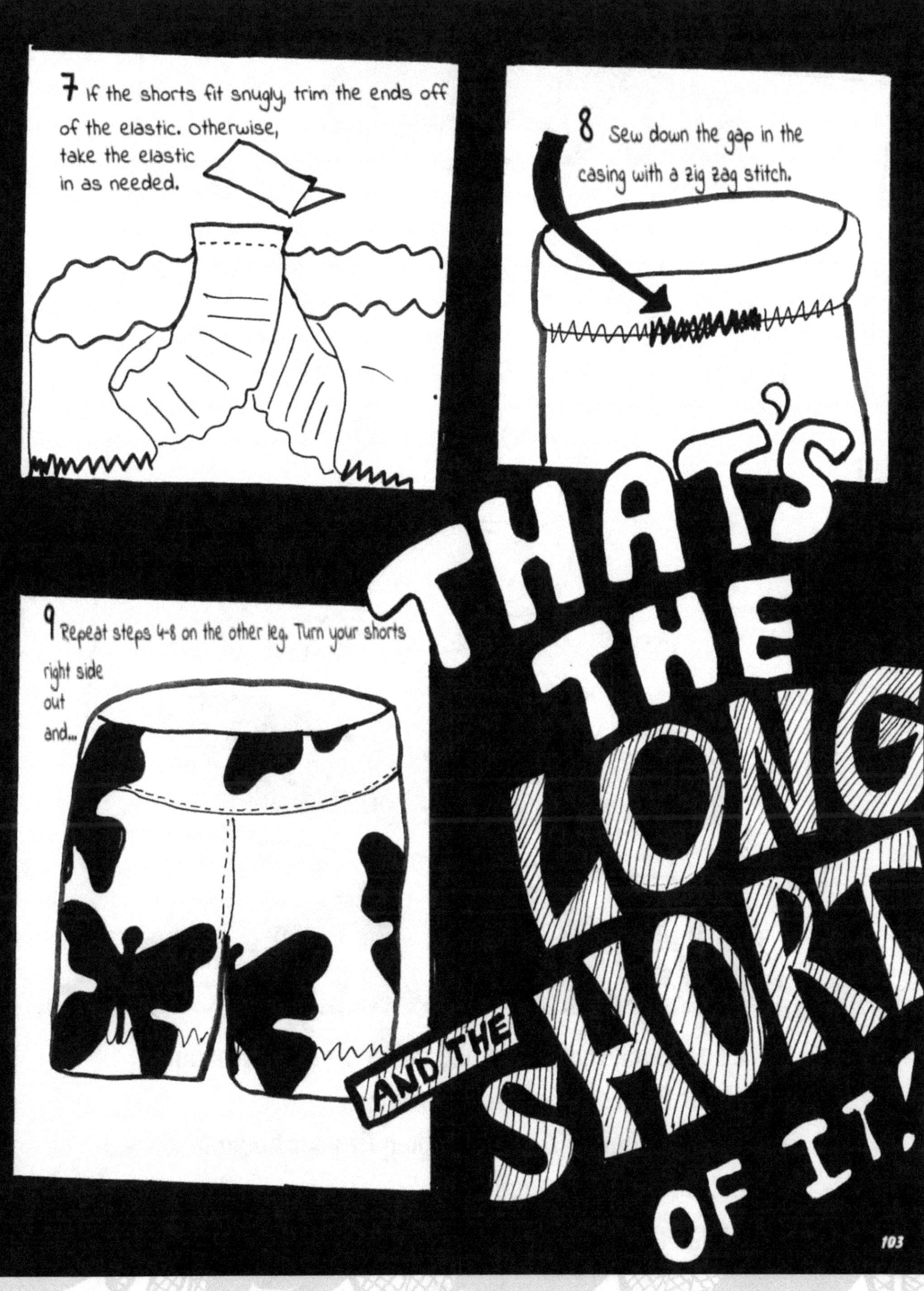
7 If the shorts fit snugly, trim the ends off of the elastic. otherwise, take the elastic in as needed.
8 Sew down the gap in the casing with a zig zag stitch.
9 Repeat steps 4-8 on the other leg. Turn your shorts right side out and...
THAT'S THE LONG AND THE SHORT OF IT!

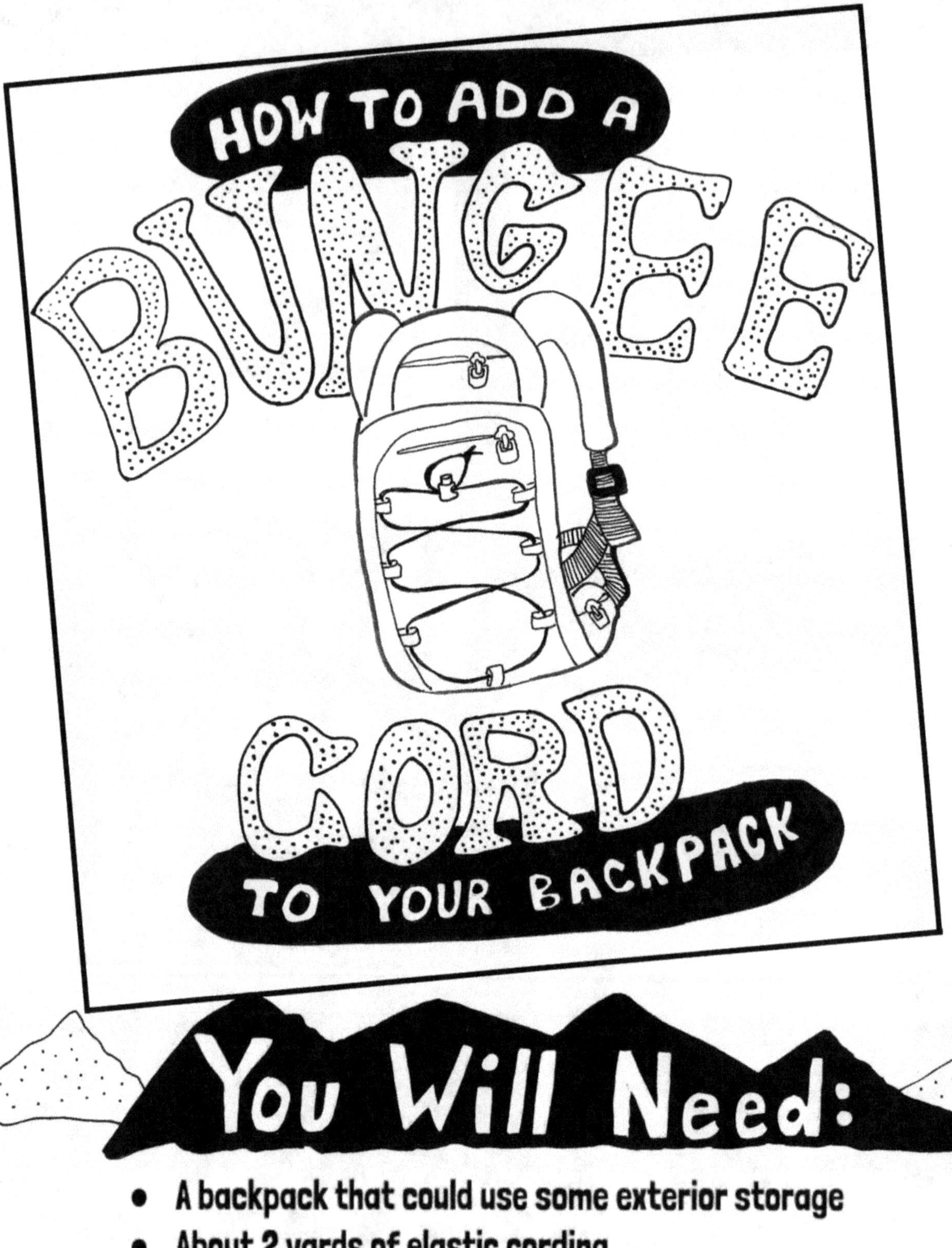

HOW TO ADD A BUNGEE CORD TO YOUR BACKPACK

You Will Need:

- A backpack that could use some exterior storage
- About 2 yards of elastic cording
- About 2 feet of ½ inch webbing (if your backpack does not already have loops)
- A toggle 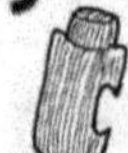

1. Cut the webbing into 3 inch long pieces. Sew them in half about ¼ inch away from the ends.

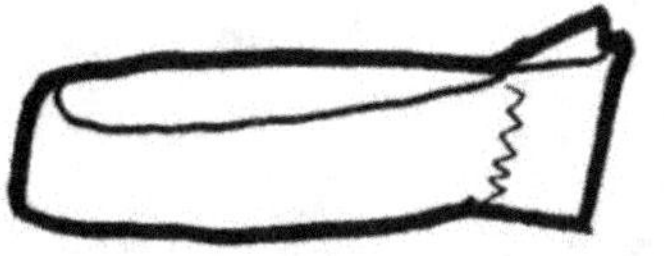

2. Mark where you will put your loops on your backpack. Make sure to put a loop on the bottom, too.

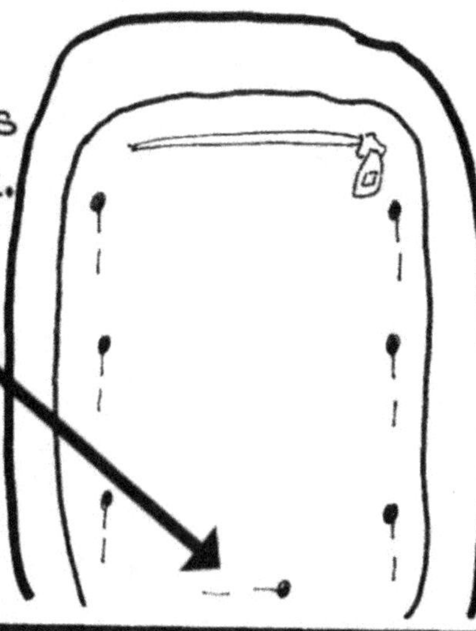

3. ***FOR EACH LOOP:*** Turn rightside out. Move seam to the bottom of the loop.

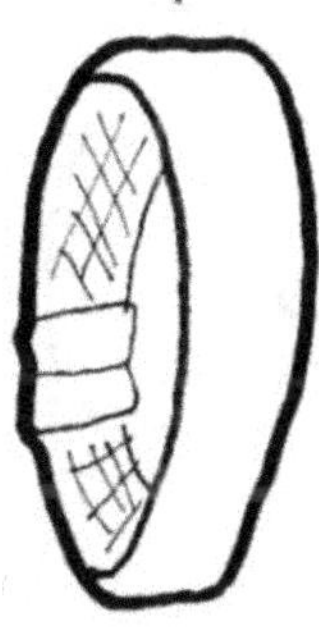

4. Fold in half and pin to backpack at a mark. Be careful not to pin shut any openings or pockets.

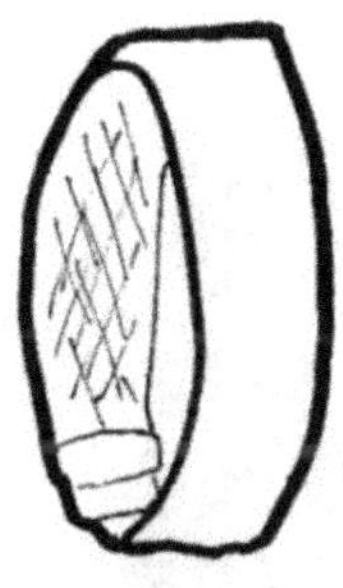

5. Sew loop to backpack at a mark. Sew about ½ inch from the fold. Sew again as close to the fold as possible. *Be careful not to sew anything together that is not supposed to be!*

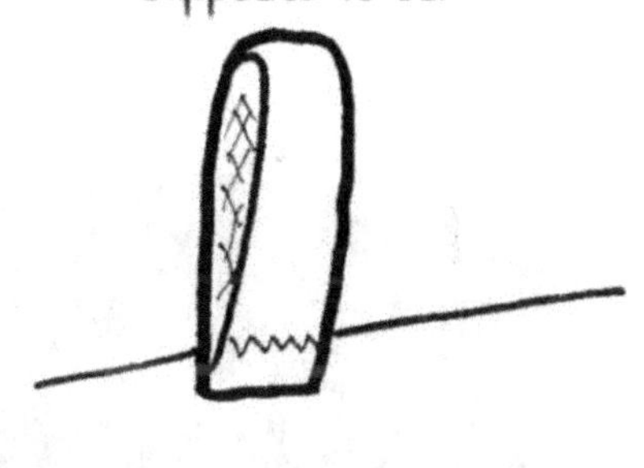

6. Center elastic at bottom loop. Continue to thread elastic like a shoelace (see numbers).

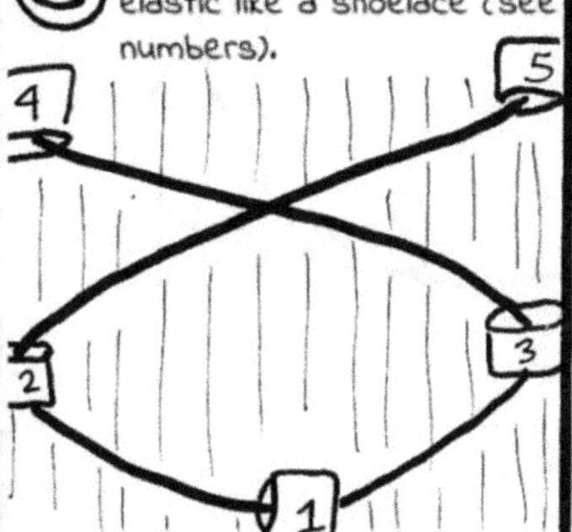

7. Lace both ends through the toggle thing like so.

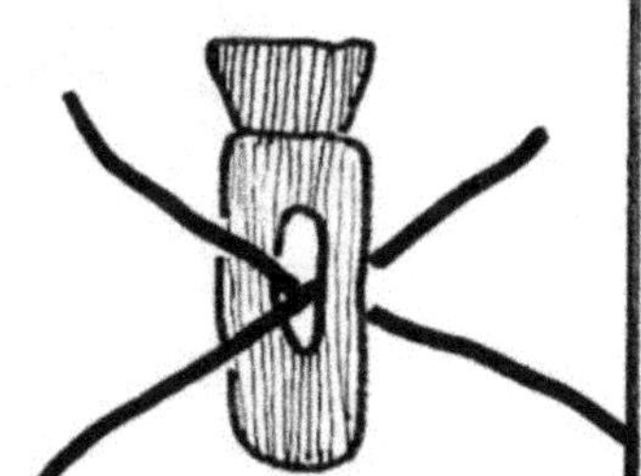

8. Tie the ends together.

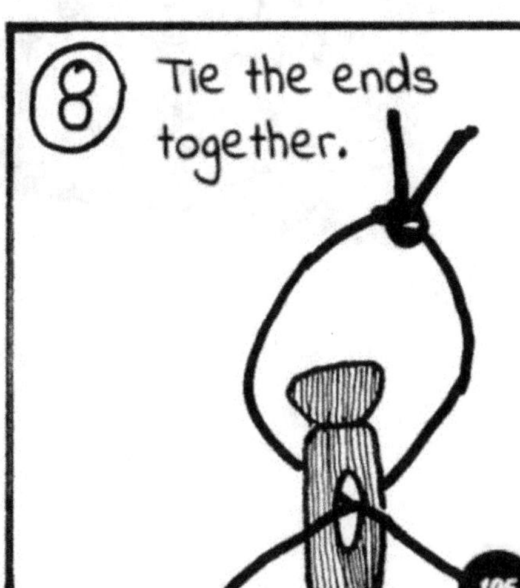

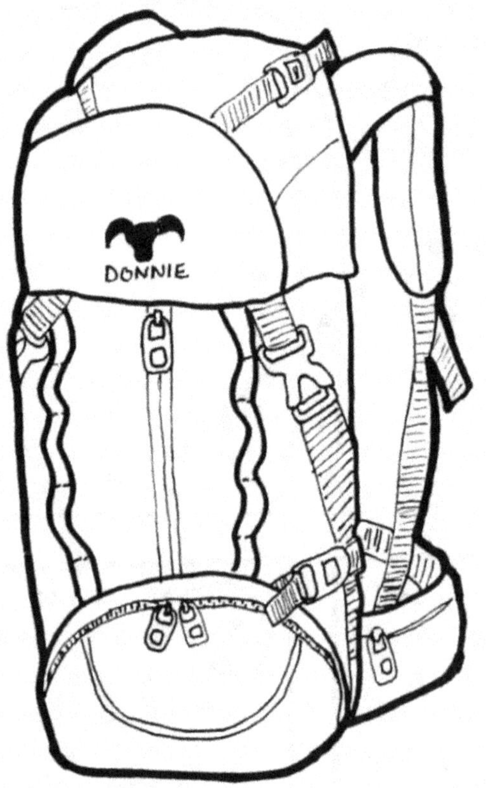

If your backpack does not have a bottom loop, pretend it does :) and lace it the same way.

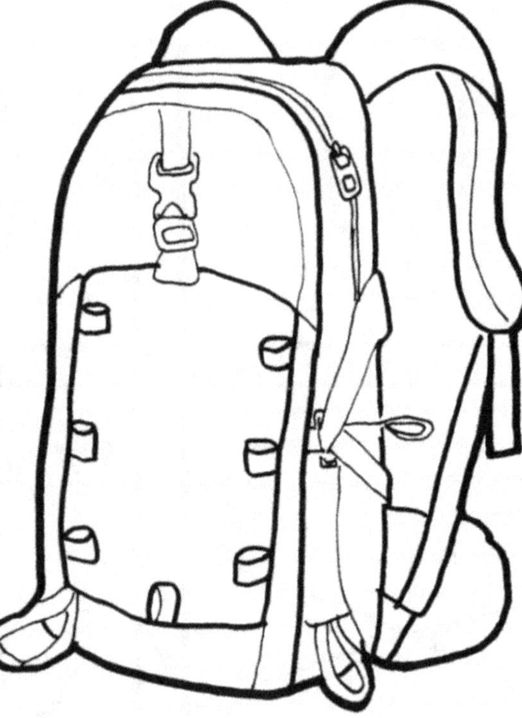

If your backpack already has loops, start with Step 6.

ADDING A SNAP TO A BUTTON-UP TO MAKE A TURTLENECK FOR UNEXPECTED COLD SNAPS

You Will Need:

- **A flannel/button-up that has a collar that is big enough to overlap when turned up**
- **A snap**

2. Flip up your left collar. Sew the outtie part of the snap to your left collar.

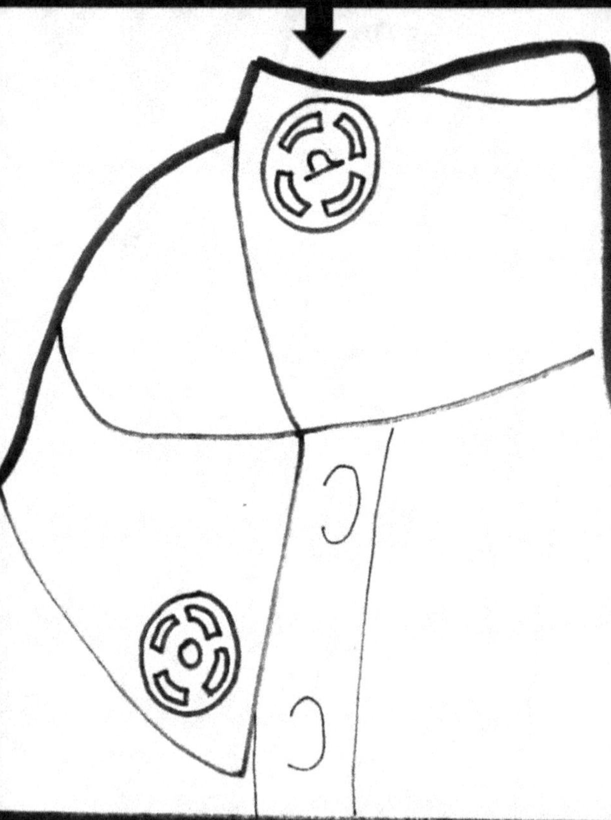

1. Sew the innie part of the snap to your right collar. *It should be facing out as shown.*

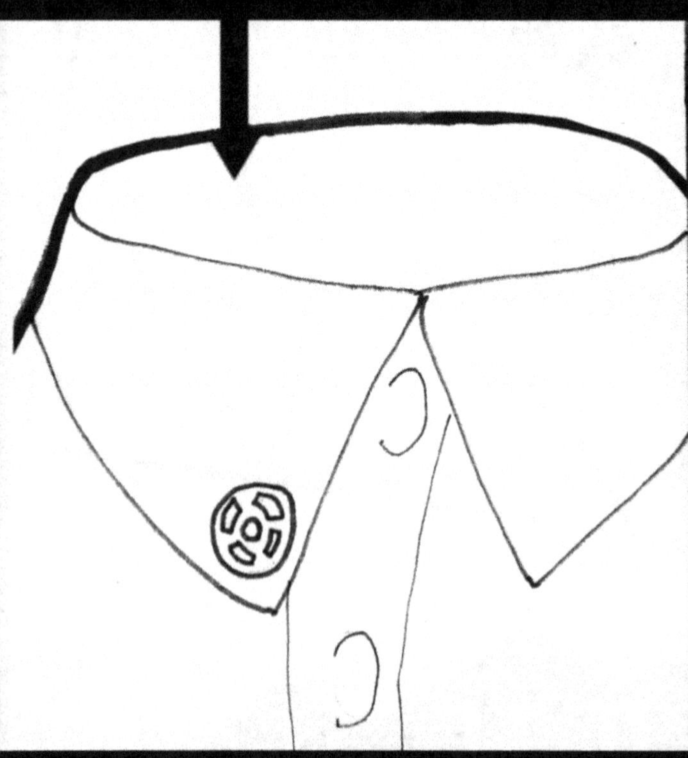

3. Flip up the right collar, snap and enjoy a warm neck on an unexpectedly chilly day.

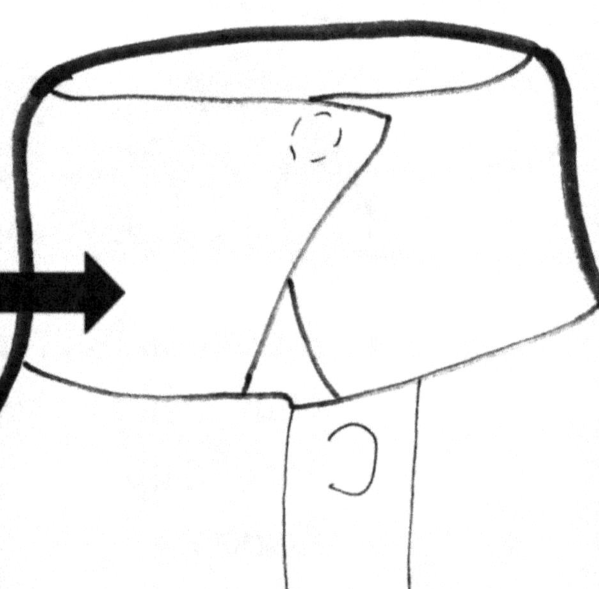

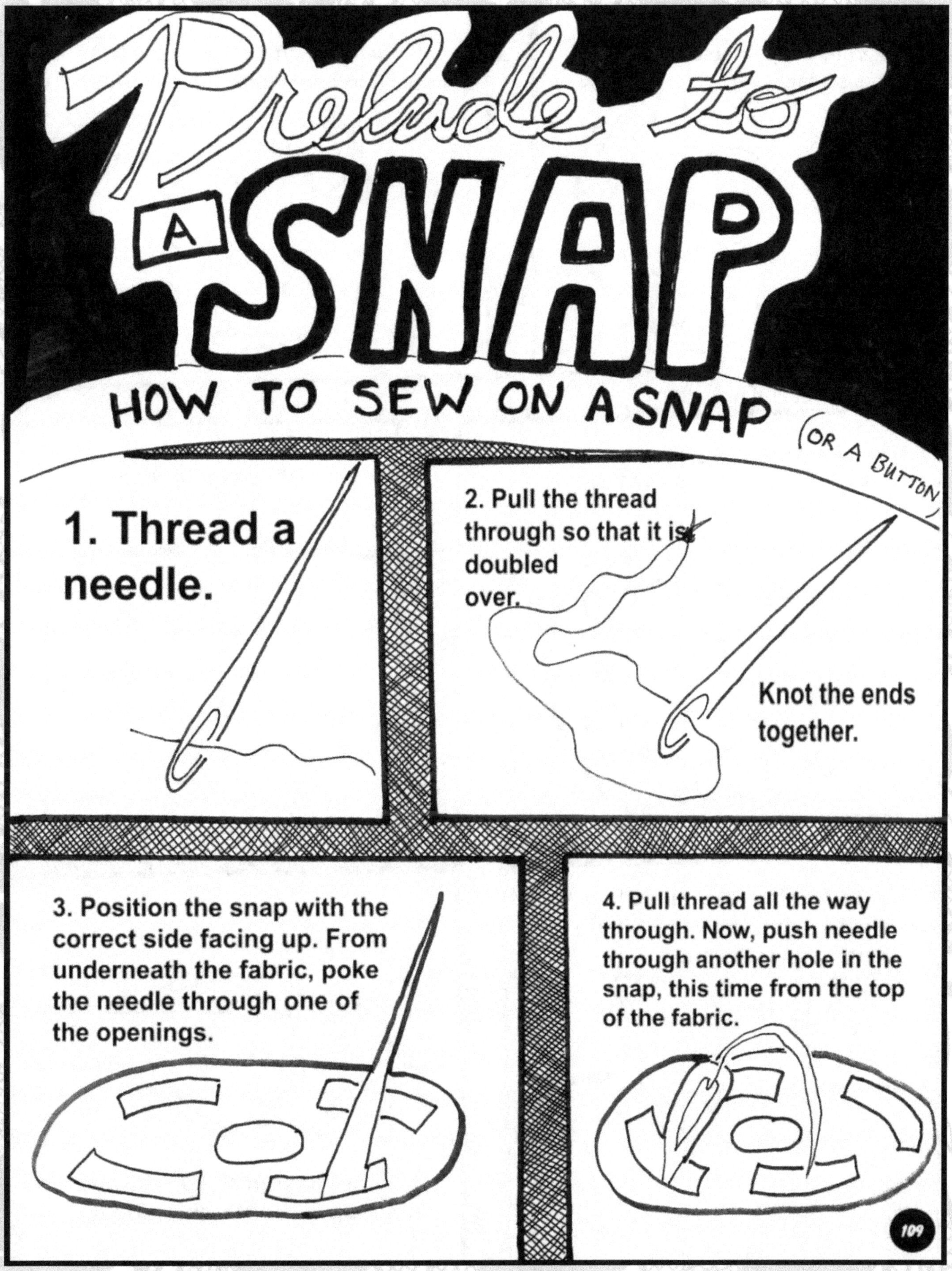

Prelude to A SNAP

HOW TO SEW ON A SNAP (OR A BUTTON)

1. Thread a needle.

2. Pull the thread through so that it is doubled over.

Knot the ends together.

3. Position the snap with the correct side facing up. From underneath the fabric, poke the needle through one of the openings.

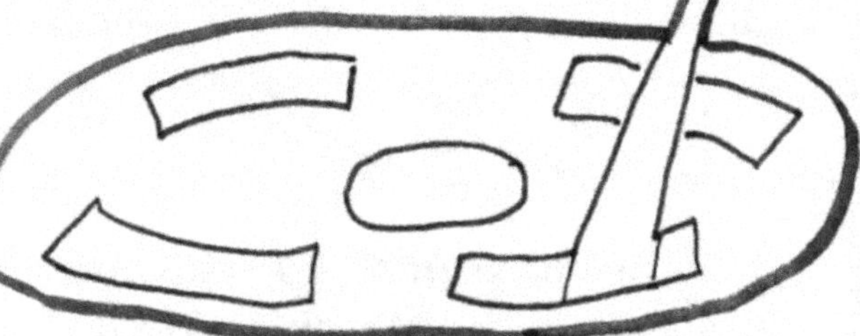

4. Pull thread all the way through. Now, push needle through another hole in the snap, this time from the top of the fabric.

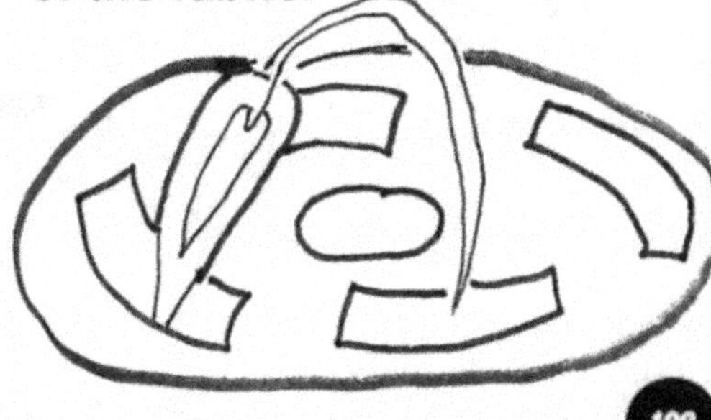

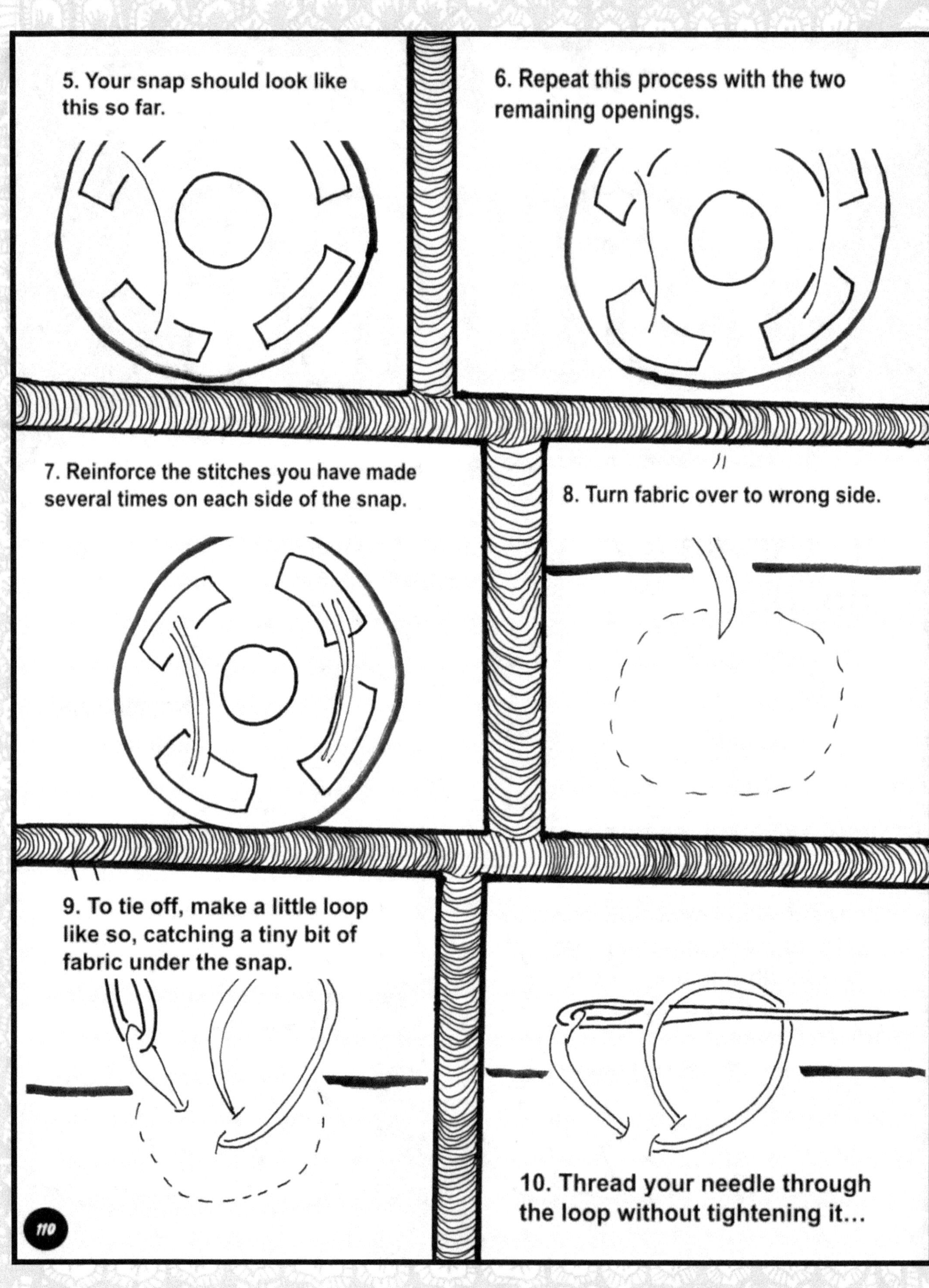
5. Your snap should look like this so far.
6. Repeat this process with the two remaining openings.
7. Reinforce the stitches you have made several times on each side of the snap.
8. Turn fabric over to wrong side.
9. To tie off, make a little loop like so, catching a tiny bit of fabric under the snap.
10. Thread your needle through the loop without tightening it...

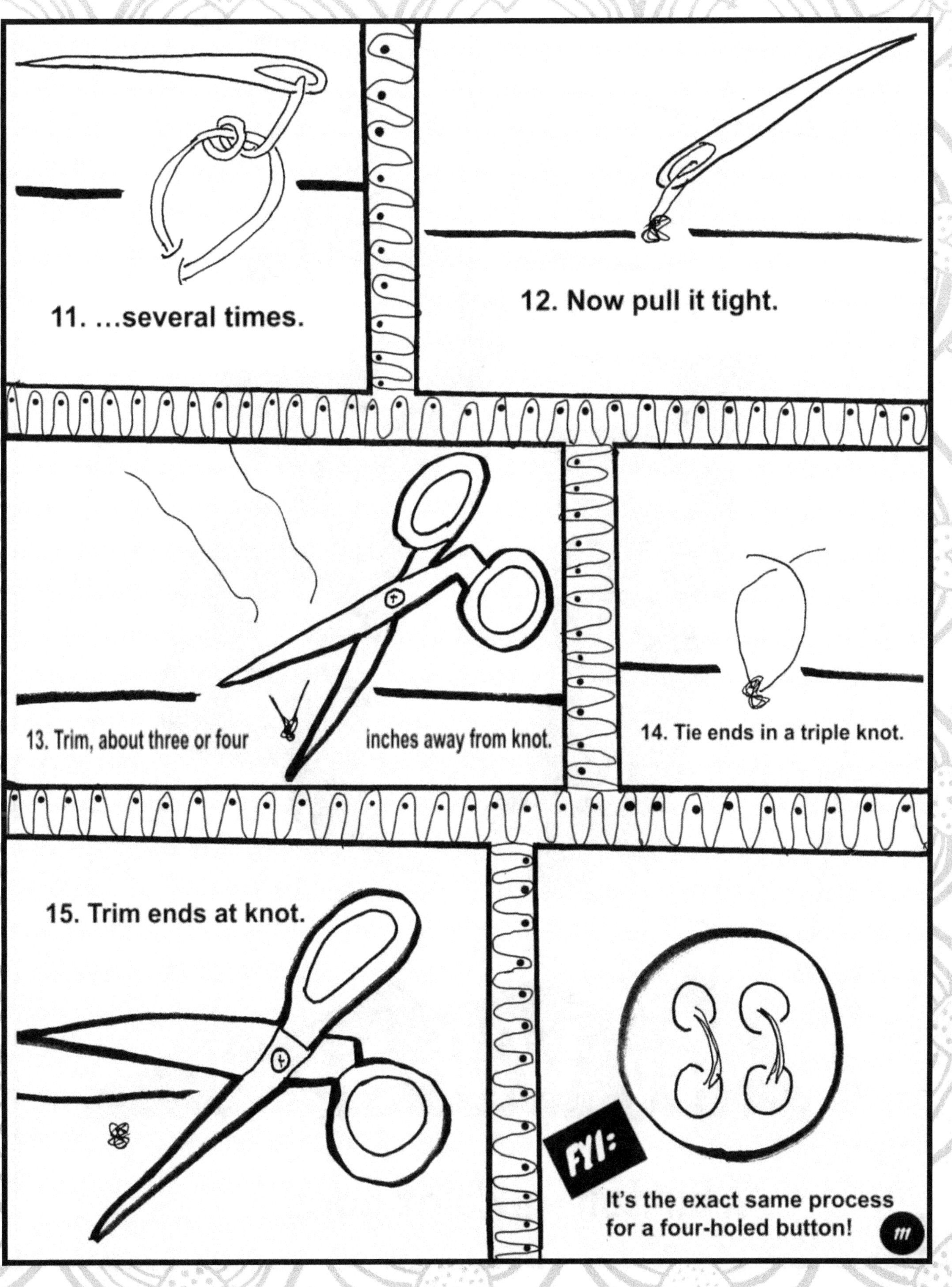
11. ...several times.
12. Now pull it tight.
13. Trim, about three or four
inches away from knot.
14. Tie ends in a triple knot.
15. Trim ends at knot.
FYI:
It's the exact same process
for a four-holed button!
111

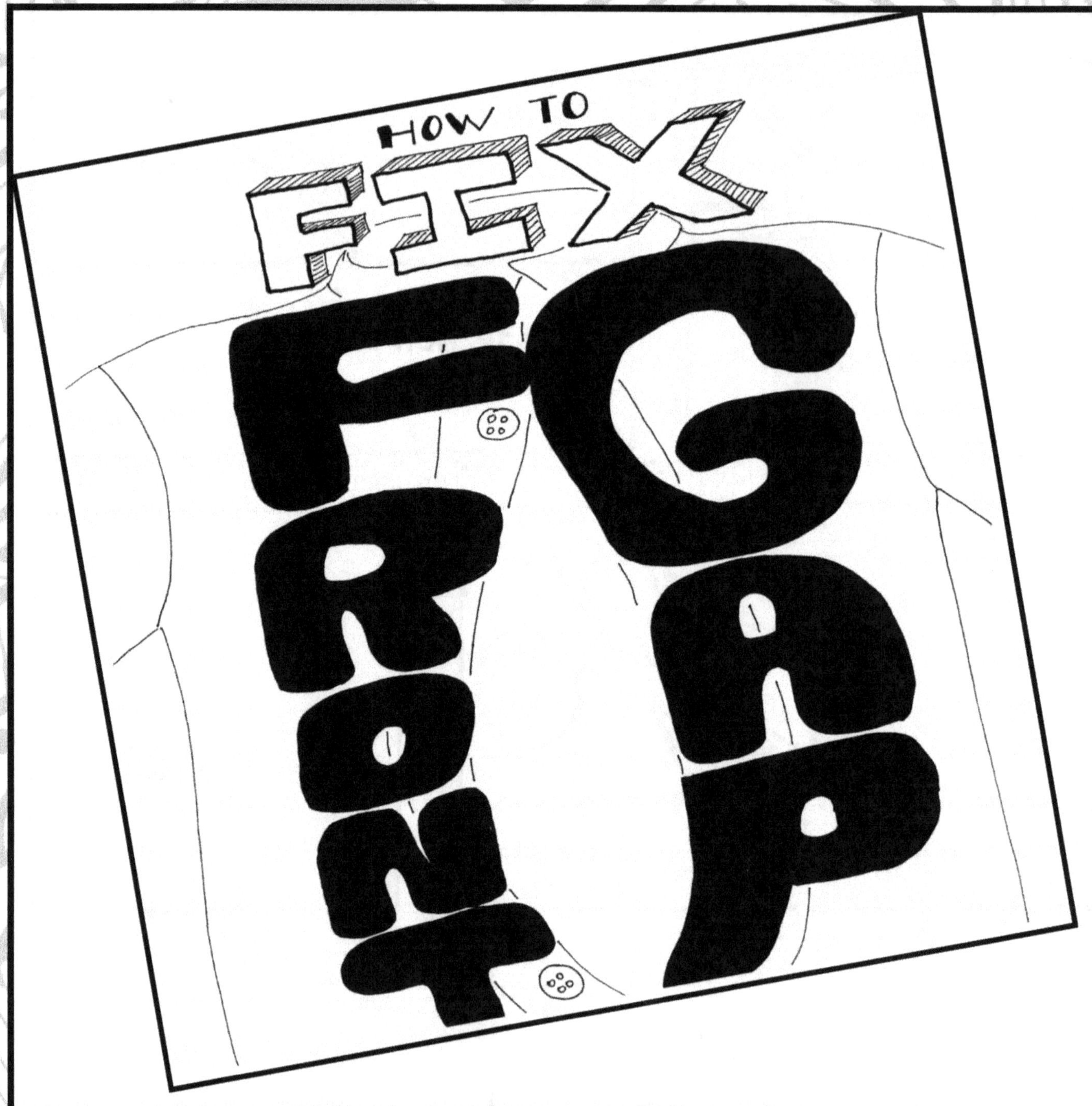

You Will Need:

A button-up that gaps

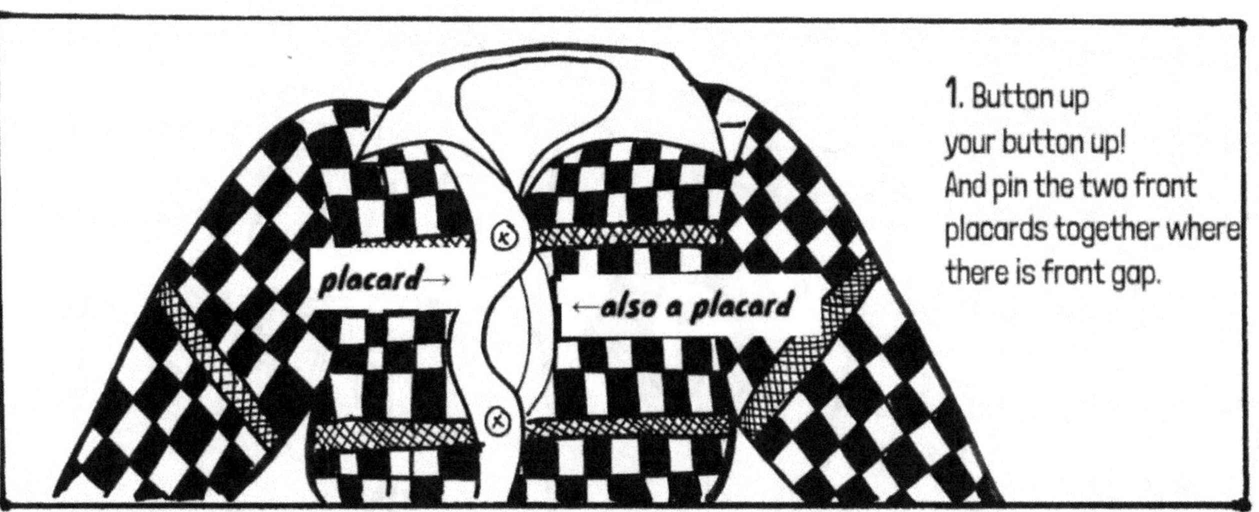

1. Button up your button up! And pin the two front placards together where there is front gap.

2. Adjust your sewing machine needle to the left.

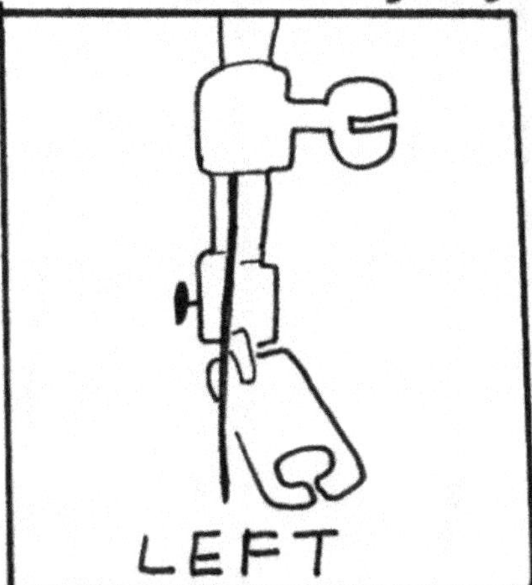

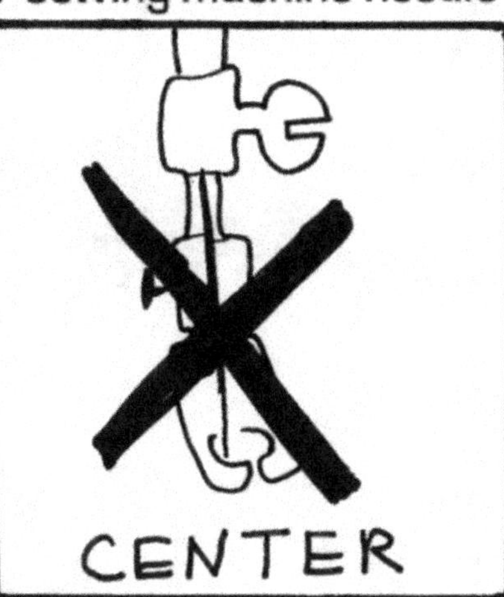

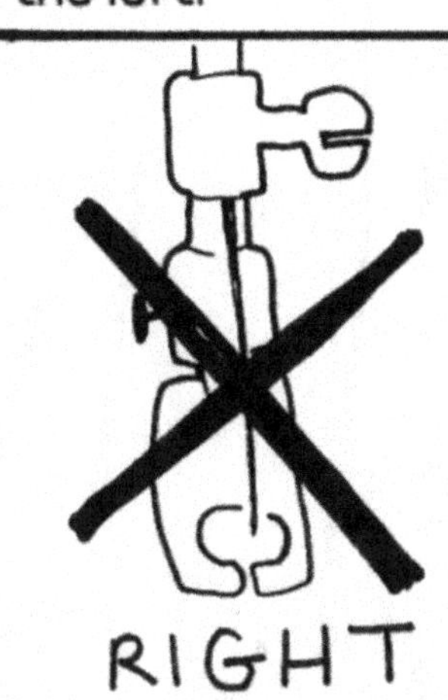

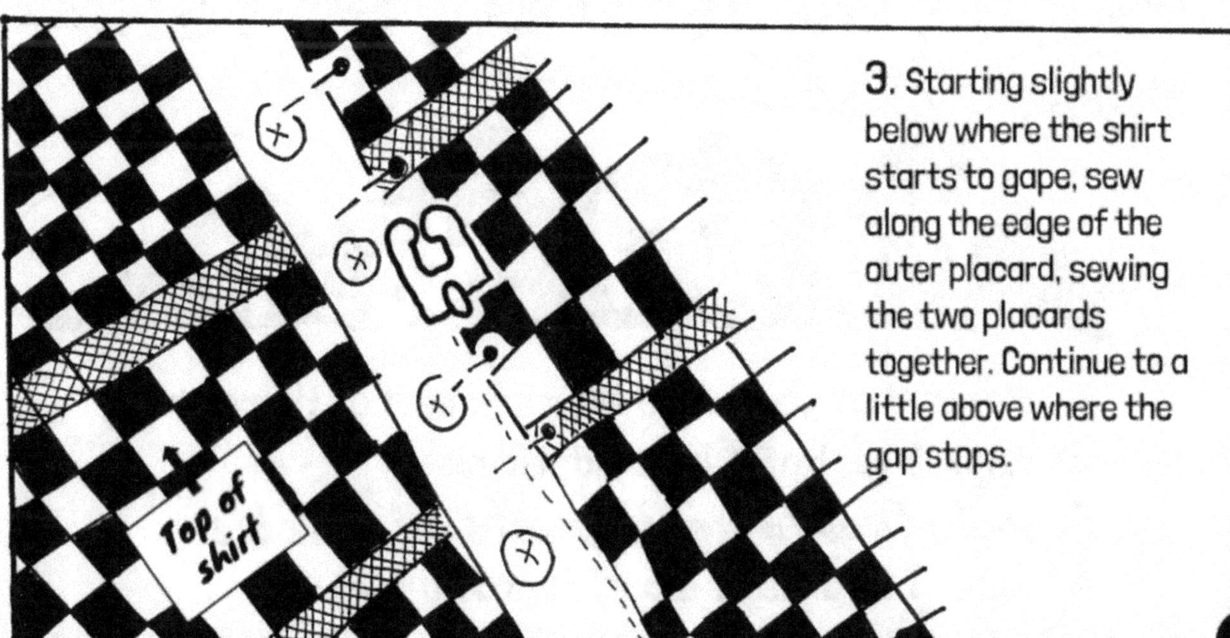

3. Starting slightly below where the shirt starts to gape, sew along the edge of the outer placard, sewing the two placards together. Continue to a little above where the gap stops.

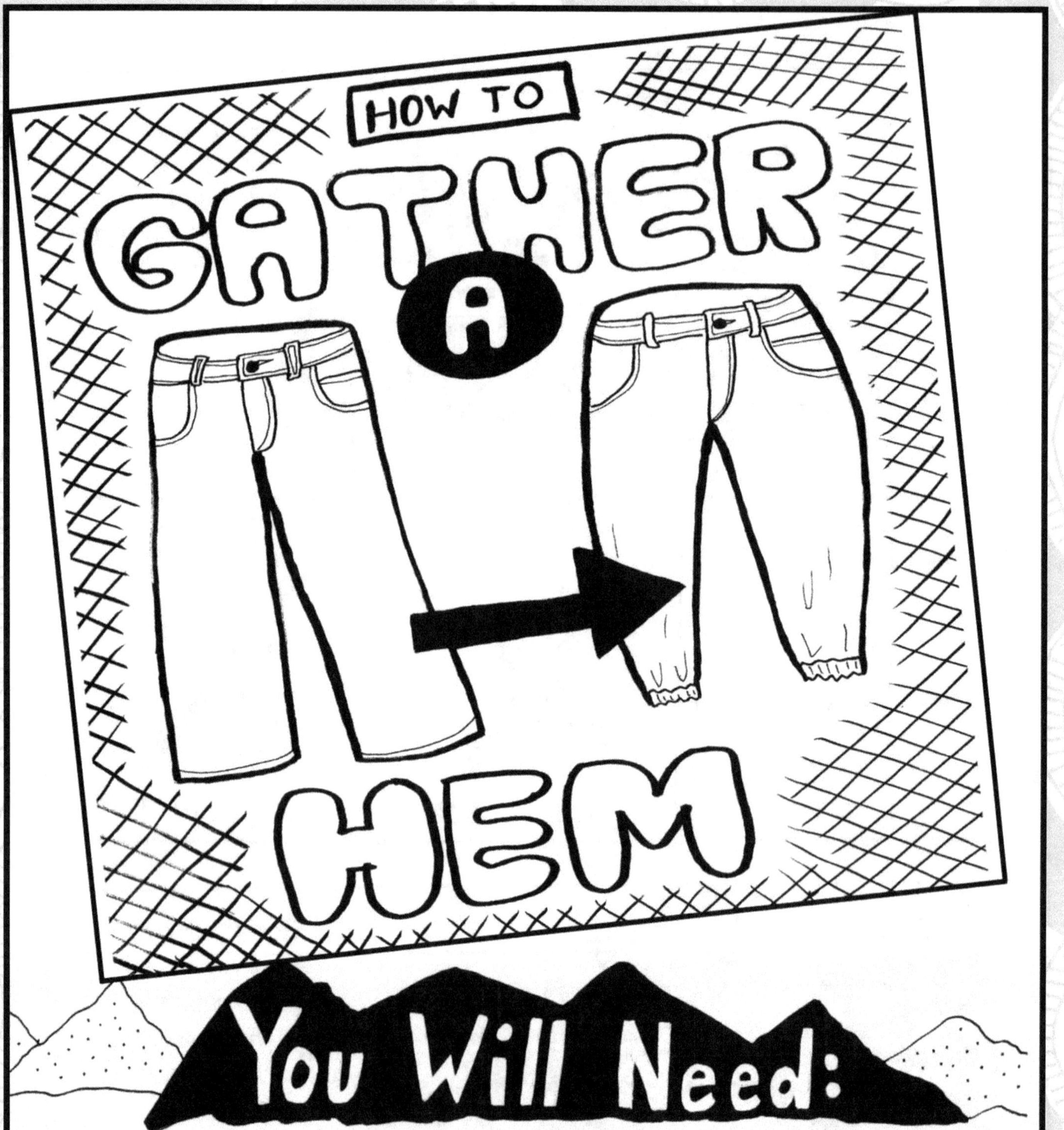

HOW TO GATHER A HEM

You Will Need:

- Pants that you would like to have a gathered hem
- Appx. 2 feet of ¼ inch elastic or

To make (lightweight) pants adjustable:

- Appx. 1.5 yards of elastic cording
- A toggle that fits the cording

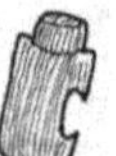

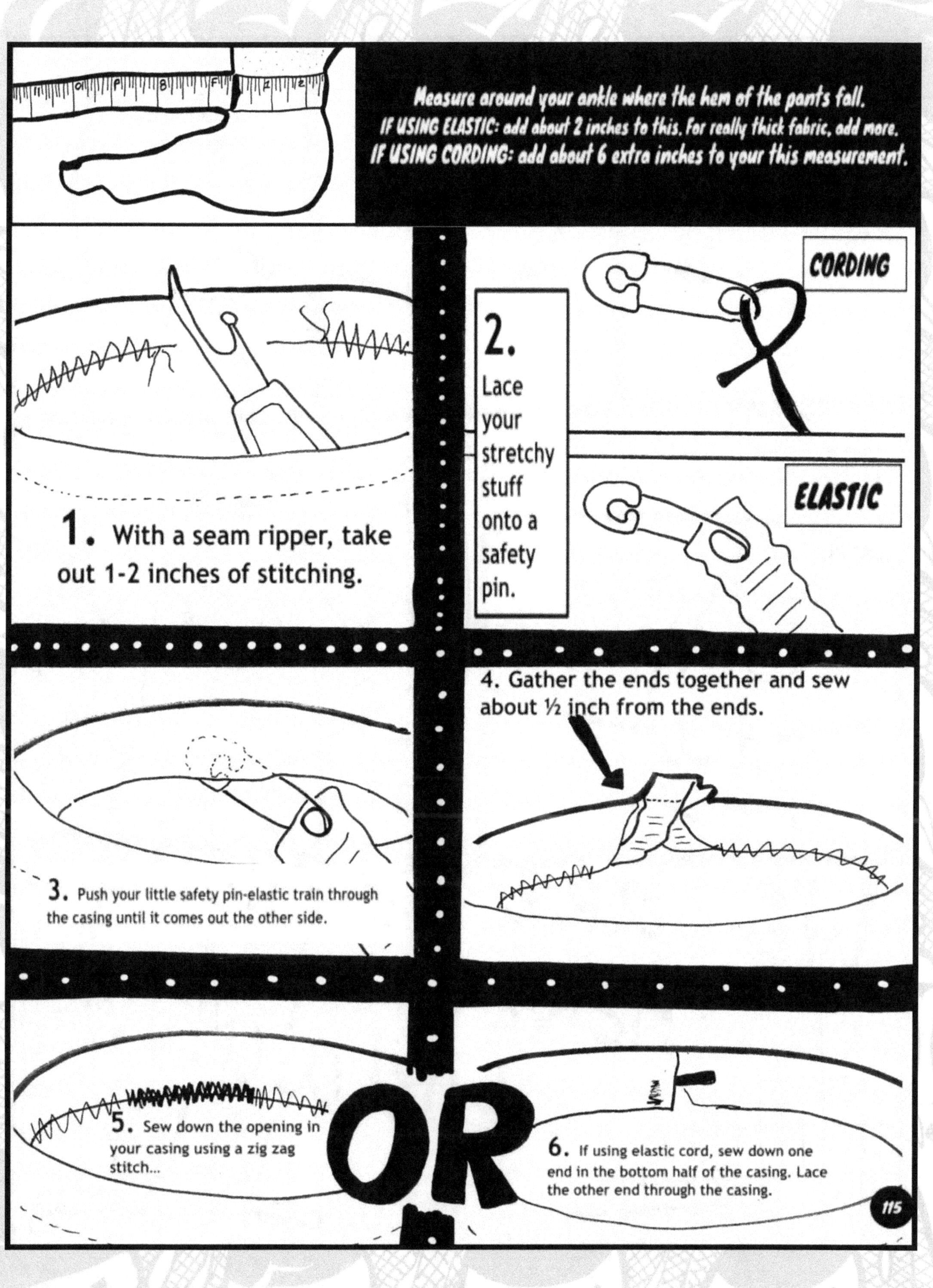
Measure around your ankle where the hem of the pants fall.
IF USING ELASTIC: add about 2 inches to this. For really thick fabric, add more.
IF USING CORDING: add about 6 extra inches to your this measurement.
1. With a seam ripper, take out 1-2 inches of stitching.
2. Lace your stretchy stuff onto a safety pin.
CORDING
ELASTIC
3. Push your little safety pin-elastic train through the casing until it comes out the other side.
4. Gather the ends together and sew about ½ inch from the ends.
5. Sew down the opening in your casing using a zig zag stitch...
OR
6. If using elastic cord, sew down one end in the bottom half of the casing. Lace the other end through the casing.

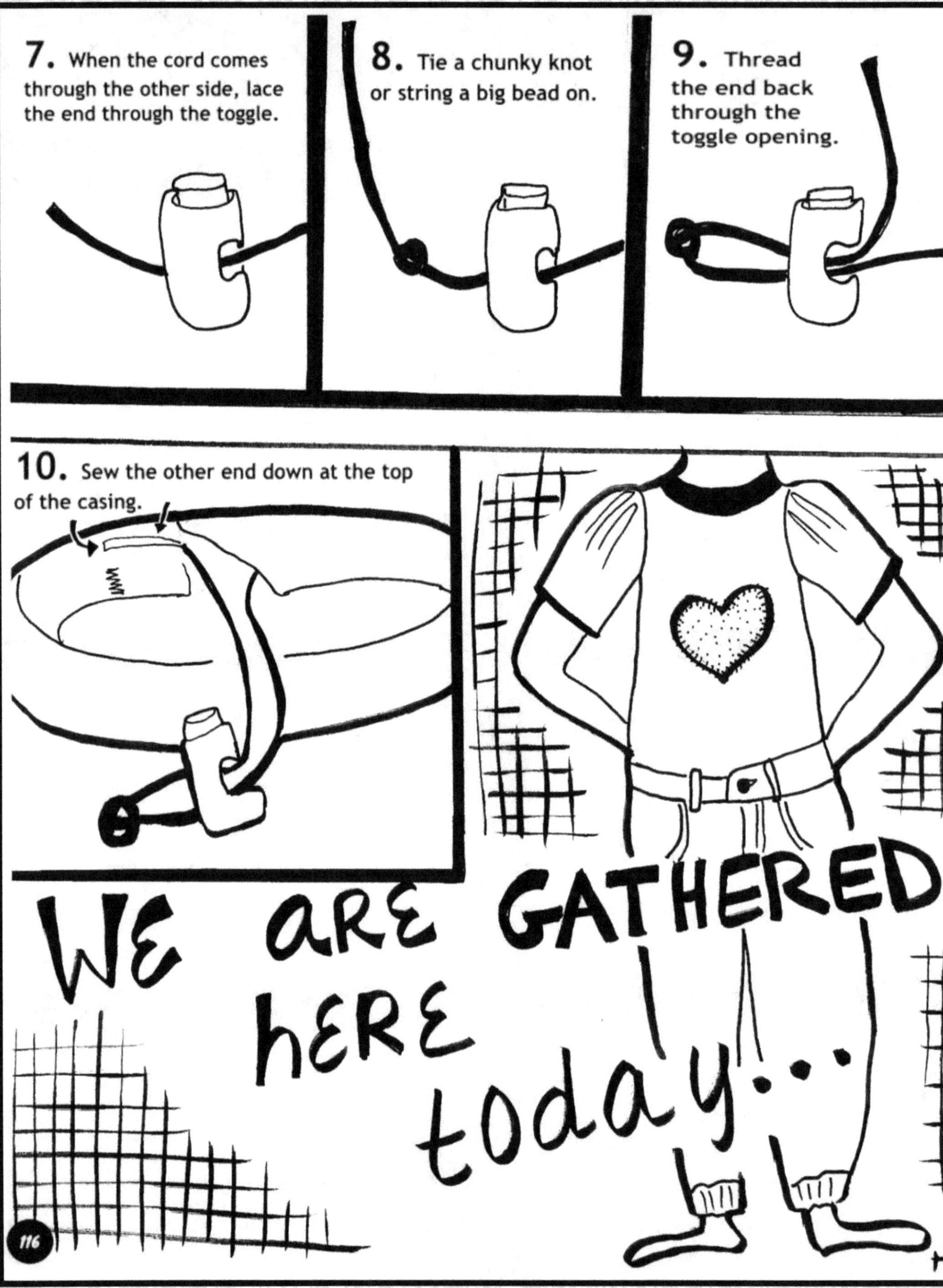
7. When the cord comes through the other side, lace the end through the toggle.
8. Tie a chunky knot or string a big bead on.
9. Thread the end back through the toggle opening.
10. Sew the other end down at the top of the casing.
WE ARE GATHERED
HERE
today...

HOW TO MAKE POCKETS BIGGER

YOU WILL NEED: SCRAP COTTON FABRIC, A GARMENT WITH A TOO-SMALL POCKET, SEWING SUPPLIES

1. PULL THE BACK OF THE POCKET AWAY FROM THE FRONT OF THE POCKET.

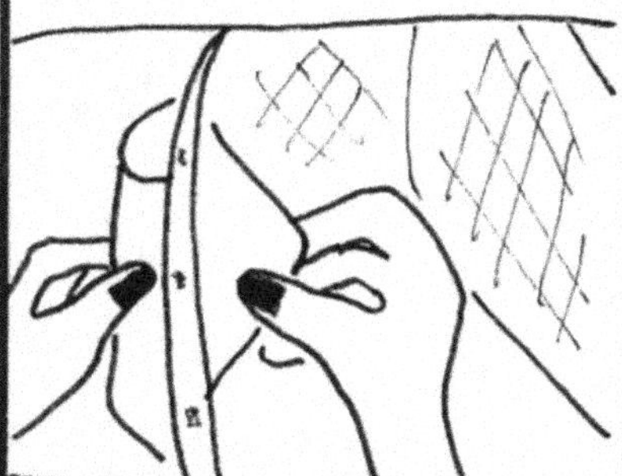

2. CUT A SMALL SLIT IN THE BACK NEAR THE BOTTOM (WITHOUT NICKING THE FRONT LAYER).

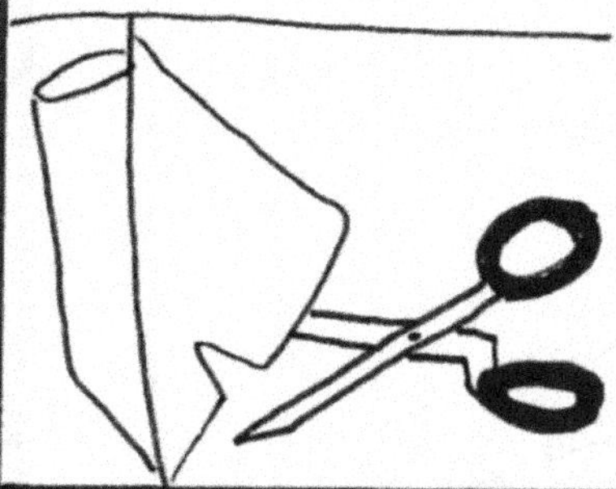

3. CONTINUE THE SLIT ALL THE WAY ACROSS THE WIDTH OF THE POCKET (STILL ONLY CUTTING THROUGH THE BACK LAYER).

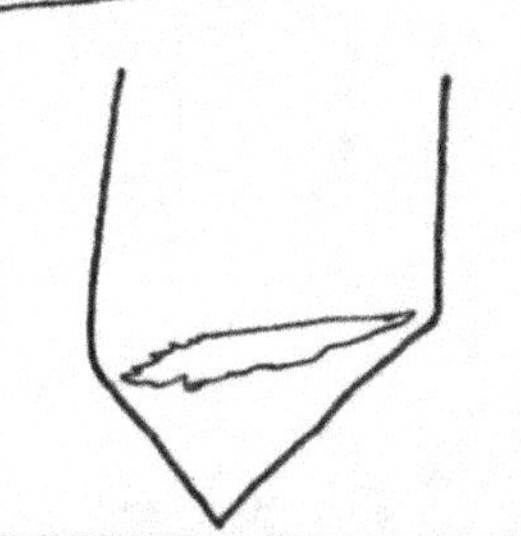

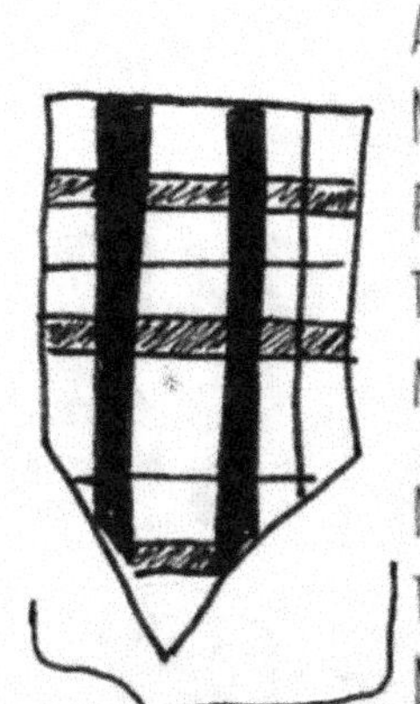

4. MEASURE THE WIDTH OF YOUR POCKET. ADD 1 ½ INCHES. THIS IS MEASUREMENT A. NOW, MEASURE FROM THE TOP OF THE POCKET TO WHERE YOU WANT YOUR POCKET TO END. ADD 1/1/2 INCHES. THIS MEASUREMENT IS MEASUREMENT B.

NOW, CUT A SCRAP FROM AN OLD T-SHIRT THAT IS: MEASUREMENT A x MEASUREMENT B.

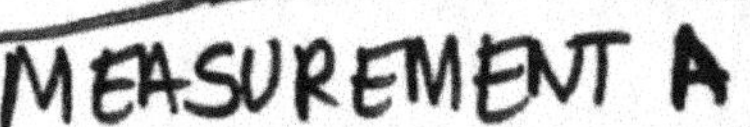

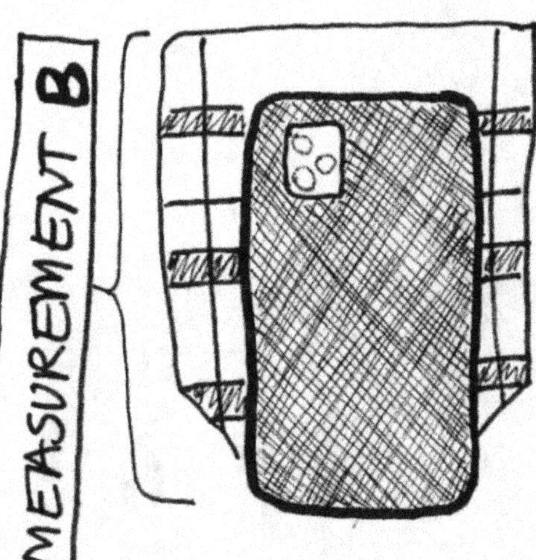

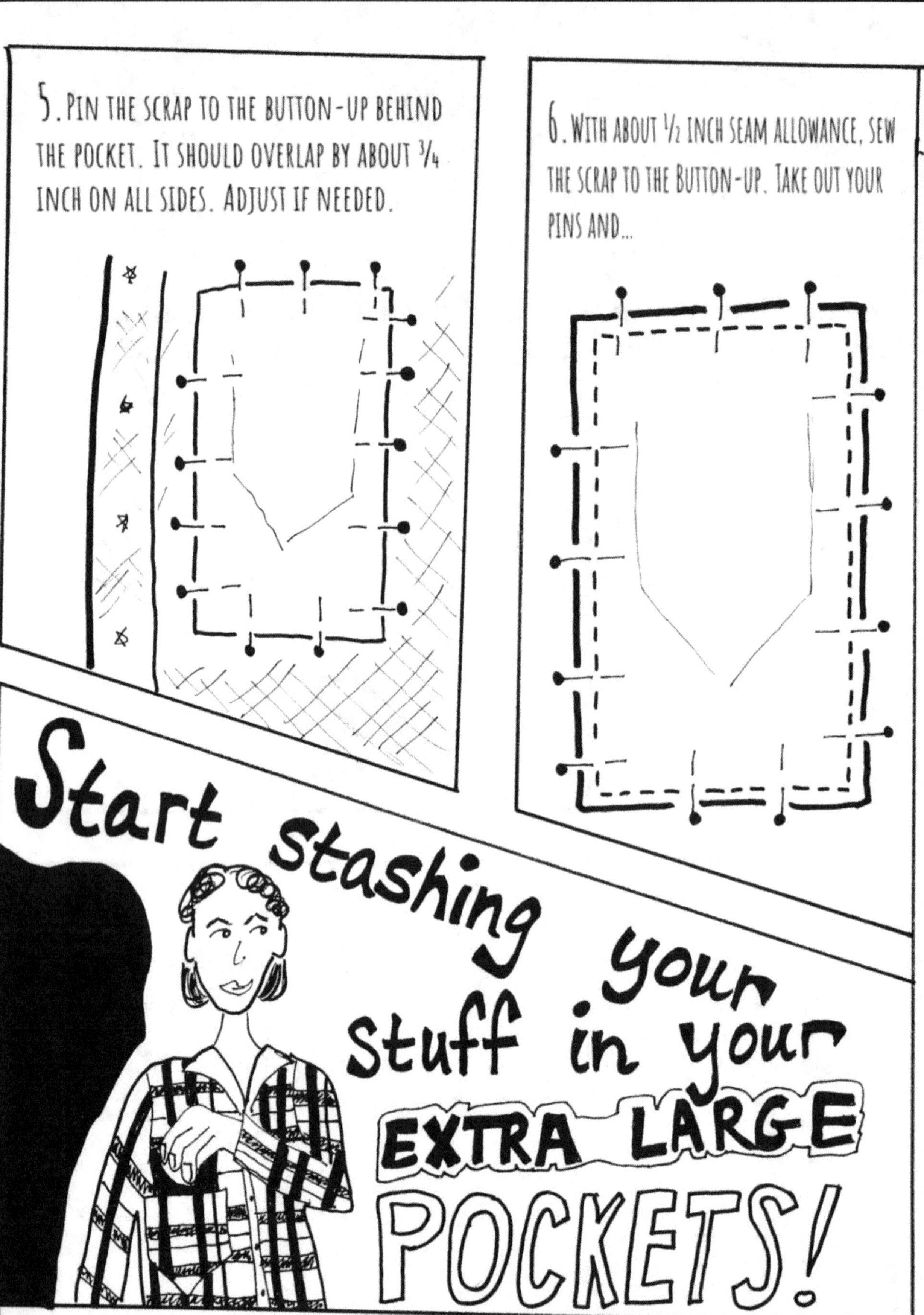
5. Pin the scrap to the button-up behind the pocket. It should overlap by about 3/4 inch on all sides. Adjust if needed.
6. With about 1/2 inch seam allowance, sew the scrap to the Button-up. Take out your pins and...
Start stashing your stuff in your
EXTRA LARGE
POCKETS!

CONVERTIBLE PANTS

You will need:

- Hiking pants that are too long or two pairs of hiking pants
- Two separating zippers. They should be slightly longer than the circumference of your pants at the thigh

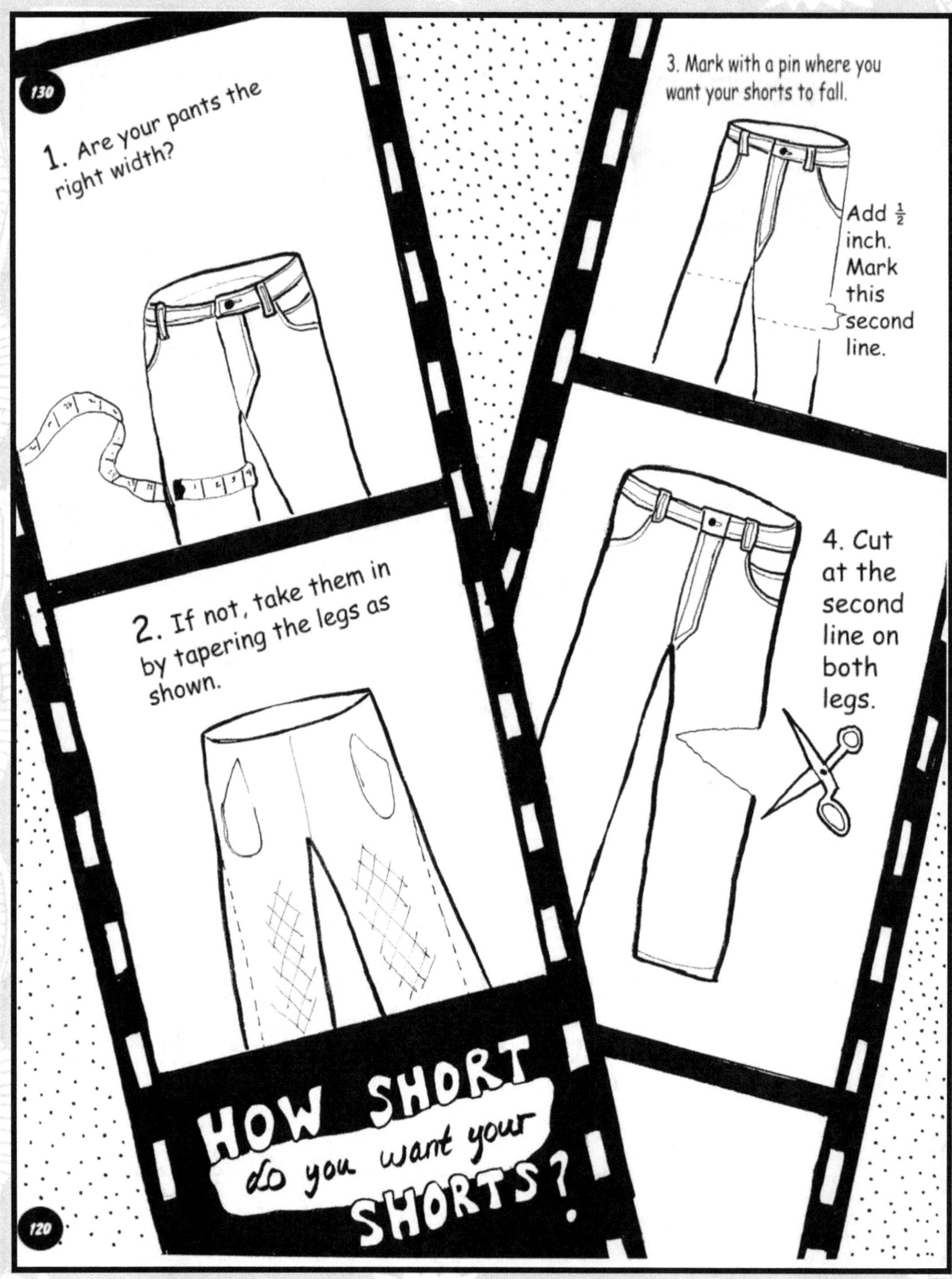
130
1. Are your pants the right width?
2. If not, take them in by tapering the legs as shown.
3. Mark with a pin where you want your shorts to fall.
Add ½ inch. Mark this second line.
4. Cut at the second line on both legs.
HOW SHORT do you want your SHORTS?
120

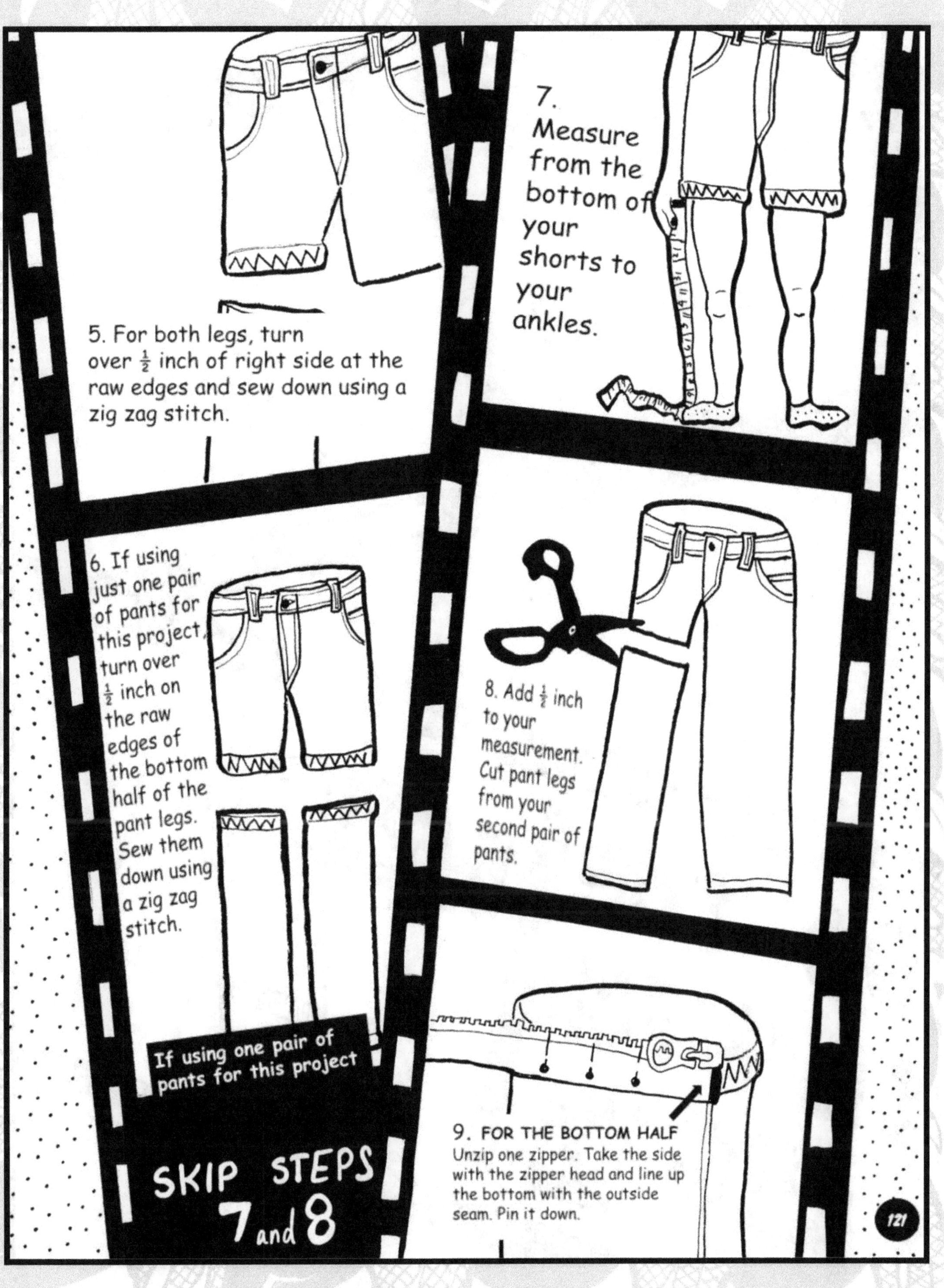
5. For both legs, turn over ½ inch of right side at the raw edges and sew down using a zig zag stitch.
6. If using just one pair of pants for this project, turn over ½ inch on the raw edges of the bottom half of the pant legs. Sew them down using a zig zag stitch.
If using one pair of pants for this project
SKIP STEPS 7 and 8
7. Measure from the bottom of your shorts to your ankles.
8. Add ½ inch to your measurement. Cut pant legs from your second pair of pants.
9. FOR THE BOTTOM HALF
Unzip one zipper. Take the side with the zipper head and line up the bottom with the outside seam. Pin it down.

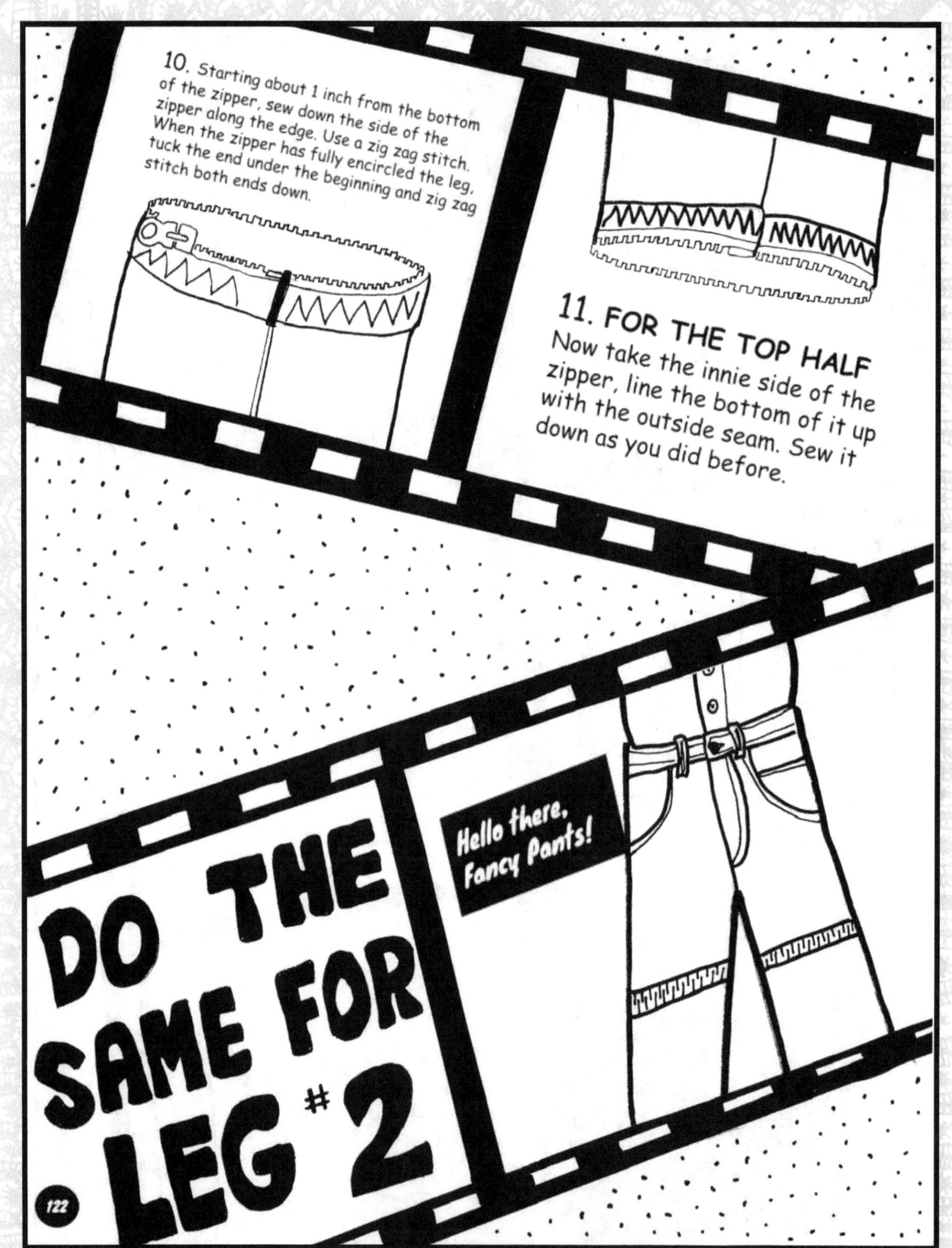
10. Starting about 1 inch from the bottom of the zipper, sew down the side of the zipper along the edge. Use a zig zag stitch. When the zipper has fully encircled the leg, tuck the end under the beginning and zig zag stitch both ends down.
11. FOR THE TOP HALF
Now take the innie side of the zipper, line the bottom of it up with the outside seam. Sew it down as you did before.
DO THE SAME FOR LEG #2
Hello there, Fancy Pants!

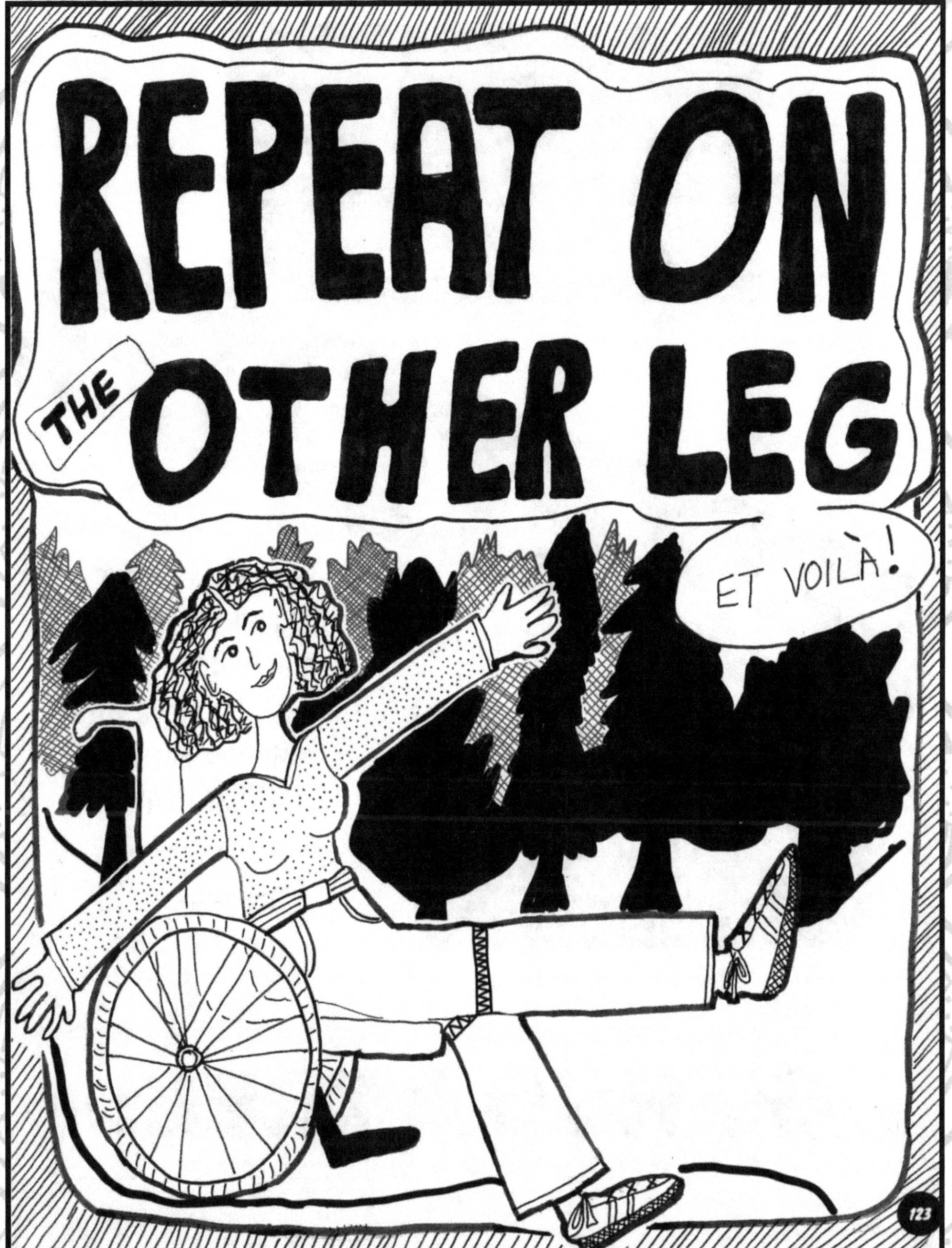
REPEAT ON THE OTHER LEG
ET VOILÀ!

Never underestimate the power of a small group of committed people to change the world. In fact, it is the only thing that ever has.

~ Margaret Mead

TOUCH GRASS

We need to move beyond the idea of 'environment' and fall back in love with Mother Earth.

~Nhat Hanh

We do not inherit the earth from our ancestors; we borrow it from our children.

~Chief Seattle

GO HUG A TREE!

OUTDOOR FABRICS

FIBER CONTENT

FIBER CONTENT refers to the type of material used to make a fabric. Understanding what a garment is composed of can guide how it may be reused or repurposed. If the fiber content label is still intact on a piece you are upcycling, it will indicate the types of fibers used and their respective percentages. Often these tags are found in the bottom left side seam.

Sometimes content information is printed directly onto the fabric. Take the time to look for some of the following properties often found on outdoor/sports clothing.

- Anti-chafe (doesn't rub or irritate your skin)
- Anti-bacterial
- Anti-mold
- Anti-stink
- UV Protection
- Hypoallergenic
- Breathable
- Cooling
- Moisture-wicking
- Evaporates quickly
- Does not retain water
- Durable

If your garment no longer has fiber content information, you can still learn a great deal by handling the fabric.

- FEEL ON THE SKIN: Will the item sit directly against your skin? If so, consider how it feels in those areas—soft, rough, breathable, or irritating.
- FABRIC DENSITY AND WEIGHT: Does the thickness and weight suit your intended use?
- STRETCH: Does your project require flexibility? Consider how much stretch you need, and whether it should extend in one direction or multiple.

Lastly, the information in this FIBER CONTENT section can help you make informed guesses about what a garment is made from. Over time, as you upcycle more and become familiar with different materials, you'll develop a stronger intuition for identifying fiber content by what material looks like and how it feels.

I got my love of sewing from my mother. Mom also passed along to me her love of thrifting. By the time I was a teenager, I knew enough about fabric that we would play a game while visiting our local Salvation Army: She would find a garment with a very distinct fabric (think shantung silk, bumpy wool or stiff cotton). And then I, using only my sense of touch, would guess the fiber content. I highly recommend this game with someone you love. 🩶

COTTON

Cotton is a material that holds a lot of water (hydrophilic) and takes a long time to dry. Wet cotton can-at best-be irritating and-at worst-life threatening. For this reason, it is often recommended to avoid cotton fabrics for activewear or sportswear garments. Personally, I like a cotton/spandex blend for anything touching my face, neck and head because it is soft; also I am not usually trouncing around in the rain.

Cotton is also breathable and easy to care for.

SPANDEX

Contrary to popular belief, spandex is NOT a brand name. It is an elasticized fabric made from polyurethane. If you have ever put on a pair of leggings, you know what spandex feels like. Spandex is often blended into newer sportswear to add stretch/comfort. Check labels; you will be surprised where you find spandex!

PROS	CONS	OFTEN FOUND IN
• stretchy • easy to care for (although tumble drying reduces elasticity)	• not always breathable • inability to biodegrade	• sweaters • socks • some base layers such as long underwear stocking • caps

WHY USED SPANDEX IS BETTER THAN NEW SPANDEX

Because spandex is not recyclable or biodegradable, upcycling keeps it out of landfills.

SILK

I know, silk seems so boujee, yet it is a great fabric for all seasons and you CAN find it in secondhand stores. Silk is usually very thin and smooth to the touch. Sometimes some synthetics like rayon and polyester can feel like silk.

PROS	CONS	OFTEN FOUND IN
• breathable • good insulator (for all seasons) • feels delightful • strength/ durability	• can weaken with sun's rays	• scarves • blouses/ tops • dresses

WHY USED SILK IS BETTER THAN NEW SILK

Making silk requires the boiling of worm larva-an inhumane practice. New silk is also expensive.

My Favorite Use of Silk:

I have been known to take an oversized silk button up with me camping in the summer. With just one garment I have:

- sun protection for my shoulders
- a bathing suit cover up
- something to throw on when I get out of the tent to pee in the middle of the night
- a sleep mask against the early summer sun
- an extra layer for the cool evening

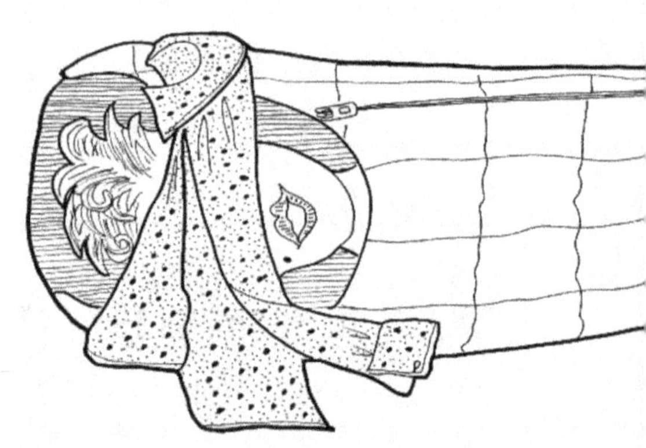

POLYESTER

Polyester is hard to avoid, especially in sportswear. Its feel ranges from almost silk-like to uncomfortable to plasticky (think: 1970s vintage).

PROS	CONS	OFTEN FOUND IN
• strength, flexibility • moisture resistance • ease of care	• not always breathable • inability to biodegrade	• sweaters • socks • some base layers such as long underwear stocking • caps

WHY USED POLYESTER IS BETTER THAN NEW POLYESTER

First off, polyester is petroleum based which means it is made from a non-renewable fossil fuel. Secondly, polyester does NOT biodegrade. All polyester that is created is with us forever!

Thirdly, the making of new polyester takes a lot of energy and consumes a lot of water. And its production creates a lot of pollution.

If you have to buy new polyester, consider a "greener" polyester called PET which is made from plastic bottles.

WOOL

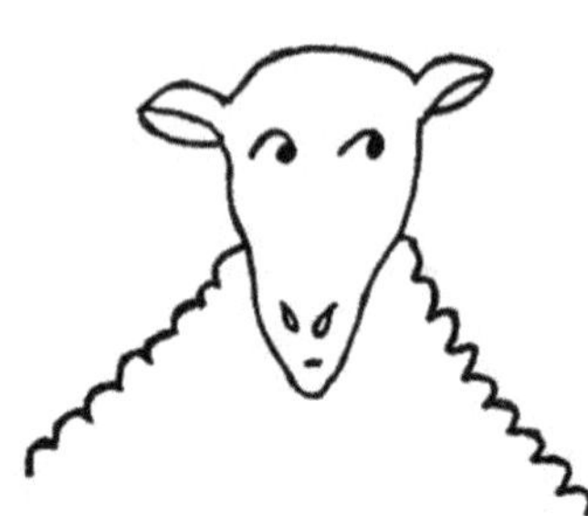

Wool is a natural, renewable material. Using wool in clothing is great for the environment as long as it is not mixed with plastic microfibers. Many people associate wool with being itchy but a lot of wool-such as Merino-is naturally soft or blended with other fibers to feel lovely against the skin.

PROS	CONS	OFTEN FOUND IN
• highly breathable • moisture wicking • anti-stink • warm even wet • great insulation • lightweight for the warmth it provides	• often cannot be tumbled dry • may snag • some farmers use practices for obtaining wool that are inhumane	• sweaters • socks • some base layers such as long underwear • stocking caps

WHY USED WOOL IS BETTER THAN NEW WOOL

Some farmers use practices to obtain wool that actually cut the sheep; they are not humane. New wool can also be expensive.

FABRIC TYPES

FABRIC TYPE refers to how a fabric is constructed. If you're a fabric nerd like me, you might find fabric construction endlessly fascinating—there are so many ways to create fabric! With constant innovation in outdoor materials—whether to improve comfort, performance, or reduce environmental impact—it can be tough to keep track of all the options out there. Below are a few fabric types you're most likely to encounter on your journey of creating upcycled outdoor gear.

As you begin your deep dive into fabric types, two useful terms to know are knit and woven. Remember weaving those *weird paper placemats as a kid? Woven fabrics are made in a similar way, but with fine threads on large industrial looms.

Knit fabrics, on the other hand, are constructed the way you might knit a scarf—by linking loops of yarn together—just at an industrial scale.

Fabrics are often described using both their fiber content and their construction type:

COTTON JERSEY

COTTON = FIBER CONTENT; JERSEY = FIBER TYPE

*No judgment: not weird because YOU made it just weird because we were making placemats out of paper!

JERSEY

Also known as 'single knit,' jersey fabrics are one of the most basic forms of large scale knitting. They are a commonly used, highly diverse popular choice for clothing in the fashion industry. Known for its stretchiness and close knits, the lightweight fabric is highly absorbent and breathable, making it a great choice for activewear, t-shirts, underwear, and baby clothes.

PROS	CONS	OFTEN FOUND IN
• stretchy • versatile • wrinkle-resistant • lightweight yet durable	• prone to pill or snag	• sports bra • tank tops • leggings • bike shorts • tracksuits • running tops

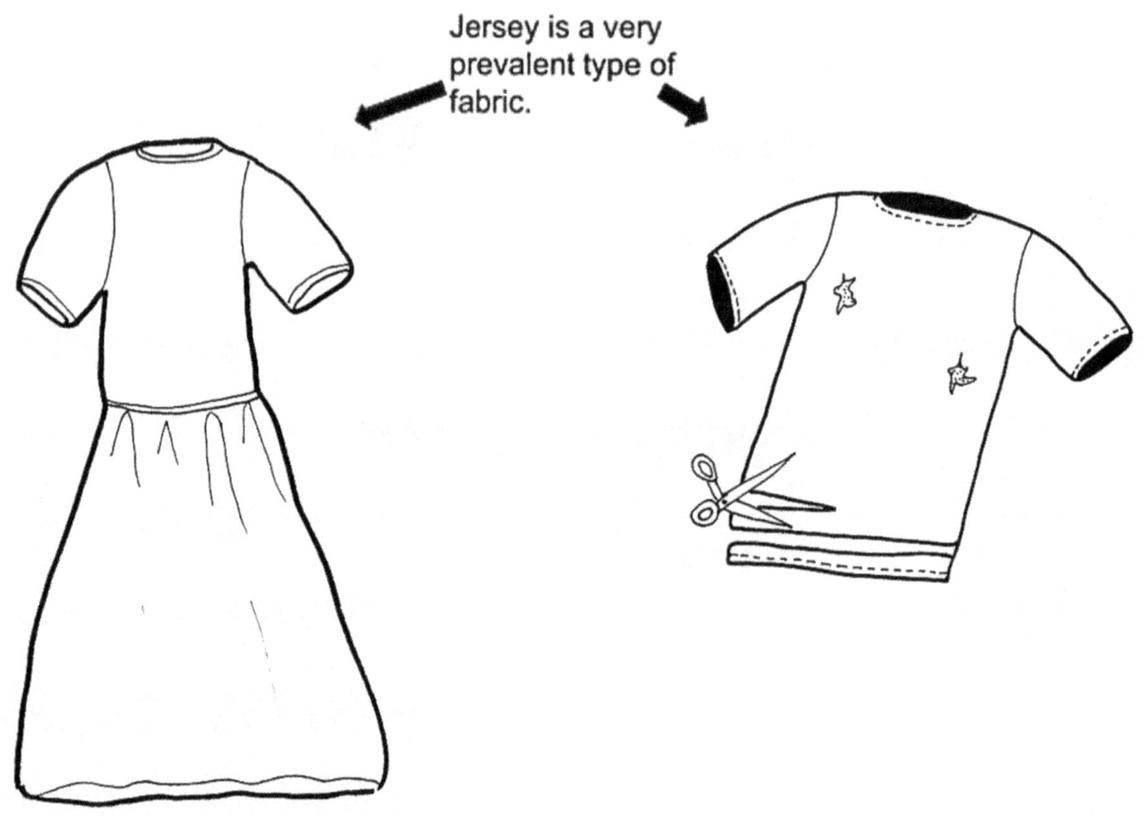

DOUBLE KNIT

The doubleknit's construction results in a thicker fabric than jersey. It is soft, a good insulator, firm, and absorbent. Although it is heavier, thicker, and firmer than single jersey, it remains breathable and feels soft and light.

PROS	CONS	OFTEN FOUND IN
• soft and comfortable • reversible and smooth • thicker fabric type • naturally stretchy same • texture on both sides does not roll and curl at • the edges	• may tend to snag, fuzz, or pile	• sports bra • tank tops • leggings • tracksuits • running tops • hoodies • jackets

RIBBED KNIT

This fabric's unique look comes from its lowered rows which, it turns out, also help with its elasticity.

PROS	CONS	OFTEN FOUND IN
• elastic and durable • interesting ribbed texture	• fabric may fray if unraveled	• stocking caps • dresses • leggings • cuffs → of sweats

NEOPRENE

Essentially a form of plastic made from petroleum and usually sandwiched in between knit fabric. Anyone who has ever wrestled themselves into a wetsuit knows that this fabric usually has some stretch but NOT A LOT.

PROS	CONS	OFTEN FOUND IN
• holds shape very well • insulating • provides a structured fit and silhouette • provides support • weather and stretch-resistant	• can feel hot in warmer, tropical climates • made from petroleum • contributes to microplastics in ocean • stiff/ bulky	• wetsuits • computer cases • women's swimwear

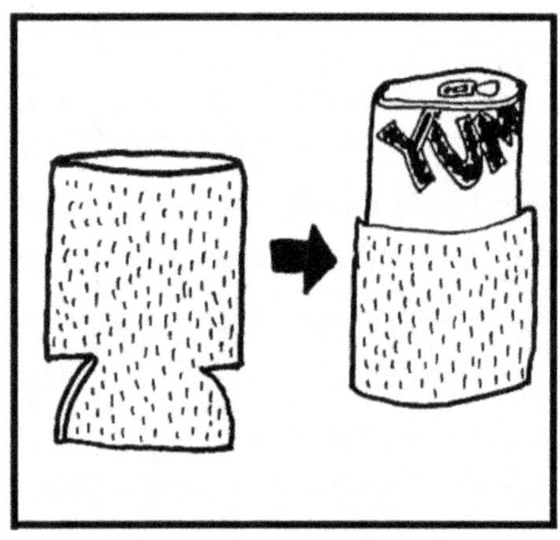

Upcycled Neoprene Cold Drink Coozie.
Or is it Cozy? Or koozie??

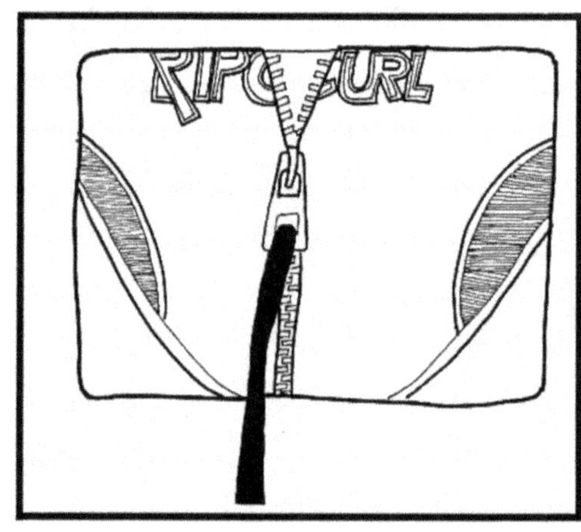

Upcycled Neoprene Computer Case

MICROFIBER

Microfiber can be woven or knit. Its name comes from the microthin fibers used in its production. Durable, absorbent, and water-repellant, the nature of microfiber wicks moisture away from the skin while keeping you cool and dry from perspiration, making it a popular choice in athletic wear.

Microfiber is always made from synthetic materials and almost always has elastic in it. As such, microfiber also allows movement and mobility during workouts, allowing stretch and elasticity while providing comfort.

PROS	CONS	OFTEN FOUND IN
• lightweight yet durable • moisture-wicking and water-repellant • wicks sweat away from skin	• tendency to accumulate static • picks up dust easily • most does not biodegrade	• wick-away shirts • gym towels • sports jerseys

POLAR FLEECE

There are MANY types of fleece found in outdoor wear, but polar fleece is the most common. Polar fleece is a warm, soft, and lightweight fabric often used for clothing, outdoor gear, and blankets. It is made by knitting the fabric, then brushing it to create a fluffy, fuzzy surface that helps trap warmth. Polar fleece is typically constructed from lightweight polyester fiber although many conscientious brands use PET which is made from recycled plastic bottles.

POLAR FLEECE

PROS	CONS	OFTEN FOUND IN
• plush and soft • cozy, warm, and provides insulation • quick-drying • lightweight and durable • can be worn year-round	• brushed fleece side has tendency to pill • contributes to microplastics in our waterways (through washing and disposal)	• jackets • hoodies • vests

CANVAS

Canvas is a durable, heavy-duty woven fabric commonly used in backpacks and outdoor clothing for its toughness and longevity. Canvas is traditionally made from cotton, but producers also use linen or synthetic fibers like polyester.

PROS	CONS	OFTEN FOUND IN
• durable • warm • easy to clean • often wind and water resistant (if tight-weave canvas)	• can fray	• jackets • backpacks • duffle bags • tents

RIPSTOP

Typically used for tactical gear and outdoor products, ripstop was originally designed to prevent ripping and tearing (get it? Rip Stop). Highly versatile and durable, the balanced square weave is made with an extra layer of weaving which creates reinforcement and tearing resistance.

PROS	CONS	OFTEN FOUND IN
• durable/ strong • interesting square texture and appearance • lightweight and smooth • moisture-wicking • can resist and repel water	• abrasion can cause holes to open along seams	• windbreakers • tents

Every aspect of our lives is, in a sense, a vote for the kind of world we want to live in.

~Frances Moore Lappé

One individual cannot possibly make a difference, alone. It is individual efforts, collectively, that makes a noticeable difference—all the difference in the world!

~Dr. Jane Goodall

IT'S GETTIN' HOT IN HERE, SO TAKE OFF ALL YOUR COAL.

To leave the world better than you found it, sometimes you have to pick up other people's trash.

~Bill Nye

PRESERVE
THE PLACES
YOU LOVE

FOLLOW THE RULES

Always follow the posted rules anywhere, they could surprise you. For example, while many outdoor areas encourage visitors to stay on the trails, I was surprised when I visited Dennali National Park in Alaska. Ranger requested that hikers refrain from making trails as they could cause erosion, compromising the fragile ecosystem! Rules can vary so make sure you check if there are any that are specific to where you are visiting.

However, there is a rule of thumb for when you are outdoors and it is unclear which rules to follow or there are no posted rules. According to the National Park Service a good guideline is to default to the **Leave No Trace Seven Principles**:

1. Plan Ahead and Prepare
2. Travel and Camp on Durable Surfaces
3. Dispose of Waste Properly
4. Leave What You Find
5. Minimize Campfire Impacts
6. Respect Wildlife
7. Be Considerate of Others

LEAVE NO TRACE

GIVE TO ORGANIZATIONS

ENVIRONMENTAL ORGANIZATIONS

There are many global and national environmental organizations you can donate money to if you are so inclined. Here are a few that I recommend:

- Greenpeace
- Native American Traditional Food Systems
- National Audubon Society
- Nature Conservancy
- One Percent for The Planet
- The Jane Goodall Institute
- World Wildlife Fund

Also, check out local organizations and nonprofits that speak to you. Your reasoning for giving doesn't have to make sense to anyone but you. For example, in Massachusetts I donate to The Trustees of Reservations (a land preservation group) because I spend a lot of time on their trails.

I also give Sustainable Cape because I am a big supporter of food access, local produce and also because I worked there for a spell and I love the people who work there. See, kinda random.

As far as giving your time, there are a variety of ways that you can volunteer. It's okay (and more sustainable) to pick something you enjoy doing! If you join the newsletter/mailing list of your favorite local environmental nonprofit you can learn about all kinds of ways you can volunteer. Depending on the organization you might be asked to: be a docent or a tour guide, teach a class, stuff envelopes or staff a booth/ info center.

You can also inquire about volunteer opportunities at: local schools, scout groups, gardens, food banks, immigration resource centers and community groups (including houses of worship).

TRAVEL RESPONSIBLY or TRY A STAYCATION

Go to bed in your own home and enjoy the sound of your alarm NOT going off in the morning. A "staycation" can be so much more than "just staying at home." First of all, congratulate yourself for having a carbon emission-free (or reduced carbon emissions) vacation!

Secondly, how do you want to use your time on your staycation? Some people love having no agenda, some people think of a staycation as a time to accomplish a long forgotten task or see their town as a tourist. Once, a friend from out of town visited me for a long weekend and we had a self-proclaimed "Writer's Retreat." We worked on writing projects we had been putting off and gave each other feedback; we stopped short of having nametags!

SOME STAYCATION IDEAS

- Check out a museum you have never been to before
- Check out your friend's shop/garage/cafe that you never have time to go into
- Take a walk down a new street
- Visit a new part of town
- Go to a thrift store
- Volunteer
- Go to a park and read
- Sit on a bench
- Take a bike trip, train or bus to a nearby town

PLAN A STAYCATION

TRAVEL RESPONSIBLY

LIVE YOUR VALUES

There is *so* much going on in the world right now. It's overwhelming. It's tempting to put our collective heads in the sand and hope someone else will fix everything while we watch a soothing nature documentary.

But here's the good news: you don't have to save the planet alone. You *can't*, actually. What you *can* do is live in a way that aligns with your principles—and that matters more than most of us realize.

Living your values can:

- Make an impact in your community
- Make you feel calmer and more grounded
- Give you back a sense of control
- Inspire others to do the same

Here are a few of my every day go tos (check out the QR code for more):

• Bring a reusable mug to a coffee shop
Pro tip: it can literally be the ceramic mug from your cupboard. It does not have to be a "travel mug." It just has to be clean-ish.

• Bring a tote bag to the grocery store
Or a backpack. Or a basket. Or the giant canvas bag you got for free at some conference in 2014.

• Walk (if safe) for shorter errands
BONUS: exercise, fresh air, possible dog sightings.

• Plant a garden
A yard garden, a container garden, a windowsill herb garden, or even a community garden plot. Watching things grow is very grounding.

• Limit your spending on new things
Try borrowing, making, mending, or buying used when possible. Your future self and your future budget will thank you.

•Check Your Thermometer
In the winter, try keeping it around 65–68°F during the day (and a little lower at night). In the summer, aim for 76–78°F if you have AC. And remember: in winter you can always add a sweater, and in summer you can always use an electric fan… or channel your inner Victorian and carry a hand fan dramatically

GO LOCAL

SHOP LOCALLY

You see the word *LOCAL* bumper-stickered on so many electric vehicles these days that it could be the subject of a Portlandia episode (wait… maybe it is). But what does *local* even mean? And why is it so important?

First of all, "shopping locally" is a slippery term. Is it within 10 miles? Twenty? What if you live on an island—does anything off-island still count?

I try to think about *local* as **"the closest source possible to me for the thing I'm trying to obtain."** That definition shifts with the seasons, geography, and what I'm buying.

Here's *why* shopping locally matters:

• It keeps money in your community
Every dollar spent locally circulates through your town—supporting your neighbors, strengthening small businesses, and shaping the kind of community most of us actually want to live in.

• It reduces environmental impact
Less fuel, fewer trucks, fewer shipping miles, and way less packaging. Local choices shrink your carbon footprint.

• It supports actual humans, not faceless corporations
Buying from local makers, farmers, repair people, and shop owners means you're literally helping your neighbors stay afloat.

• It builds community
Shopping locally becomes part of your life story. You run into familiar faces. You learn the barista's dog's name. It feels human—and grounding.

• It keeps unique places alive
Local establishments and artisans are what make a town unique and not just another mini mall wasteland (this was the not-so-affectionate name we called the town that I grew up in).

• It encourages more sustainable habits
Local produce is often in-season. Local goods tend to use fewer new materials. Local thrift stores keep items out of landfills and often support local charities. Every choice has a ripple.

Food hasn't been shipped for days. Handmade and upcycled items are created with care. My favorite part is if something's off, when you shop locally you can talk to an actual person who can actually help. Anyone else hate spending hours on the phone with customer service, over-enunciating "speak to an agent?"

BUILDING COMMUNITY BEYOND BUYING

Investing in your community also means showing up, participating, and actually knowing the humans who live around you. Here are some other ways to connect with your community that require nothing but a little curiosity:

•Meet your neighbors
Yes, even the ones whose lawn signs confuse or anger you. Community starts with simple connection.

• Get involved with local government
It sounds intimidating, but it's literally just regular people making decisions that affect your daily life. I joined the bicycle committee in my community and I LOVE it!

• Find out who serves on your local town board

• Go to town meetings
I know, I know. Town Meetings aren't known for their riveting content. Bring crochet. Bring a sketchbook if you need to. But pay attention, vote, ask questions. This is YOUR community!

• Explore your community like a participant, not a passerby
Show up for a local concert, a school play, a winter festival, or an open mic. Join a parks and recs class, show up to a local pick up sports game, try trivia night or a book club at the library!

MARVEL AT THE BEAUTY OF NATURE

Put down your phone.
Lay down on some moss.
Get lost in the clouds or the intricate pattern of the tree bark.
You've got this.

Isn't nature f@#$ing magnificent?!!

BIBLIOGRAPHY

FIBER CONTENT

Downing,Suzanne."Anatomy of Outdoor Gear: The Materials That Help Us Adventure." *ActionHub*, 29 Feb. 2024, www.actionhub.com/outdoors/anatomy-outdoor-gear-materials-allow-us-adventure.

Koerner, Brendan. "Is It Better for the Environment to Wear Leather or Pleather?" *Slate Magazine*, Slate, 4 Dec. 2007, slate.com/technology/2007/12/is-it-better-for-the-environment-to-wear-leather-or-pleather.html.

Lamri, Geoffrey. "What Are the Advantages and Disadvantages of Silk ?" *The Oversized Hoodie®*, the-oversized-hoodie.com/en/blogs/blog/quels-sont-les-avantages-et-les-inconvenients-de-la-soie. Accessed 3 July 2025.

Mathews, Donovan. "The Useful Activewear Fabrics Guide." *Bryden Apparel*, 1 June 2024, brydenapparel.com/activewear-fabrics-guide.

Sewport Support Team. "What Is Spandex Fabric: Properties, How Its Made and Where." *Sewport*, Sewport, sewport.com/fabrics-directory/spandex-fabric. Accessed 3 July 2025.

"What Is Neoprene Fabric: Properties, How Its Made and Where." *Sewport*, Sewport, sewport.com/fabrics-directory/neoprene-fabric. Accessed 13 Nov. 2025.

"Why Wear Wool?" *Outdoor Gear Exchange*, www.gearx.com/knowledge/technical-outerwear-apparel/why-wear-wool?srsltid=AfmBOopgpowfgX9YJKqoW2U04zpYgvFk5zKHqJ_n1d2YbSep13kkXvgy. Accessed 13 Nov. 2025.

PRESERVE THE PLACES YOU LOVE

25ThingsYouCanDotoHelptheEnvironment - Wonderlab, wonderlab.org/25-things-you-can-do-to-help-the-environment/. Accessed 12 Nov. 2025.

Chayne, Kaméa. "35 Environmental Organizations and Nonprofits for a Sustainable Future (List and Ways You Can Get Involved)." *Green Dreamer*, Green Dreamer, 29 Sept. 2023, www.greendreamer.com/journal/environmental-organizations-nonprofits-for-a-sustainable-future.

"Have an Environmentally Friendly Vacation." *WWF*, wwf.panda.org/act/live_green/travel/on_vacation/. Accessed 12 Nov. 2025.

"Leave No Trace Seven Principles (U.S. National Park Service)." *National Parks Service*, U.S. Department of the Interior, www.nps.gov/articles/leave-no-trace-seven-principles.htm. Accessed 12 Nov. 202

It’s me, Hi!
I’m the octopus,
It’s me!

Hold your phone camera to the QR code to access a resource.

Also, if you want to give a (GLOWING!) review of this book you can leave one on GoodReads or at Amazon!

I appreciate you!

BUY MY FIRST BOOK
WEBSITE
FREE PROJECTS
INSTA
NEWSLETTER
TIK TOK
YOUTUBE

Thank you!

To those that proofread my book and gave me feedback: Ben Stich, Michelle Whelan, Yamani Levitsky, Ben Levitsky, Lois Gearson, Pam Stich and Kat Steckbeck. Your taking the time to look at something so near and dear to my heart means the world to me.

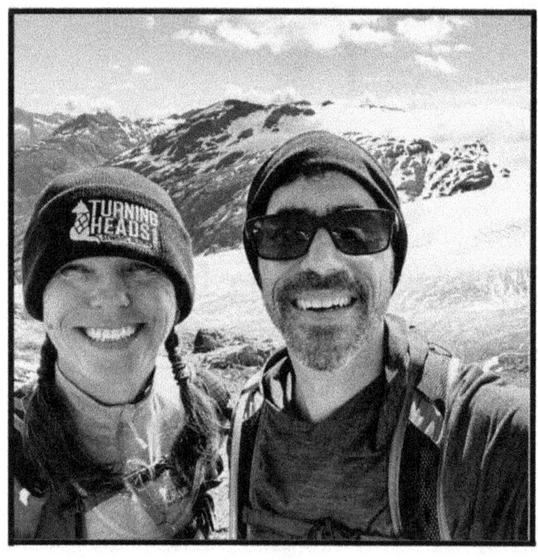

Thank you to Ben Stich for your unflagging and absolute support. The outdoors is 1000% more fun with you!

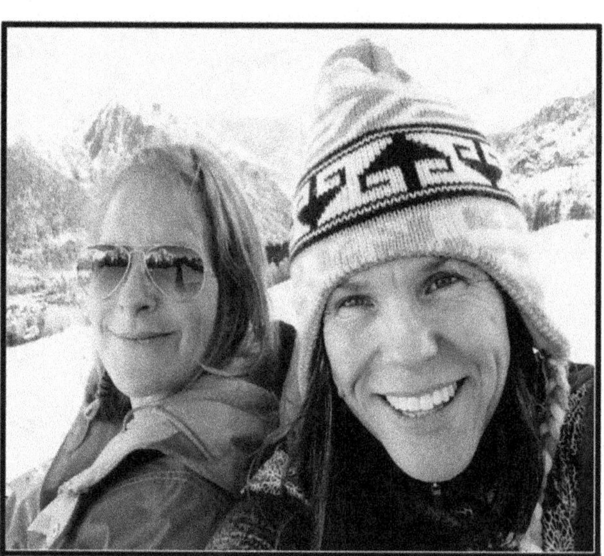

Thank you to Jennie Duke for a lifetime of support and adventure. And for your willingness to rollerskate any time, any place.

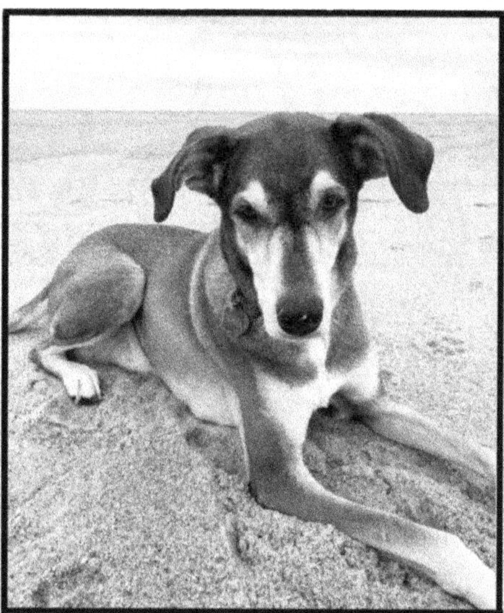

And to my sweet Donnie Boy.

ABOUT THE AUTHOR

Calin Duke is an author, illustrator, and storyteller. Two things she loves wholeheartedly are upcycling and spending time outdoors.

That's why she wrote this book for you!

This is her second book in the *How To Upcycle Nearly Everything* series. However, her ADHD propels her to write books in many genres. Look out for her upcoming children' s book on wild foraging as well as her novel centered around her family's fascinating (and traumatic!) intergenerational stories. Calin also loves spending time with loved ones, reading or busting goofy dance moves in the kitchen when it's time to make dinner.

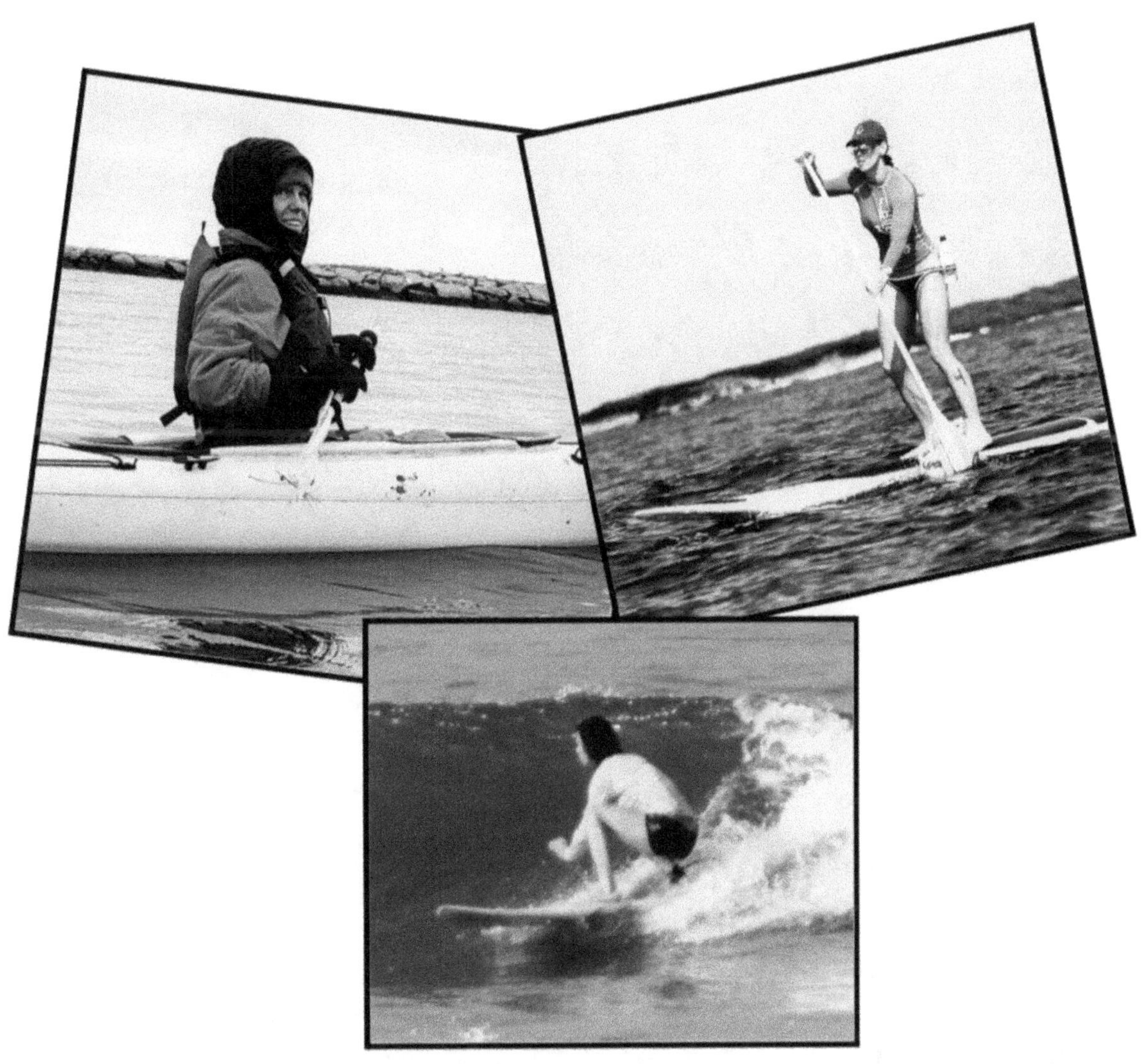

www.ingramcontent.com/pod-product-compliance
Lightning Source LLC
LaVergne TN
LVHW061203120826
845149LV00011B/1891

* 9 7 8 1 9 6 0 3 6 7 0 4 4 *